FOILING
THE
SYSTEM
BREAKERS

FOILING THE SYSTEM BREAKERS

Computer Security and Access Control

Jerome Lobel

McGraw-Hill Book Company

New York   St. Louis   San Francisco   Auckland
Bogotá   Singapore   Johannesburg   London
Madrid   Mexico   Montreal   New Delhi
Panama   São Paulo   Hamburg
Sydney   Tokyo   Paris
Toronto

Library of Congress Cataloging-in-Publication Data

Lobel, Jerome.
    Foiling the system breakers.

    Bibliography: p.
    Includes index.
    1. Computers—Access control. I. Title.
QA76.9.A25L6 1986   005.8   85-24161
ISBN 0-07-038357-X

1234567890   DOC/DOC   89876

ISBN 0-07-038357-X

The editors for this book were Stephen G. Guty and Nancy Warren, the designer was Mark E. Safran, and the production supervisor was Sally Fliess. It was set in Aster by The Saybrook Press, Inc.

Printed and bound by R. R. Donnelley & Sons, Inc.

To Carrie, Jana, and Linda
and in memory of my mother and father
also to my special friends, Mary, Gordon, and Hal

Contents

Preface

This book was written for all the people who are interested in what can be done to protect computer systems and the vital data and programs stored in them against an increasingly common form of abuse—unauthorized access.

This book was also written for those people who want to believe that unauthorized computer access may not invariably bring about a bad result and, therefore, is harmless. I am hopeful that this book will change their minds. It is my opinion that, at the very least, unauthorized system and information access creates the opportunity for someone to do harm to someone else.

I believe this book is different from other books on computer security and privacy because the problem of computer access control is given greater attention. Although access control is certainly not the entire computer security problem, I think it is the main beam upon which many other computer security safeguards depend for support. Therefore, this book attempts to cover the subject of computer access control in a comprehensive fashion.

It is my hope that the basic flow and organization of the ideas presented here will give readers a better insight into not only why, but how, to go about achieving systems access control. The sequence in which the material is covered is therefore important.

Specifically, the information in the six major sections of this book should help the reader do the following:

- Determine the need for computer access control in a system
- Establish a coherent information security and access control policy
- Evaluate the available tools that can help achieve system access security

- Select the right combination of security products and techniques that will satisfy a system's design requirements
- Implement and monitor access security during the life cycle of the information system
- Gain the insight required to anticipate future access control requirements that will be mandated by the arrival of new generations of computer and communications systems

The level of technical information presented in this book is designed to meet the needs of computer users, data processing staff members, and system designers. Others who might find the material of benefit include commercial software developers, EDP auditors, law enforcement personnel, attorneys, computer scientists, engineering and business students, and people in all levels of management whose responsibilities include computer applications. Considerable material may also be of value to the new owners of personal and home computers and even to the latest generation of computer hackers (who I hope are open to reform).

It took almost sixteen years, the length of time I have been dealing with computer security problems on almost a daily basis, to decide to write this book. As many of you already know, one of the most difficult of all computer security and access control problems is constant change, or the "moving target" syndrome. This book is my attempt to cope with at least part of this problem.

Another influence that led to my writing this book is that for the past several years I have taught part-time a course in computer security in the Computer Science Department at Arizona State University. In a way, this book is a tribute to the extremely fine and unusually gifted students who have helped to hone my appreciation of the problems, both technical and moral of computer access control.

Finally, I have certainly gained a wealth of knowledge about this problem during the past twelve years as Manager of Computer Security for Honeywell Information Systems. Naturally, this experience is revealed in many ways throughout the book. I do take full responsibility for the contents of this book, however, and thank Honeywell for the opportunity to study this problem in a multitude of environments.

JEROME LOBEL

Introduction

Computer Access Control—An Overview

Sometime during August 1983, America was rudely awakened to learn that another wholesale breach of computer security had just taken place. The accomplishment of a group of about a dozen youths between the ages of 15 and 22 would go down in computer history.

They called themselves the 414s, after the Milwaukee, Wisconsin, telephone area code number. What they had achieved put to shame the celebrated sequence of computer-penetration events accomplished not long ago by several 13-year-olds attending an east coast school. That group had initially tried to cheat Pepsi-Cola out of a few free cases of soda pop, but they eventually moved on to bigger game—a Canadian time-sharing company, including twenty-two of its commercial customers.

According to news reports, the 414s had broken into more than sixty prestigious computer installations including Los Alamos National Laboratories, Security Pacific Bank, a Dallas consulting firm, and a Canadian cement company. What added fuel to the fire was that the youths were able to gain access so easily to systems through the Telenet national communications network. The scope of their penetrations was shocking. For example, it was reported that they had illegally entered the Sloan-Kettering computer eighty times, using the equipment a total of ten hours. Sloan-Kettering is the world famous cancer center in New York, and its computer contained 6,000 therapy records on current and former patients. The malicious "hacking" of the hospital's computer, widely covered by the news media, brought the entire 414 incident to the attention of almost every household and business in the United States.

One result, according to the news media, was that it looked like authorities had finally decided that the "games" that some youthful computer experts played were no longer to be considered innocent pranks. Breaking and entering someone else's computer files should not be condoned, according to the authorities. It did not matter whether harm had actually been done. Instead, the issue coming to the forefront was that information and communications

1

systems must be made safe, and if technological safeguards cannot get the job done, then the law and its enforcement will.

To the chagrin of those who watch movies such as *War Games* and *TRON*, their heroes may not be heroes any longer—at least not in the eyes of corporate officers, government officials, and law enforcement agencies. Although many may escape the new computer dragnets initiated by the FBI, those old enough to get indicted and convicted may be given plenty of time to think about their misdeeds.

Although in the past youths have escaped serious punishment (as is also possible for the 414s), there is little doubt that the responses to their actions that will be taken by the government, the computer industry, and system users will have long-term consequences. Primarily, experts predict tougher laws, more severe punishment, and an increasing interest in computer system access control and security.

How tough will the courts get with system hackers? Only time will tell. Computer system access control and security, however, is finally getting the attention it deserves. The purpose of this introduction, therefore, is to provide an overview of the present state of the art in this area and to offer some insights into how computer access control technology might be improved.

History of Unauthorized Access

There has been a need for system user identification since the installation of the first-generation computers. Accountability and user service charges were the main reasons for wanting to know who was using the computer. The limitations of batch processing, running only one user job at a time, and physically taking most work to the computer resulted in very little concern about unauthorized usage.

User access control concerns began to appear when remotely located direct access devices were connected to second-generation computers via cables and telephone lines. However, the amount of work submitted to computers in this way was so small and the sensitivity of the data files was generally so low, that access control was still not a high-priority problem in most organizations. In addition, there were less than 50,000 mainframe computers in the United States in 1970.

The installation of the third- and fourth-generation computers dramatically changed the picture. Remote user access to computers increased significantly as organizations began to implement such new system concepts as time sharing, multiprogramming, and multiprocessing. The introduction of typical fourth-generation applications such as transaction processing, networking, and distributed processing accentuated the problem of unauthorized system usage.

Eventually, it became obvious that as the system became capable of more "resource sharing," the more vulnerable it became to illegal entry and use.

Insiders versus Outsiders

There are several ways to classify unauthorized computer access. One simple approach states that unauthorized access may be accomplished by an "insider" or an "outsider." This rather elementary approach is of value because it helps us to examine the differences between the types of internal controls and hardware and software mechanisms that are needed to guard against unauthorized system activity from two different positions of attack.

For example, there are the trusted employees who use the computer to get their jobs done. There may be, and probably should be, limitations placed upon their system usage. Normally, a good password system and a careful examination of system accounting logs suffice to provide adequate access control for an organization's employees—if the data and programs do not contain extremely valuable or secret information or financial records that lend themselves to manipulation.

A procedure for personnel clearance and data classification needs to be implemented on the more vulnerable computer system in order to restrict the access of legitimate users to only the data and programs that they need to do their jobs. The U.S. Department of Defense formalizes this concept by calling it an individual's *need to know*.

Unfortunately, the insider access control problem can become very serious if the system is extremely sensitive, and if the potential benefit from compromising its operating system is particularly high. This is because in most computer systems the access or permission control mechanisms are usually implemented in software as part of the operating system. Insiders with normal system access privileges are in a prime position (with enough technical expertise) to use computers for illegitimate purposes.

Protecting against unauthorized access by an insider is therefore normally much more difficult than securing the system against an outsider, as will be discussed later in more detail.

It has been claimed that some computer systems using dial-up or nondedicated common carrier communications lines with poor password access control can be compromised almost as easily by an outsider as by an insider. Obviously, a truly sensitive or valuable information system that has been implemented with so little regard for security should be reimplemented or changed as quickly as possible.

However, user inconvenience, together with high costs, is often given as the reason for allowing weak communications protection and inadequate password control. This is unfortunate because these are generally the two primary areas used by outsiders to break into computer systems.

It should be much easier to prevent unauthorized access by an outsider than by an insider. In simple terms, it should be more a matter of barring the gate against an outside intrusion at the system front end or at a communications node before the outsider even has a chance to access the host computer operating system.

Unfortunately, many dial-up systems do not have a way of clearly differentiating between an insider or an outsider if there is an inadequate password system and if no basic precautions have been taken, such as the purchase of special terminals or the implementation of some form of a "dial-up–answer-back" system.

The possibility of collusion between an insider and an outsider would appear to add to the access control problem. However, a system that is carefully safeguarded against unauthorized insider access should also be less vulnerable to an attack by an outsider.

Communications Security

Most recent computer compromises that attracted national media interest in the United States involved gaining unauthorized computer usage by first accessing some part of a common carrier and/or telecommunications network.

Many critics believe that if the communications part of a computer network can be secured, compromises such as hacking would be much more difficult. The two communications aspects of computer security problems are (1) communications as a gateway to compromise and (2) communications interception.

Communications—A gateway to Compromise

Even though it is illegal to use the telephone system to commit a computer fraud or carry on other illicit activities, the law, in itself, has not sufficiently deterred the use of the telephone or other carrier systems by unauthorized computer users.

Unfortunately, it is easy to abtain unlisted data telephone numbers as well as the password(s). The fact that hackers and others have not been stopped by a host computer's password identification system is a sad commentary on computer system designers and managers and should not be considered part of the data communications problem.

For example, in the case of the 414s it was reported that members of the group had simply dialed a local telephone number to connect their computer to a leased telephone line operated by a major communications corporation. The company provides access to about 1,200 computers across the country for approximately 150,000 authorized subscribers. Apparently when the 414s located a computer, they would initially attempt to enter it by typing in familiar passwords. If this did not work, they would proceed to more sophisticated compromise techniques.

Unfortunately, there are no simple solutions to the types of problems revealed by the computer compromises of the 414s. The complexity of most data communications systems and computer networks is such (Figure I-1) that only a comprehensive analysis of the potential weaknesses of each system can provide feasible solutions.

Finally, the communications weaknesses described above are not liable to disappear. The problem is threefold: user convenience, cost, and overall

Network or system characteristic	Types of or characteristics of unauthorized access	Possible protection mechanisms	
		Active	Passive
1. Dial-up capabilities	1. Game or challenge	1. Access control software	1. Better use of system accounting data
2. Standard hardware and software (products)	2. Communication capabilities (terminals, modems)	2. User and password ID: Request both at once	2. Access control software
3. Easy access by design for authorized users	3. Access to telephone numbers (electronic bulletin board)	3. Change ID/password more frequently	3. Better database reports
4. Poor protection and lack of security planning in systems design	4. Password accessibility (searches)	4. Encryption	4. Warnings
5. Lack of adequate monitoring	5. Execution of some type of unauthorized activity	5. Dedicated lines	5. Disabled IDs
6. Access ID and/or password too available	6. Age: young, students (maybe gifted)	6. Better authorization mechanism	
	7. Time availability	7. Automatic call-up and answer-back	
	8. Repeated successes	8. Personal positive identification (characteristic matching)	
	9. Use off-hours to advantage	9. Telephone trace	
	10. No guilt	10. Smart card or magnetic-stripe ID	
	11. Ego		
	12. Network access		
	13. No fear of punishment		

Figure I-1 414 problem analysis.

system vulnerability. Solutions will require independent action by computer user organizations that recognize their vulnerabilities. Computer security experts tend to support this approach, because few solutions to access control problems have been offered by the carriers themselves.

Communications Interception

The possible interception of data communications traffic is an area of distinct risk to computer network users. The clandestine nature of such activity and its illegality have prevented computer user organizations from recognizing this problem.

Government agencies, communications carriers, and private industries have approached the problem of data communications interception with a wide variety of solutions, where prevention or detection was deemed worthwhile or essential.

Wiretapping, radiation recording, and microwave interception are all well-known threats to private communications. The technology to detect and prevent such activity is relatively well known because it has been so thoroughly researched as a result of the historically critical needs to protect certain classes of voice communications and military data. The application of state-of-the-art solutions to commercial and private data communications problems, however, lags because many computer users do not perceive a need for a solution.

Need for an Action Plan

The time is quickly coming when the need for solutions to the problems of information system access control will require action. In fact, for many computer users the time has already arrived. But to make important system security decisions without a plan of action can be costly.

This book attempts to respond to this need. Specifically, the organization of the book's six sections constitutes a form of an action plan that encompasses the following topics:

- Understanding the need for computer access control
- Establishing a system security policy
- Selecting access control tools and technology
- Completing a secure system design
- Implementing and monitoring access control
- Coping with change

Access control, of course, is only one of the major elements of a total computer security program, as shown in Figure I-2. The other elements of a security program—a physical security plan, disaster recovery plan, computer audit plan, and operations security plan—are beyond the scope of this book.

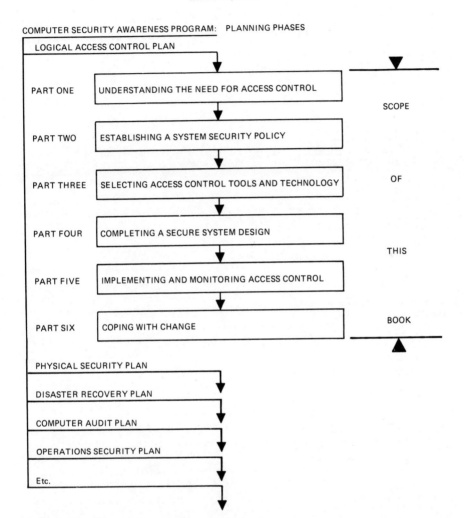

Figure I-2 Computer security program.

Understanding the Need for Computer Access Control

COMPUTER SECURITY AWARENESS PROGRAM

PLANNING PHASES

LOGICAL ACCESS CONTROL PLAN

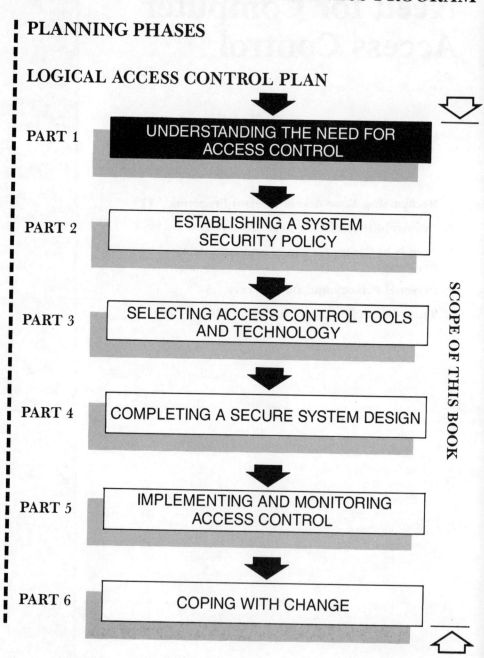

PART 1 — UNDERSTANDING THE NEED FOR ACCESS CONTROL

PART 2 — ESTABLISHING A SYSTEM SECURITY POLICY

PART 3 — SELECTING ACCESS CONTROL TOOLS AND TECHNOLOGY

PART 4 — COMPLETING A SECURE SYSTEM DESIGN

PART 5 — IMPLEMENTING AND MONITORING ACCESS CONTROL

PART 6 — COPING WITH CHANGE

SCOPE OF THIS BOOK

1. Recognizing Your Access Control Problems

Slowly but surely, people who use computers are beginning to realize that they cannot take for granted the protection of their systems and the information contained therein. In this regard, the horror stories that have been repeated so many times may possibly have done some good. On the other hand, to really deal with the problem, we must understand the vulnerabilities of the specific information systems we have come to rely upon. We must also recognize that an information system will probably never be more secure than the people who design, implement, maintain, and use it want it to be. So, how secure do you want your system to be?

In this chapter we will try to help you develop your answer to this question by addressing three basic questions:

- What is computer access control?
- Why is computer access control needed?
- How do you recognize access control problems?

What Is Computer Access Control?

Computer access control refers to the combination of logical, physical, and administrative protection capabilities that are associated with a computer system or information network. The subject of this book is primarily logical systems security. Physical and administrative security will be covered only to the extent that is is necessary to demonstrate how logical protection must be supported.

Logical access control is the protection afforded to data stored or processed in a magnetized format in a computer or communications system and the associated software and electronic hardware.

Logical access control is just one major part of an organization's total computer security protection program. Total computer security includes the following: a need to protect the data and programs stored or processed in a computer or network against any form of loss or unauthorized access or modification; the different capabilities that might be used to provide information confidentiality and privacy, including hard-copy or document protection; the need to protect system users against any interruption or stoppage of computer processing or communications; and the capabilities of disaster recovery or contingency plans, backup procedures, and numerous administrative controls and physical safeguards designed to minimize other classes of system threats. An example of a major security component is a fire prevention and extinguishment system.

Computer access control requirements are also influenced by the type, size, and functionality of the computer(s) and communications system. In a communication-oriented system, for example, access control should consider such factors as typical users, terminals (or microcomputers), and type of carriers used. An evaluation of a stand-alone computer system with no communications capability might have to consider other potential problem areas. Even a single stand-alone computer that allows multiprogramming or several user jobs to run cooperatively and simultaneously could have user access control problems that are similar to and just as serious as those of a communications-oriented system.

Access control also considers more than unauthorized data access problems because many different resources can be connected directly and indirectly (i.e, via communication) to a particular computer. Local and remote printers, terminals, tape and disk drives, and buffered and communications devices, all under logical control, can be used to compromise or abuse a system.

It is important to note that logical access control as defined in this book includes all the above potential compromise areas because access to many physical subsystems can be attained through the manipulation of system logic in both hardware and software.

Finally, there is the legal definition of access control. The proposed State of Minnesota Computer Crime Bill [MI 1982] defines unauthorized access, and then discusses penalties that can be applied to computer abusers who have gained unauthorized access.

Access defined by the bill means "to approach, instruct, communicate with, store data in, retrieve data from, or otherwise make use of any resources of a computer, computer system or computer network."

The bill provides for severe penalties for anyone who:

1. Knowingly and willfully, directly or indirectly accesses, causes to be accessed or attempts to access any computer, computer system, computer network, or any part thereof for the purpose of:

   a. Devising or executing any scheme or artifice to defraud, or

   b. Obtaining money, property, or services, for himself or another, by means of false or fraudulent pretenses, representations of promises; and

2. Intentionally and without authorization and with intent to injure or defraud directly or indirectly accesses, alters, damages or destroys any computer, computer system, or computer network, or any computer

m or data contained in such computer, computer sys-
network. [MI 1982]

that provides for penalties for violations states that
... [above] is guilty of computer abuse and may be
nt for not more than ten years or to payment of a fine
r both." A logical conclusion might be: If enforced, a
e one of the more effective access control solutions

Control Needed?

...tion system access protection is needed to protect computer users
against a number of potential abuses. Past experience tells us that the methods
or the extent to which they are used to breach a system are not nearly so
important as why the system was compromised and how much damage was
done.

Generally speaking, there are three classes of information systems abuse:
(1) a criminal attack for personal gain, (2) a malicious attack for revenge or
some other personal or political purpose, and (3) a partially or totally nondestructive attack perpetrated as a game or challenge.

Criminal attacks for gain are intended to produce a profit or some other
material benefit for the perpetrator. Violations may range from the use of
someone's computer without permission for personal benefit to a carefully
planned major fraud or the theft of valuable trade secrets.

Malicious attacks can potentially cause more harm (i.e., where loss of life
could occur) than certain criminal attacks. Past incidents have ranged from
destroying someone's files, to "crashing" a system (resulting in denial of
system services), to eliminating critical financial data or important computer
programs.

Partially or totally nondestructive attacks may be represented by some of the
hacker intrusion incidents. These can range from entering someone's system
without authorization to causing serious disruption or data loss problems.

Other forms of computer-oriented abuse do not clearly fall into one of these
three categories. Noteworthy examples include the compromising of an individual's personal privacy by some type of unauthorized information access
(see Chapter 4) and the copying of proprietary software (see Chapter 5).

Unfortunately, almost all computers, including personal and home systems, are susceptible to abuse precipitated by unauthorized system access.
Furthermore, as computer use increases, the potential for abuse will increase
to the extent that users become more dependent upon their computer(s).
In other words, as users learn more about how to use their systems, they
are inclined to put more sensitive data or applications on their systems. In
addition, as their volume of transactions and file storage increases, their
ability to back up their system with redundant files and equipment often
becomes inadequate. And finally, in most cases the typical users' ability to

revert back to a former manual system (if there was one) becomes extremely difficult, if not impossible.

None of these descriptions of possible conditions is intended to downgrade the importance of data and system backup. The point is that most computer users will need better system access controls as they put more applications on their computers.

How Do You Recognize Access Control Problems?

People have trouble recognizing access control problems because they ask the wrong questions. For example, they ask, What kind of protection does my system need? A better question might be, What do I have that needs protection?

This question provides a good approach to access control problems whether you are considering the vulnerabilities of an international network of large-scale host computers and distributed databases or your new personal computer. In any case, you might also want to ask the following questions:

- What is the value of access to the data and programs that are stored or processed in the system to its user(s)?
- What would the value of access to the same data and programs be to someone else?
- What is the value of continued normal service from the system? Or put another way, what losses would be sustained from the interruption, discontinuance, or denial of service?
- What would result if system service and data processing results (i.e., integrity) could not be depended upon as a result of intentional sabotage or modification of some part of the system?
- Am I legally obligated to protect access to the data?
- Would the loss of the data result in a serious problem?
- Would the divulgence of the data compromise some individual's personal privacy?
- Would the data reveal information about another organization that could be used to harm that organization?
- Could the use of the data cause innocent parties to suffer losses because of the nature of the data or because of its possible lack of integrity?
- Would unauthorized access to the data result in the loss of some future opportunity?
- Could unauthorized access to the data bring about some form of financial loss or other embarrassment to its legal owner?

These kinds of questions will help point you in the right direction. The only procedure that might be better would be to ask the question during the design phase of the system. The cost of solutions might be considerably less. Many after-the-fact (after implementation) security improvements or changes tend to be economically prohibitive. In certain instances the desired security protection may not even be technically practical or possible after a system has gone on-line.

Classic examples of security problems that should be dealt with early include vulnerabilities associated with operating systems, terminals and workstations, and communications networks, because access control changes often affect basic system capabilities. Often, a major change can only be implemented in conjunction with a total system redesign and reimplementation.

Asking the right questions, therefore, may involve not only the correct problem identification but also the right timing.

The Right Question: What Do I Have to Protect?

How you answer this question will normally depend upon who you are, what data is in your computer, what use or application you make of your computer, and how you identify and value your system-related assets.

Who you are is important because if you are an individual using a personal computer in your home, your protection requirements may only be governed by your own personal preferences. On the other hand if you represent a government agency or a public corporation, you may have a formidable set of regulatory, legal, or corporate policy guidelines to follow.

As an example, FIPS (Federal Information Processing Standard) publication number 102 [GU 1983] says that a computer security requirement for a federal agency should "derive from governmental policy, agency mission needs, and specific user needs." Computer security, the publication states, is "the quality exhibited by a computer system that embodies its protection against internal failures, human errors, attacks, and natural catastrophes that might cause improper disclosure, modification, destruction, or denial of service."

Unauthorized data or system disclosure, modification, destruction, and denial of service are interpreted to be unacceptable by FIPS publication number 102. So, what do you have to protect? In a government agency, each computer system and network would have to be analyzed for unacceptable loss potentials from legal, regulatory, and practical viewpoints. System threats that could result in welfare fraud, compromise of national security information, or the disabling of an air traffic control system might be examples of major computer system protection requirements.

In the private company or corporate sphere, the determination of information system protection requirements might take a slightly different approach. This would be particularly true of a public corporation that must abide by regulations administered by the U.S. Securities and Exchange Commission (SEC).

A public corporation needs to protect its information system because of the economic necessity of protecting its essential assets. Its data and communications systems represent company assets in at least three ways. It is (1) an essential component in the asset creation part of the business, (2) the storage vault of company data, and (3) a part of the physical and intellectual assets of the company.

Legally and otherwise, public companies need to protect and effectively and efficiently utilize all their major assets. This includes their information and communications systems. Most potential threats to the confidentiality, security, or continued operation of these systems can, therefore, be avoided by some form of access control.

In the first analysis, computer security is good business. Unauthorized information system access has had devastating effects on the profitability of many companies. Private companies have an obligation, therefore, to implement system access control in order to minimize the impact of potential losses. Examples of losses include financial fraud, trade-secret theft, and unauthorized divulgence of company plans, proposal data, financial transactions, or customer lists.

National Bureau of Standards Technical Note 809 [GO 1974] takes a somewhat different approach to the identification of computer system threats. It classifies threats as "threats to individual privacy" and "technological threats." The technological threats include the problem of controlled access to computer-based record keeping systems.

This publication establishes four classes of users who may attempt some form of unauthorized access to a system:

Consumers: a term applied to the authorized recipients of information (products) of a computer-based record keeping system . . . .

Producers: a term applied to the analysts and applications programmers who design and implement specific record keeping systems which produce information products for consumers. . . .

Services: a term applied to the computer operations staff; includes operators, systems programmers, data entry services, etc., responsible for availability and maintenance of the computer system resources. . . .

Intruders: a term applied to individuals or organizations who have no authorized access to a computer system or its products and have a possible malicious interest in obtaining unauthorized access to data or a system. Intruders are generally thought of as not belonging to any of the above categories. . . . [They are] outsider[s].

The NBS Technical Note 809 [GO 1974] states:

The threat to data confidentiality or system security is related to the capabilities of each class of individuals in dealing with a system and the existence of an asset (data or system) that is supposed to be protected from some or all members of one or more classes.

Included in the report is a matrix-type diagram that attempts to correlate possible system threats with the various classes of individuals who might have

access to the system. The sixteen possible entries were grouped into ten classes of threats, as shown in the accompanying table.
Although the matrix is an extremely simplified approach to threats from unauthorized access, it provides a systematic way to isolate specific system threats and the possible sources of compromise. Specific questions related to

| Access capability | Type of system | | | |
| | Local (off-line) batch | | Remote (on-line) | |
	Dedicated	Shared	Dedicated	Shared
Intruder	T1	T1	T2	T2
Consumer	T3	T4	T5	T6
Producer	T7	T8	T7	T9
Servicer	T10	T10	T10	T10

T1	Intruder versus batch	Threat is a function of physical security measures and their enforcement. High degree of risk of exposure to intruders.
T2	Intruder versus remote	Greatly expanded threat of unauthorized access due to potential vulnerability of communications. Low risk of exposure. Potential for masquerading as any of the authorized users quite high.
T3	Consumer versus dedicated batch	Threat to data confidentiality primarily that of misusing data otherwise authorized for access. Access control based on personal identification.
T4	Consumer versus shared batch	Same as T3 plus risk of misdirecting data; control of access to data (products) generally based on personal identification by operations staff. Procedures to assure proper data handling must be available and strictly enforced.
T5	Consumer versus dedicated remote	Somewhat expanded threat because of substitution of automated methods of personal identification. Also must validate identity of terminals. Requires either physical access controls for terminal area or authenticated identification of user. Increased costs of administration to control physical access to terminals and/or authenticated identification method.
T6	Consumer versus shared remote	Same as T5 with increased opportunity to masquerade if identifier/authenticator is compromised. Risk of data misroute present.
T7	Producers versus dedicated systems	Producers constitute roughly the same threat as consumers except that they have the technical capability to siphon off data through corrupted programs. Degree of threat is a function of where they reside organizationally. If under same management control as consumers, threat is about the same as the consumer threat.

(continued)

T8	Producers versus shared batch	An increased threat to data over T7, but generally dependent on the operating system design. Can frequently spoof the operating system to gain unauthorized access to data.
T9	Producer versus shared remote	Same as T8 (and T7) except greatly reduced risk of exposure plus increased opportunity for anonymous bypass of masquerading depending on organization and physical set-up of remote sites.
T10	Servicer versus all systems	Maximum threat. Generally unrestricted access to any program or data on the system. Greater opportunty and technical capability to access data due to direct physical access to the computer system.

possible risks to informational assets would have to be created and studied on a system-by-system basis in order to identify access protection requirements.

Individuals and very small companies or offices need to identify their computer access risks in much the same manner as larger organizations. The answer to What do I have to protect? may be more a personal matter with the absence of legislative or regulatory constraints or external financial obligations.

Do not make the mistake, however, of disregarding the vulnerability of personal or home computers. The possibility of physical system theft or unauthorized physical access is significantly greater for these users. The problem is that the residence or small office can seldom afford the elaborate physical security measures usually taken by a large business enterprise or government agency.

However, the loss of important information might be even more calamitous to an individual or a small company. Consider, for instance, the impact of vital data or program loss to an independent consultant, a software company, an author, a teacher, or a physician. Adequate system backup, of course, would protect against many possibilities but would not be a solution to the harmful use of the stolen data by the perpetrator of the crime.

Losses from unauthorized logical access to such systems should also not be ignored. This is particularly true for small companies that keep sensitive financial inventory or other highly proprietary data on a computer.

More than one physician, for example, has realized weeks, months, or even years later that a trusted bookkeeper, who also happens to be in charge of the office computer, has absconded with enough money for the practice to incur a devastating loss.

The problem of unauthorized access to a small or personal computer may escalate significantly if, for some reason, it is connected to a communications network. Remote access by an unauthorized user to the database of an on-line personal or home computer can be damaging to all the other users of that network.

Even videotex systems are candidates for information security breaches.

Without encryption, or coding to prevent unauthorized access, there is little to prevent unauthorized message or transaction interception and even modification. Your videotex-oriented purchases or stock transactions may not be as confidential as you assumed. (It may not be confidential anyway if the videotex sponsor receives proprietary rights to all network transaction data for commercial exploitation.)

Another access problem with the personal computer is in its use as a stand-alone (i.e., no communications) system in an office in a large organization. Even if the physical security is adequate, access control may not be. The personal or small computer's programs and databases used by a scientist, engineer, or office worker for local processing can contain extremely sensitive applications and data. Unless locked up in a vault when not in use, the vital data can be accessed and compromised. Copying a floppy disk or transferring data from a fixed disk to a floppy disk is an easy task. The unauthorized modification of data or the addition of extraneous information to the file is not difficult either. Intentional sharing of the computer with others increases the possibility of unauthorized access.

A variation of the personal computer vulnerability problem that is becoming more common occurs when employees are allowed to take data or software home to perform some work on a compatible personal or home computer. Even if unauthorized communications access is not a problem, the potential problems of the office have now been moved to the home.

So, in general, the questions that should be asked about what needs to be protected are not determined necessarily by computer size, location, or communications capability. Access control is dependent upon the value of the information, its availability, and the importance of its integrity.

Finally, access control may be difficult and expensive to attain. However, the consequences of not giving it proper attention may be even more costly.

2. Vulnerabilities of User-Friendly Systems

Improvements in home computers, personal computers, personal workstations, communications networks, and related host computer functions are putting "computer power" into the hands of millions of new people every year. As a result, we are experiencing dramatic changes in the makeup of computer users and the amount of resources available to them.

User-friendly systems are produced by making specific improvements to hardware, software, and administrative procedures. The result is supposed to produce certain benefits for potential computer users. And, in fact, the new computer systems do produce significant benefits, not the least of which is a dramatic improvement in user convenience.

User convenience is a two-edged sword, unfortunately. Many problems of unauthorized computer access can be attributed to the extent to which systems are user-friendly. What is missing from the standpoint of security is a balance between user satisfaction and systems access control.

In order to justify the implementation of proper computer access control, it should be demonstrated that any reduction of user capabilities would be greatly offset by the benefits of having a safer and more secure system.

One way of doing this would be to identify the important benefits proclaimed for the new systems, the risks that might be associated with the benefits, and finally the security strategies that might help balance benefits, risks, and security costs (Figure 2-1). Viable security strategies will result from an overall appraisal of benefits and risks. The strategies will dictate the types of solutions, technical and otherwise, that should be implemented.

Increased Productivity and the Bottom-Line Peril

New information technologies and applications that promise increased productivity force management to focus on cost reductions and simultaneous profit improvements. Concurrent with new system implementation projects are new budgets. The budgets in a way are a form of justifying the cost of the new system.

21

System benefit	Peril resulting from benefit	Description of peril	Security strategy
Increased productivity	The bottom-line peril	The promise of increased productivity focuses attention on cost reduction, which means that budgets for security-oriented controls will not be given proper priority.	Some form of formal risk management programs should be initiated which includes the balancing of potential losses against security costs.
Ease of use	The convenience peril	Intentional elimination of internal controls in order to increase productivity or simplify user procedures.	System designs should be more carefully evaluated for security weaknesses before implementation.
Reduced complexity	The peril of invisibility	Many system functions are concealed from the users, resulting in their ignoring major security problems.	System users must understand enough about the functions and technical components of their system to appreciate the role they play in supporting system security.
Shared system savings	The people peril	Increase in number of people with computer and terminal access.	Users must be more involved in systems design and implementation in order to appreciate and correct for shared system weaknesses. They must take their "ownership" responsibilities more seriously.
System flexibility	The decentralization peril	Too much information resource for too few people with too little internal control.	More attention needs to be paid to adequate staffing, job separation, and size and location of remote offices in order to provide for adequate system security.
Reduced personnel requirements	The peril of uncertain responsibility	Poor job separation and no formal security function for small workstation, project, or office components.	Every terminal and computer location should have someone responsible for administering system security functions and responsibility.

Figure 2-1 Typical attributes and perils of a user-friendly system.

22

Adding new and additional system protection costs to these development and operating budgets is not particularly pleasant, and so our new system encounters the risk we call the *bottom-line peril*.

For example, when the banking community first examined the benefit of the automatic teller machine (ATM), certain cost improvements, such as the ability to process more customer transactions more conveniently, twenty-four hours per day, with fewer employees, had considerable influence on a bank's decision to automate.

Often, however, potential risks and system perils were not sufficiently analyzed; therefore, neither were the costs of needed security protection measures. Without fully considering necessary security protection measures, those who watch the bottom line (and competition) told the banks to go ahead with ATM.

Losses from abused ATM systems quickly hit the front pages. ATMs were conned, kicked, pried open, shot, and literally dragged off. Customer losses ranged from armed holdups at the ATMs to card thefts and more sophisticated forms of fraud and impersonation.

Improvements in security involved the "hardening" of the ATM, improving the generation, distribution, and use of the personal identification number (PIN), making the plastic card tamperproof, and adding some form of encryption, or coding, to both the communications line that carried transaction data and the "enabling bit" that was required for final approval of each transaction.

ATMs are now in common usage throughout the United States and in many other parts of the world. After a potentially disastrous introduction, financial institutions became more adept at balancing the improvements promised by new system technology with related risks, perils, and security costs. And, apparently, the cost of modifying the ATM systems to improve their security has not negatively affected either customers' convenience or the bottom line.

Security strategies to offset the bottom-line peril require that new system projects include a review of potential risks and security protection measures and costs. The implementation of some form of risk management program should be assured by proper budgeting. Profitability and computer system security are not incompatible.

Ease of Use and the Convenience Peril

System designers strive in almost every way possible to make computer systems easy to use. The assumption is that if less effort is required to use the system, the user will be more interested in utilizing the system.

The *convenience peril* refers to the intentional reduction of internal controls (including access controls) for the purpose of increasing productivity such as system throughput or turnaround time or of simplifying a user procedure. Designing systems strictly for user convenience can result in critical vulnerabilities such as the following:

• Poor password control (shared passwords or passwords that are too short, too easy to remember, or infrequently changed)

- Inadequate terminal control (vulnerable physical locations permitting unauthorized access or inadequate terminal identification procedures)
- Weak input and output controls, user authorization permission, or system and program change control
- Inadequate system backup or disaster recovery capability
- Poor audit capability including inadequate error reporting procedures
- Weak access control resulting from auto-dial/auto-log-on

Proper security strategies should compensate for the inclination to make systems overly convenient. Ideally, system designers should be required to consult with system users and management concerning areas where they believe they can trade off security and access control for convenience without jeopardizing system safety.

Reduced Complexity and the Peril of Invisibility

There is a strong tendency in the design of computer systems to mask or hide as many technical hardware and software functions as possible. This is done in order to reduce the user's perception of the complexity of the information system. Simplicity in design of user interface functions is also supposed to reduce user training and technical skill requirements.

This results in systems that contain many functions or technical capabilities of which users are never aware. The claim is that "what users can't see can't hurt them." The truth is that this type of system design can in fact come back to haunt both the users and the designers.

Specifically, the security or protection requirements for such system components as terminals, communications lines, passwords, networks, databases, and many other user interface functions may be highly dependent upon the "invisible" or "transparent" features of the system.

Ideal security strategies will not necessarily increase system complexity or require major changes to hardware, software, or communications components. User-oriented solutions require that the users participate in the system design process. Given understandable information on how technical system functions operate, users can then understand the justification for, and implementation and careful operation of, required internal controls, including the access control mechanisms.

Shared System Savings and the People Peril

The trend toward increasingly large numbers of people having some form of computer access is an important part of the "information revolution" now taking place. Even if only 50 percent of the U.S. work force will require computer access and know-how in their jobs by 1990 (as many experts predict), the growth in computer access is going to have profound effects on our society.

One of the effects certain to be of concern is: How shall we control unauthorized computer access when so many individuals will have the capability to do wrong? The very size of the potential problem makes it difficult to develop a clear perspective.

With personal computers selling at a rate in excess of 3 million systems per year, the potential growth of unauthorized computer access through dial-up systems becomes monumental. Will unauthorized access problems increase in proportion to the growth of user-friendly access that is being given to people? Nobody really knows the answer to this question.

A good security strategy with which to combat the shared systems or people-peril problem would be to initiate security planning as part of every system design and system acquisition project. In addition, computer users must learn to accept more responsibility in the future for the security of their own systems. Solving this problem will require a more careful analysis of which security and access control problems are primarily "people-driven" as compared to "technology-driven." The result should be the implementation of a combination of people-oriented administrative controls and technology-oriented computer and communications access controls.

System Flexibility and the Decentralization Peril

Decentralization of computer resources for efficiency and flexibility improvement results in more information access for more people. In addition, improvements in data communications, shared systems, and databases result in even further decentralization. A classic example of this is the *distributed system*, which includes a number of information processors that cooperate through message exchange facilities in order to improve information sharing and system capabilities. *Decentralization* requires the acceptance of more responsibility at remote computer and terminal locations. Unfortunately, the size of the organizations and the experience and educational qualifications of the people given these new responsibilities are often inadequate. This is particularly true with regard to information system access and other internal controls.

Security strategies to prevent unauthorized access and other forms of computer abuse at minimally staffed remote offices will require internal control principles applied in sound and yet ingenious ways. For example, job separation in a one- or two-person office can be a dilemma. In such cases the application of special technological developments such as positive user identification mechanisms, encryption, call-up and answer-back systems, TV monitors, and software security monitors might provide solutions. Another, but possibly less acceptable, alternative would be the reorganization or relocation of vulnerable offices to eliminate problems of inadequate job separation or insufficient numbers of qualified personnel.

Reduced Personnel Requirements and the Peril of Uncertain Responsibilities

Uncertain responsibility for computer security is a by-product of the decentralization problem. Small remote offices ordinarily cannot justify a trained full-time or even part-time system security officer. Asking operational employees to take on this function can succeed *if* the internal control—i.e., *job separation*—can be applied and if the demands of the office, including system access control, can be satisfied.

Security strategies that address this problem will also be needed for very large corporations. A remote computer or terminal location could be only as far away as the office down the hall or in a reception area. The primary solution to this problem is the elimination of uncertain security responsibilities by the implementation of a computer security awareness program for all employees. The physical protection of terminals, minicomputers, and internal communications lines as well as user identification codes and passwords should be the responsibility of all employees—both personally and organizationally. These solutions can and should be supplemented with various levels of security audits and, if appropriate, programmed controls at all available system resource locations.

Summary

It can be difficult and time-consuming to prove that certain computer user benefits or conveniences which may have to be given up can be offset by the advantages obtained from implementing better access controls. As a result, many organizations and computer users are in too much of a hurry and implement the latest state-of-the-art systems technology without allowing enough time to evaluate the accompanying risks or vulnerabilities. Even so, as we have seen, the losses sustained by many organizations from inadequate access control have had little effect on the continuing implementation of the latest computer products.

The array of available solutions to unauthorized system access are covered in other chapters in this book. Unfortunately, most of these safeguards can be compromised by the people who design, implement, or operate the system, *if* basic people-oriented controls are neglected. Both technical and administrative security and access controls require the education, assistance, and proper management of the people involved with the system if the result is to be a trustworthy system.

3. Trends in Computer Fraud and Industrial Espionage

There is a question of whether a crime perpetrated against or with the help of a computer system deserves a classification separate from the category often referred to as white-collar crime. The American Bar Association defines a *white-collar crime* as "any non-violent, illegal activity which principally involves deceit, misrepresentation, concealment, manipulation, breach of trust, subterfuge, or illegal circumvention" [FE 1978].

At present, even the authoritative Uniform Crime Report (UCR) published by the Federal Bureau of Investigation (FBI) does not distinguish computer fraud as being in a special crime category. We, therefore, do not have a reliable statistical base against which we can measure trends in computer abuse of a criminal nature.

Eventually, we will probably develop statistics by adding up the crimes prosecuted under the various state computer crime statutes (about twenty-three states now have such laws) and prosecutions under certain federal laws. Experts tell us that even these numbers will probably not indicate what is really happening, because the vast majority of computer-oriented or computer-associated crimes are prosecuted under existing laws covering such crimes as theft of property or trade secrets, embezzlement, and fraud.

In order to identify the trends in computer fraud and industrial espionage, three key problem areas related to the impact of unauthorized information systems access on computer-oriented crime must be addressed:

- The opportunity for computer crime
- The relationship between access control and computer crime
- Computer crime prevention planning

The Opportunity for Computer Crime

It has been clearly demonstrated that as more financial records are stored on computers, more computer-oriented crimes are committed. The reason for this is simple: Criminals simply go where the money is.

This observation is supported by many criminal justice experts. The only argument to this conclusion is that not only might financial records attract the criminally inclined but probably *anything* of value may command their attention. This includes trade secrets, proprietary software, or national security information.

The often repeated comment "computers don't steal, people do" is altogether appropriate. Therefore, what should our expectations be *if*:

- Fifty percent of the U.S. work force has computer knowledge and access by 1990.

- A twelvefold increase occurs in electronic mail messages between 1980 and 1995.

- We experience an annual increase in the installation of personal computers to approximately 3 million systems a year beginning now and continuing some years into the future. (This does not take into consideration increases in system upgrades, intelligent terminals, "dumb" terminals, minicomputers, and all forms of medium- and large-scale host computers.)

The point is that even if we do not have good statistical crime data upon which to base our expectations of computer abuse, we do have extremely reliable (if conservative) estimates of the number of new people who will have direct access to computers and data communications networks in the next decade.

If crime follows opportunity (and when does it not?), then the future should be a reflection of what has happened in the past and what is happening today. To help our extrapolation, let's examine a few of the published (or alleged) cases of computer crimes. Figure 3-1 contains a brief description of eight alleged computer crimes that took place between 1969 and 1973.

A review of the primary characteristics of these cases (and many others not included here) that occurred between the late 1960s and the middle 1970s results in the following observations:

1. The majority of early computer crimes were perpetrated by an employee of the organization.

2. Many of the computer crimes involved some form of physical or administrative security breach in order to facilitate or complete the compromise.

3. Only a few cases involved the compromise of some part of the data communications facilities of an information system.

4. In many instances the same procedures could be used to compromise systems today.

Computer Crimes of the Present

Figure 3-2 contains a sampling of computer crime cases reported by the national news media from 1981 to 1984. (Cases occurring between 1973 and

Date reported in media	Victim	Crime description and dollar loss, if identified	Nature of compromise	Problem source
June 1969	Bank	Overdraft on bad checks not reported: $1,357	Computer program was changed to prevent overdraft report	Bank computer programmer
June 1969	Brokerage company	Embezzlement: $250,000	Created unauthorized punched card input	Vice president
June 1969	Antipoverty agency	Phony payroll checks issued: $1.75 million	Print unauthorized payroll checks	Data center employee
September 1970	Bank	Misapplication of deposits: $5 million	Deposit manipulation and recycling of cashier checks	Bank president
March 1971	Service bureau	Unauthorized system use and data compromise	Time-sharing terminal and public telephone lines	Competition of a time-sharing service bureau
March 1971	Service bureau	Unauthorized removal of computer programs from system: $5 million suit	Time-sharing terminal and public telephone lines	Competition of a time-sharing service bureau
April 1973	Bank	Issued dividend checks to accomplice: $33,000	Input false information	Employee
July 1973	Computer manufacturer	Stolen trade secrets: $1.6 to $3 million	Copy information on new disk systems and sell to competition	Employee

Figure 3-1 Examples of alleged computer crime cases, 1969 to 1973.

Date reported in media	Victim	Crime description and dollar loss, if identified	Nature of compromise	Problem source
August 1981	Bank	Computer "kiting scheme": $21 million	Use access to computer terminal to generate illegal deposits and credits at branch bank	Conspiracy and embezzlement by bank operations manager
February 1982	College	Unauthorized use of local college computer time for personal gain: $200,000	Enter unauthorized work into computer	Illegal use of computer by data processing director
March 1982	Bank	Confidence scheme operated through Automatic Teller Machine	Conspirator requests ATM user to "test" adjacent terminal or explain that ATM being used is "out of order." Then card or data is manipulated	Conspirators con ATM user
December 1982	Federal Reserve System	Obtain confidential Federal Reserve information to aid private investment company recommendations	Attempt to use terminal at new employer's office to access former employer's computer database	Ex-employee attempts unauthorized access
January 1983	Automobile manufacturer	Operate gambling operation on employer's computer	Use word processing terminals to print football tickets and weekly results	Clerk-typists make unauthorized use of terminals and host computers
March 1983	Computer manufacturer	Important files containing vital technical development data was intentionally destroyed	Terminal used to insert unauthorized purge instructions into host computer system's software	Disgruntled contract programmer

July 1983	Federal food stamp program	Food stamp fraud: $150,000	Terminal used to approve food stamp applications left operational (i.e., logged on) during lunch hours	Unauthorized use of terminal by federal agency employees
November 1983	U.S. government agencies; numerous universities, research organizations	Destroyed or damaged several hundred accounts in the computer files: Estimate: "hundreds of thousands of dollars to reprogram"	Used a home computer to gain access to 14 ARPANET sites	Student sabotages important computer data files
November 1983	Savings and loan company	Six-month money market accounts manipulated: $145,000	Enter transactions into teller terminal that transfers funds from customers' accounts into a personal account	Employee a compulsive gambler
December 1983	County welfare agency	Authorize illegal welfare payments or kickback arrangement: $300,000	Enter illegal input transaction directly into host computer database	Fraud by government employees

Figure 3-2 Examples of alleged computer crime cases, 1981 to 1984.

31

1981 varied only slightly from those of the 1972 to 1973 period, except for an increase in terminal-oriented abuse.) Conclusions that might be arrived at from an analysis of Figure 3-2 include the following:

1. Unauthorized terminal access to computers is playing a more important role in systems abuse and computer crime.

2. Employees still seem to be the primary source of computer crimes, particularly those involving financial fraud.

3. There may be a trend toward computer crimes being committed by lower-level (organizational) individuals as opposed to being committed by executives or managers. (This is not verified, of course, because we are viewing only a small sample of the actual cases.)

4. Malicious activity (system sabotage) by students and others may be on an upward trend (but this would be difficult to prove without more verification).

5. Overall, it would appear that the trend in the last fifteen years has been toward proportionately more system compromise through unauthorized logical access and manipulation rather than unauthorized physical access.

Computer crime in the future will probably resemble computer crime in the past. The reason for this is that even if computer abuse is technology-driven, it still is primarily people-caused. Certain crimes may be easier to commit because of the computer's more advanced capabilities and the fact that computers are designed to be more user-friendly.

Three important areas of systems abuse are fraud, industrial espionage, and malicious acts of sabotage.

Fraud

Apparently, the more we look for fraud, the more we find. A government report says that there is an emerging consensus on computer fraud in government. The consensus is:

- Computer fraud and abuse do exist. Perceptions about the size of the problem, however, vary widely.

- No data exist which define the scope of the problem either in Government or the private sector, although case histories gathered by experts describe a variety of computer-related incidents.

- While no computer system can ever be entirely secure, most systems, particularly those with non-defense related applications, lack sufficient controls to afford an adequate level of protection from computer-related fraud and abuse. [CO 1983b]

The report concludes by recommending that investigative staff be trained in automated system controls in order to improve both the investigative process and the quality of recommendations for improvement.

Industrial Espionage

There seems to be a fine line between normally and legally acceptable methods for gathering business intelligence and the unethical or illegal acquisition of information on competition. We often lack clear definitions of what constitutes unauthorized system entry, data theft, personal corruption, or blackmail.

We have many laws that deal with the theft of tangible or physical assets. The unauthorized removal of intellectual property is another matter. Specifically, the possibility of punishment for crimes involving the theft of technical design concepts, plans, manufacturing know-how, and customer data is not clear.

Until recently, high-technology secrets, particularly in the areas of computer hardware and software, seemed almost indefensible. This seems to be changing somewhat with recent court decisions involving the theft of trade secrets from the electronics industry and related industries.

Malicious Acts of Sabotage

In terms of physical or financial damage, incidents such as that involving the 414s should not rate much attention. The real importance of such incidents, however, is the fact that the compromises demonstrated all too vividly the vulnerability of our advanced computer and communications systems.

The possibility of escalation is alarming: From the seeds of small and possibly harmless intrusions can grow real threats to the integrity and survivability of systems, products, businesses, and maybe even governments. The "ounce of prevention" theme is especially appropriate in a consideration of acts of sabotage.

Computer Crimes of the Future

What form might computer crimes take in the next five to ten years? On the basis of what has already been covered in this chapter, we can be reasonably certain of the following:

1. Increased access to personal computers, workstations, and intelligent terminals means that more unethical people will be inclined to "get in on the act." In essence, we can and should anticipate an increase in computer-oriented crimes (including malicious attacks) for economic, personal, and even political reasons.

2. As businesses, government agencies, and individuals have access to more powerful user-friendly systems, we will see far more sensitive and confidential data stored in computer databases. The targets will be more tempting. The result will be a need for improvement in fail-safe protection and access control to prevent an escalation in system compromises.

3. Our increasing dependence upon almost 100 percent system uptime and availability is going to make safeguarding and backup more critical than in the past. Attacks against systems in order to destroy all or part of their capabilities or to render them even temporarily unavailable to users will increase.

If the above is not enough to cause alarm, consider the additional problems we will probably experience as a result of trying to link almost everyone's computer with everyone else's (i.e., first the telephone and now the total communications utility). The advantages to culprits who may wish to compromise sensitive communications systems must be considered, especially since communications will most likely remain the weakest link in the majority of systems.

The Relationship between Access Control and Computer Crime

Unauthorized access to computers or communications systems is not a prerequisite to the commission of computer fraud or other criminal acts. On the other hand, people with perfectly legitimate access authorizations can and will perform fraudulent manipulations through computer systems. Once an employee, or insider, is given access to the system for whatever purpose, only four things prevent the person from attempting a nonauthorized or criminal activity. These are:

1. Fear of getting caught and receiving some form of punishment
2. Internal system controls implemented through administrative or automated procedures
3. Knowledge that careful exhaustive audits of past system activity are conducted
4. Accidental discovery, by another employee or administrator, of the crime before it is committed

The point is that once organizations grant the keys to the lock, the combination to the vault, the password, or permission to access data or other system resources, they must rely heavily on the basic honesty of individuals.

Access controls are designed not only to stop unauthorized access but to permit and control legitimate access by people to sensitive objects or system resources. Once given this access, the person can perform all the activities (and unfortunately sometimes more) that are possible within the available system environment.

Need for Overall Internal Control

Access control is one of the most important tools that can be used to implement overall internal control for the information system in order to prevent computer crime.

Unfortunately, many people regard internal control principles as something strictly out of the world of accounting theory. This is a mistake because there is nothing in the accounting books that says that internal controls must be implemented on only a manual, physical, or administrative basis.

Consider, for instance, the primary principle of internal control: separation of duties and responsibilities. This principle actually consists of two parts:

- No single individual must have responsibility for the complete processing of any transaction or group of transactions.
- The perpetration of a fraud must require the collusion of at least two individuals.

This principle can be implemented in many ways depending upon the nature of the computer applications and the hardware, software, and administrative environment that comprise the system.

Essentially, both logical and physical access controls, described in Part 3, should be considered as mechanisms that can be used to enforce the basic internal control principle. In many cases, the actual implementation will consist of a combination of hardware and software logic.

Computer Crime Prevention Planning

Probably the most important step an organization or an individual can take to prevent unauthorized system compromises from turning into major financial or personal disasters is to recognize that computer abuse is a dynamic, constantly changing problem. The mechanisms that can protect your system today may not be able to handle the risks of tomorrow. The reasons for this include the following:

- Changing technology results in new system implementations and therefore new vulnerabilities.
- Any defense a person can think of today, someone else, given enough time, may figure out how it can be compromised.
- Unless tight management control is exercised, employees may circumvent or disable security controls in order to eliminate what appears to be a nuisance or an unnecessary obstacle to getting work done.

Overcoming Obstacles to System Security

First, system users need to know what it is they need to protect and to review their conclusions periodically. They may need to remind themselves that any change (i.e., hardware, software, communications) they make to their system may require some form of new access control protection.

Second, users need to establish a set of guidelines for unauthorized access control procedures for prevention, detection, and correction.

Third, users need to make access control a design criteria or specification to be included with any change, addition, or deletion to their system. Access control should not be an afterthought if a system is really to be secure.

Fourth, users should document their access control plan for management budget approvals and for operational control and compliance reviews.

Fifth, system users should periodically test their system against their access control specifications.

Finally, users need to address the human-factor problem. They need to ensure that all employees, and others who might want access to their system, know the rules that have been established and the penalties for noncompliance or criminal behavior. [5]

Summary

Gradually, we can expect to see better computer crime data and statistics. Computer users cannot wait, however, for absolute proof that their information and communications system vulnerabilities are increasing before implementing protective measures.

A better approach is to assume that dramatic increases in access to computers and communications networks by more people will lead to an equally significant rise in computer fraud, industrial espionage, and possibly system sabotage.

In addition, even if we do not expect the basic nature of crimes (i.e., fraud, embezzlement, industrial espionage) to change, what will change is the possible seriousness of the compromises.

Vulnerabilities will probably increase as we see an expansion of more sensitive computer applications and system resource sharings. For example, the penetration of new systems used for electronic fund transfers, computer-aided design and manufacturing, word processing, and electronic mail will probably result in heavier losses than those experienced by the victims of earlier abuses.

Finally, system security and access control planning should be considered an ongoing activity. Computer abuse driven by constant technological change is a moving target. It must be challenged by an equally new and formidable security technology.

4. Personal Privacy and Data Access

Computer privacy refers to the concern that individuals have with regard to who might be given access to vital or sensitive information about themselves which is contained in a computer system. The terms *private* and *privacy* are used to distinguish data about individuals from data that is of primary concern to an organization. Protection of confidential data, trade secrets, and business or financial information would normally be classified as an organizational security problem.

People have many reasons to be concerned about how data regarding their personal lives is handled and made available to others. The accuracy, completeness, currency, and availability of personal data can have a serious and long-term impact on an individual's well-being and lifestyle. Consider, for instance, how data contained in computer files somewhere can influence a person's employment possibilities, or the ability to buy a house or a car, gain admission to a college or university, buy insurance, drive a car, fly an airplane, or even get elected to a political office.

In this chapter we are concerned with the access control problem of personal data for primarily four reasons:

- The consequences to an individual of unauthorized access to sensitive personal data
- The legal consequences to organizations and computer users of unauthorized access to personal data in information systems
- The changing international situation with regard to the communication of computer-oriented personal data across national borders
- Privacy concerns arising from a great increase in electronic fund transfers and home videotex systems

The Consequences to Individuals of Unauthorized Access to Sensitive Personal Data

It does not seem to be an exaggeration to say that there is probably very little about an individual's history and habits that is not stored in a computer somewhere.

People usually give up information about themselves to gain something of value (e.g., driver's license, employment, credit). In the past, this data, even when stored in computers, was generally inaccessible to other people unless they had a legitimate need to see it. The wide physical and geographic distribution of data generally protected from compromise most personal data.

There are many reasons why an individual might not want personal data such as salary, medical history, scholastic grades, asset records, or military service files made available to people (other than those to whom it was given originally) without the individual's consent. In the past, when most computer systems were either stand-alone systems or were not capable of much resource sharing or communications connections, the problem of computer privacy compromise was one of conjecture more than of fact. (There are exceptions, of course.)

Today the problem is much different, and most people already know this or will soon find out. Computer and terminal proliferation and extensive data communications connections not only make access to personal data easier but make its total access and integration much simpler.

The problem, therefore, grows from a personal problem to conceivably a major social issue. People may decide (legally) not to provide accurate personal data to businesses and government agencies. As a result, the basic services and benefits that would normally be derived from the exchange will be greatly constricted. The continual hassles over use of social security numbers and the proposed national ID card system are manifestations of this problem.

And where will all this lead, and what will it mean to individuals? The answer is that organizations and individuals have it within their capabilities to be discriminating and careful. Personal data that could be collected but does not have a high need or use priority should not be collected in the first place. Also personal data, when obtained, should be granted the same access control protection that the most valuable trade secrets or financial data receive. A balance can thereby be obtained between the value and sensitivity of data and the amount of protection provided for it. Most individuals would probably find it easy to cooperate under these circumstances.

The Legal Consequences of Unauthorized Access to Personal Data

Although there was no specific provision for "right to privacy" in the U.S. Constitution or Bill of Rights, numerous pieces of legislation granting such rights have been passed in the United States since 1970. Today there are many important legal precedents in the area of personal privacy. Furthermore the development of legislation regarding personal privacy has occurred not only in the United States but also in many other countries in the western world.

The impetus to provide legislation to protect the privacy of personal data was an outgrowth of two congressional hearings held in 1966 to 1967 to consider the establishment of a national data center for statistical research and to review the operations of commercial credit bureaus [WE 1972]. The following are just a few of the federal laws that resulted from these and subsequent hearings:

- Federal Privacy Act of 1974
- Freedom of Information Act
- Fair Credit Reporting Act of 1971
- Fair Financial Information Practices Act
- Bank Secrecy Act

Certain laws are addressed to government agencies, while others mostly affect commercial organizations such as banks, insurance companies, and credit bureaus. In addition to the federal laws, about thirty states have passed privacy and freedom of information laws and other statutes that relate to personal privacy.

A number of the statutes pose certain conflicts for some systems operators, such as how to comply with a privacy law and a freedom of information law at the same time.

A number of the laws carry severe civil and criminal penalties. For instance, laws that apply to agencies that maintain criminal justice records often prescribe jail sentences for people who allow unauthorized access to, or modification of, criminal justice records.

In addition to the above special-purpose laws, most commercial organizations are quite vulnerable to civil litigation depending upon the type of access they provide to their employment, salary, and personnel records.

The most important of all the privacy legislation passed in the United States thus far is the Federal Privacy Act of 1974. This legislation applied primarily to federal government agencies and private contractors who maintain information systems on behalf of the government. According to a government report:

The major provisions of the Privacy Act which most directly involve the use of a computer system/network control are Section 36 which limits the disclosure of personal information to authorized persons and agencies and Section 3e (10) which requires the use of safeguards to insure the security and confidentiality of records. In this context, the principal technological concern revolves around computer systems and networks which are shared by many users and where access to the system is provided though remote terminals. Although the Act sets up legislative prohibitions against unauthorized disclosures, technical controls are also needed to assure that the authorizations are properly invoked and that intentional or accidental violations of security and confidentiality do not occur.

These controls include techniques for providing positive identification of the authorized user of the system, authenticating his right to have access to specific data in a system shared by others and preventing him from gaining access to data or programs to which he is not entitled, and finally, providing a system of internal audits for monitoring compliance with the stipulated security and confidentiality requirements. In some cases involving the automated transfer of personal data between terminals and a computer system or among systems, the confidentiality requirements may be sufficiently strong to warrant the use of data encryption techniques. [CO 1975]

The following are the penalties that can be assessed for violations of the Federal Privacy Act of 1974:

1. Criminal Penalties. Any officer or employee of an agency, who by virtue of his employment or official position, has possession of, or access to, agency records which contain individually identifiable information, the disclosure of which is prohibited by this section or by rules or regulations established thereunder, and who knowing that disclosure of the specific material is so prohibited, willfully discloses the material in any manner to any person or agency not entitled to receive it, shall be guilty of a misdemeanor and fined not more than $5,000.

2. Any officer or employee of an agency who willfully maintains a system of records without meeting the notice requirements of subsection (e) (4) of this section shall be guilty of a misdemeanor and fined not more than $5,000.

3. Any person who knowingly and willfully requests or obtains any record concerning an individual from an agency under false pretenses shall be guilty of a misdemeanor and fined not more than $5,000. [PR 1974]

Nongovernment (i.e., private sector) computer system managers and employees who operate under contract a record system for a federal agency are equally liable to receive sanctions or penalties imposed by the act.

In addition to specific federal and state privacy-related laws, commercial or private organizations may be vulnerable to civil litigation, depending on how personal data is handled in the companys' internal information systems.

Almost all of the latest business information systems have vulnerabilities, according to an article by Professor Alan Westin.

In a recent national study he directed involving about 100 major companies, Westin found that: "About half of these are beginning to adopt security measures to protect sensitive office automation data from outside penetration. But in more than 90 percent of the organizations, management is not yet addressing the policy questions as to privacy and confidentiality that are arising as microcomputers are adopted for clerical, customer service, professional and executive activities in the office" [WE 1983].

In nine out of every ten organizations studied, it was found that management:

• Had not formulated policies specifying what data concerning the performance of individual CRT [cathode-ray tube] terminal operators should be collected and how any such records should be used for personnel purposes.

- Has not examined how personal computer record keeping might affect the organization's compliance with regulatory duties, anti-trust laws and other legal remedies.
- Is not periodically auditing or even sampling the data that employees and executives are putting into their machines.
- Has not issued confidentiality rules concerning data in electronic mail and message systems and has not issued explanatory literature or held training sessions to acquaint new groups of users with basic concepts of privacy protection for sensitive information. [WE 1983].

In general, Westin concluded that "office automation calls for many of the same rules of privacy protection that are required when organizations put sensitive personal data into DP [data processing] systems" [WE 1983]. The study, however, did reveal several very important differences between the earlier privacy violation vulnerabilities in the DP environment and the privacy threats of the new office automation systems. Four areas that seemed to need immediate attention include:

1. Professional and executive OA [office automation] applications are leading to data handling that can violate organizational and legal standards of data privacy. [One example noted by Westin was when end users, who can now decide exactly what data to put into a system, elected to mix "organizational data, personal data, and data from outside sources" in extremely dangerous ways.]
2. OA information is being handled by end users who do not understand principles of information sensitivity.
3. Information in OA files is often more finished, refined and sensitive than DP data.
4. OA creates new channels of information communications and distribution that can upset important confidentiality relationships. [WE 1983]*

Two examples of office automation applications that Westin thought extremely vulnerable to mishandling in the areas of data input, storage, and retrieval are electronic mail and word processing.

The Changing International Situation

There are tremendous worldwide political, social, and economic forces at work that are aimed at restricting the free flow of computer-oriented information between nations. The governments of individual nations and their various representative associations such as the United Nations, UNESCO, the International Telecommunications Union, the Organization for Economic

---

Cooperation and Development, the Council of Europe, the European Parliament, and the European Economic Community have been struggling for many years to resolve problems associated with computer data and its accessibility.

Personal privacy and the rights of citizens have been two of the most important issues since the transborder or transnational data flow was first recognized as a world force that required attention.

One of the first questions asked was: If it is important to protect access to personal data stored in a computer system within a country's borders, what about its accessibility from across the border? Although countries initially concerned themselves with the transmission of computer data recorded on magnetic tapes and other removable media, the problem escalated with the increased use of international communications facilities which communicate data directly to and from computers and terminals.

Although personal privacy and national security were the main topics discussed at the bargaining tables, other, and possibly even more significant, issues began to arise. Nationalism inspired countries to look more closely at the economic consequences. After all, isn't it true that countries which receive and process the most computer data acquire special advantages? Specifically, weren't they able to develop and build a stronger computer industry as a result of having to have more installations? And what about the number of people who received data processing training and the number of jobs created because there was more data to process? Also, how should a country react if it discovered it was at a competitive disadvantage because it could not access a class of demographic information from a foreign country that had access to similar data from within *its* borders?

The above arguments were important issues even to the countries that did not have the advantage of being able to accumulate important data about the businesses and social conditions in other nations.

Personal privacy was and still is a sensitive issue, particularly in Europe. Wars and, at times, coercive governments, have taken advantage of personal data record systems in the past. There is little wonder that European nations are gun-shy.

Fortunately, there has been cooperation, and realistic approaches have been taken thus far. It appears that most countries worldwide recognize that the free exchange of data, especially computer-oriented data, is to everyone's mutual advantage in the long run.

Free world trade is extremely dependent upon data exchange. The impact on foreign investment and trade could be disastrous if international companies were not able to rapidly acquire the latest data on employee performance, customer needs, and the financial status of their affiliate companies.

One of the most important results achieved to date is probably the agreement by the members of the Council of Europe to adopt the "Guidelines Governing the Protection of Privacy and Transborder Flows of Personal Data" [OE 1980]. Part Two, "Basic Principles of National Applications" (principles 7 to 14), clearly points out the member countries' awareness of the need for the free flow of personal data across national borders:

COLLECTION LIMITATION PRINCIPLE

7. There should be limits to the collection of personal data and any such data should be obtained by lawful and fair means and, where appropriate, with the knowledge or consent of the data subject.

DATA QUALITY PRINCIPLE

8. Personal data should be relevant to the purposes for which they are to be used, and, to the extent necessary for those purposes, should be accurate, complete and kept up-to-date.

PURPOSE SPECIFICATION PRINCIPLE

9. The purposes for which personal data are collected should be specified not later than at the time of data collection and the subsequent use limited to the fulfillment of those purposes or such others as are not incompatible with those purposes and as are specified on each occasion of change of purpose.

USE LIMITATION PRINCIPLE

10. Personal data should not be disclosed, made available or otherwise used for purposes other than those specified in accordance with Paragraph 9 except:

 a. with the consent of the data subject; or

 b. by the authority of law.

SECURITY SAFEGUARDS PRINCIPLE

11. Personal data should be protected by reasonable security safeguards against such risks as loss or unauthorized access, destruction, use, modification or disclosure of data.

OPENNESS PRINCIPLE

12. There should be a general policy of openness about developments, practices and policies with respect to personal data. Means should be readily available of establishing the existence and nature of personal data, and the main purposes of their use, as well as the identity and usual residence of the data controller.

INDIVIDUAL PARTICIPATION PRINCIPLE

13. An individual should have the right:

 a. to obtain from a data controller, or otherwise, confirmation of whether or not the data controller has data relating to him;

  b. to have communicated to him, data relating to him
   (i)   within a reasonsable time;
   (ii) at a charge, if any, that is not excessive;
   (iii) in a reasonable manner, and
   (iv) in a form that is readily intelligible to him;
  c. to be given reasons if a request made under sub-paragraphs (*a*) and (*b*) is denied, and to be able to challenge such denial; and
  d. to challenge data relating to him and, if the challenge is successful, to have the data erased, rectified, completed or amended.

ACCOUNTABILITY PRINCIPLE

14. A data controller should be accountable for complying with measures which give effect to the principles stated above. [OE 1980]

The struggle for equity (or advantage) with regard to the exchange of computer data through communications networks is far from over. International businesses and communications companies will need to lead the way in at least one important area, that is, information system security and access control.

Once international data exchange rules and laws are initiated and commitments made, governments will ensure that the parties involved comply with the agreement. Personal data protection and access control could easily be deciding factors for continued intergovernmental cooperation.

Privacy Concerns: Electronic Fund Transfers and Home Videotex Systems

New privacy legislation in the future will probably be in those areas where there is a heavy implementation of new communications and computer resource-sharing technologies. Areas that are particularly susceptible to legislation include electronic fund transfer (EFT) and home videotex.

As early as 1979, federal officials proposed the Privacy of Electronic Fund Transfer Act. The act proposed to apply regulations similar to the laws that protect mail and telephone calls. The proposed act would:

• Permit disclosure of transaction by an EFT service provider only to parties to the transaction; or government agencies with a court order.
• Forbid interception of a transfer except by government agents under court order.
• Provide criminal penalties for violations.
• Allow citizens to sue for damages caused by violations. [BL 1979]

Another area that is certain to require close scrutiny will be access to the private data communicated to and from home videotex users.

Videotex refers to the use of a home television set as a form of computer terminal. With the addition of a user keypad and an appropriate communications carrier (such as a telephone line), the TV set can be used to display data, instructions, and graphic presentations. This enables the user to complete numerous transactions at home which formerly required personal visits (e.g., a trip to the bank) or to exchange some form of oral or written communication. Videotex's major advantages are its speed, convenience, and potential cost savings to its users. Typical applications allow users to shop from their homes, pay bills, perform banking and investment transactions, and receive a wide assortment of special services such as stock quotations, bank statements, or special reports.

The two major vulnerabilities of videotex systems involve communications and computer record or database risks. First, since videotex systems are a form of electronic mail needing a carrier such as a telephone line, messages can potentially be intercepted or corrupted. Secondly, many videotex applications require the creation of data banks containing massive amounts of personal data.

Recently a company involved in getting into this business in a major way announced it was planning to claim proprietary rights to the data going through its facilities en route to or from the home user. It claimed that it would use the data for market research and customer prospecting.

In contrast, the Videotex Industry Association (VIA) developed a recommendation that would "limit service providers" the use of subscriber information and give subscribers the right to access and correct their records [KI 1983]. Guidelines were recommended that would apply to all subscriber records under the operator's control. The guidelines proposed that data on individual subscribers would be used for only five purposes:

- To provide service at the subscriber's request
- To maintain technical operations
- To prevent illegal or unauthorized use of the system
- To manage and operate billing and accounting systems
- To conduct market research in order to compile bulk information [PR 1983]

Summary

It is highly likely that we will see considerably more computer privacy-oriented legislation in the future, particularly laws that are directed at commercial organizations. The public has been sensitized to this issue. Wise information systems designers, operators, and users should, therefore, consider including access control over personal data records as a standard system specification and operational policy.

5. Trade-Secret Theft and Software Piracy

In previous chapters we have addressed the need for access protection for data, software, hardware, and communications facilities. Abuse problems have been examined from the standpoint of the injuries that might be sustained from data loss, manipulation, or unauthorized access and exposure. We have also touched lightly upon the need to protect computer programs (both system software and application) in order to preserve the proprietary rights of the owner.

In this chapter more light will be shed on the growing problem of protecting the right of ownership to computer programs. Three major questions relating to proprietary software losses will be addressed here:

1. How large is the problem?
2. What are the major risks to internal (nonmarketable) software?
3. What are the major risks to marketable software?

How Large Is the Problem?

The term *software piracy* came into vogue in the late 1970s with the implied meaning that there were people who would copy a legally obtained program rather than pay for a copy or create the program themselves. The term was usually applied only to the theft of marketable software. *Marketable software* refers to computer programs that are sold or leased for revenue-generating purposes, in other words, for a profit.

Nonmarketable software does not mean that the software is not valuable or that it cannot be marketed if and when the owner should so decide. Rather, the term *nonmarketable* implies that the software was developed for use primarily by an individual or within a specific organization. *Unbundled software*, i.e., software priced separately from the equipment it is designed to be used with, including application programs sold to customers by computer manufacturers, is considered to be marketable, as is software created by a software house with the intention of selling it to more than one customer.

47

Software, therefore, can be extremely valuable regardless of its marketability. In addition, the ownership of software conveys or implies certain proprietary rights. These rights are not unlike the rights to other classes of property.

When individuals or organizations are deprived of property rights, different types of legal recourse may be open to them. It is not within the scope of this book, however, to give legal advice. Suffice it to say that large financial losses can occur as a result of individuals or organizations being deprived of their legal rights to their software.

Software piracy or theft is an international problem today. We frequently read about the losses suffered by people or organizations at the hands of those who "legally" or otherwise steal, "borrow," copy, or in other ways duplicate proprietary software.

Piracy is normally distinguished from theft in that an illegitimate copy of a computer program is obtained from a legitimate, marketable (probably purchased) copy as opposed to a "copy" of a program having been physically stolen through some form of unauthorized or illegal access. The problem appears to be most serious in the area of illegal copying of microprocessor or personal computer software.

The amount of actual losses to date from illegal, or at the very least unethical, copying of proprietary software is not available. The frequent reporting of incidents in the news media and trade publications and information from other relatively reliable sources indicate a probable loss potential in the tens of millions of dollars a year.

A classic example of this loss potential was a reported incident where a computer disk that cost $2.50 containing $2 to $5 million worth of computer graphics was stolen at the American Institute of Architects' Convention in Phoenix, Arizona [CO 1984a]. The incident was reported by the owner of a Montreal company that had only recently started marketing building design information on computer disks. The software was developed for use by architects and engineers.

The owner also reported: "We have other copies, but what I'm afraid of is that someone will make copies and try to sell it. . . . Every computer-graphics company in the world would like to have software like this." When asked how the theft was accomplished, the owner replied, "It can be done in a matter of two or three seconds by opening a door on the disk-drive box and taking the disk out." The owner said he was a former professor of engineering, and that the software now represents 100 percent of his company's business [CO 1984a].*

A recent news report estimated that in 1984, "Americans will spend an estimated $65 billion on computers of all kinds. They will lay down an additional $16.2 billion for the software." It was also estimated that the majority of software sales in the country today are made to the government and industrial owners of mainframe computers. The proportion of software being sold for large versus small computers is about to change soon, however, according to the report:

---

*Reprinted with permission of *The Arizona Republic*.

While only $260 million worth was sold as recently as 1980 (to personal computer owners), sales this year (1984) are expected to reach $1.5 billion. At least 1,000 companies are making programs. . . . No one knows for sure how many programs actually exist; estimates range from 8,000 to 40,000. . . . Programmers, the people who write software, can find themselves millionaires at 20, but has-beens at 30. So-called pirates are stealing millions of dollars' worth of programs by copying them illegally. [WI 1984]*

In general, it appears that most of the losses resulting from the theft of proprietary software occur for the following reasons:

• To avoid paying legitimate costs
• To obtain a competitive advantage such as having software available for use sooner than it would be through legal or more acceptable means (internal development or a contract with a software house)
• To obtain trade secrets contained in the software logic
• To respond to a need for a challenge or entertainment

Going to court for legal redress can provide those who are successful with compensatory rewards. The avoidance or prevention of software theft in the first place, however, would obviously be of greater advantage to most individuals and organizations.

What Are the Major Risks to Internal (Nonmarketable) Software?

Compromise or outright theft of proprietary software has plagued the data processing industry and computer user organizations since the first computer programs were written. The implementation of either a new software system or a new application program usually gave an organization a competitive advantage over its competitors.

Companies that had much to lose from the compromise of important software recognized this problem quite early. A very lax atmosphere in which computer programmers could do little wrong and could and did move around from company to company with great ease made it extremely difficult for companies to protect proprietary programs. Some more enterprising programmers even went so far as to set up their own companies in the same business because they were able to avoid the startup expense of writing new software.

Victimized organizations realized that because of the complexity of the new technology and the lack of specific laws, it would be very difficult to successfully prosecute on civil or criminal charges. However, even when

---

grounds for legal action presented itself, the possibility of bad public relations or exposing management neglect made organizations avoid public prosecution and take their losses as one of the normal risks of doing business.

Growth in computer installations, including the implementation of increasingly more sensitive applications (i.e., geophysical studies, design optimization, forecasting, and business planning models), resulted in greater awareness by corporations of the need to protect their programs. The fact that their annual investment in these programs was growing far beyond expectations helped management decide to move beyond simply recognizing the problem to finding solutions for it.

In the earlier batch systems, adding physical securities such as opening briefcases and locking up the computer room and the media library were reasonably effective precautions, unless programmers were allowed to take work home (as they usually were). With the advent of time sharing and communications terminals (also taken home), the battle was on. On one hand, companies had more invested and therefore more to lose. On the other hand, how could they maximize their investment if they restricted computer access time to their programmers?

What has been said about programmers here is not necessarily meant to imply that a company's own computer programmers are the major source of software theft problems. Yet, until quite recently, the distinction between software theft and the "coincidental" creation of an almost identical program was very confusing. Blame was often directed at a programmer who had less than honorable intentions.

The picture became a little brighter as a result of court cases where juries declared purloined software to be "theft of trade secrets" and, therefore, clearly a punishable offense. The only difficulty was it had to be proved that the software was in fact treated like a secret. Unfortunately, programs which had been publicly discussed, demonstrated, or bragged about at computer conferences failed the test.

Of course, the management attitude of different companies regarding the need to protect their software and trade secrets varies considerably. As an example, an executive in a major corporation recently said that "my company is not concerned about the theft of our proprietary software because our major competition doesn't need our programs. They have their own." At a later moment, he conceded that he did not have quite the same opinion about some of his company's "lesser and more independent rivals." Unfortunately, regardless of whether this gentleman's opinion was right or wrong regarding the ethics of his rival companies, his legal responsibility to safeguard his company's assets has not been adequately considered, nor has the potential loss his company might suffer if he should be wrong.

Many attorneys now believe that trade-secret laws provide the best protection for certain classes of software. Software (particularly internally used software) can be a trade secret if reasonable measures are taken to keep the program code and documentation secret. In addition, any information (including software) that is used in a trade or business in secrecy, that is not generally known, and that is useful in competition is eligible to be a trade secret.

This position confirms that there is a need to provide adequate access control for proprietary programs that are in themselves both valuable company property and trade secrets. A company interested in obtaining the maximum protection possible for its huge software investment (and related competitive advantages) can probably do so best by implementing and maintaining its software under conditions of secrecy. The use of access control mechanisms and procedures to protect proprietary software in all forms of computer media becomes mandatory.

In addition, trade-secret protection can be used even when proprietary software is being written for, leased to, or exchanged in some way with other companies through appropriate legal contracts. The purchaser, for instance, can agree not to make unauthorized copies, and not to bootleg or divulge the contents of the program. Software producers can therefore be required to maintain secrecy for programs that reside in their facilities, or in their computer systems. They might also then be responsible for the maintenance of adequate access control while the software is in their systems.

It is important to note that the content of trade-secrecy laws may vary considerably in the statutes of different states. In addition, the handling, storage, exchange, and protection of source code versus object code have been interpreted at times in different ways. It becomes important, therefore, to seek competent legal advice in these matters.

What Are the Major Risks to Marketable Software?

The illegal copying of commercially marketed software is an act which deprives the owner(s) of certain legal rights. Theoretically, it doesn't matter if one copy or a thousand copies are made. Each illegal copy has the potential of depriving the rightful owner or owners of the income or other benefits that might have been theirs, if the illegal copy had not been generated.

One news report quoted the general counsel of a major U.S. software house as saying that "as many as 20 fraudulent copies of a program (one of their more popular word processing programs) may be made for every one sold" [WI 1984]. Other reports claim that the illegal copying of microprocessor or personal computer software is in the 30 to 40 percent range.

Since software piracy is in fact a form of theft of intellectual property, why is it tolerated? How much does it really cost, and what can be done to stop it?

Why Is It Tolerated?

The first claim as to why so much software is copied is that software is so expensive to obtain that people are justified in trying to acquire copies at little or no cost. Some claim that the amount of copying being done today does not have that much financial impact on the rightful owners (i.e., they can afford the losses). Others claim that software copying is necessary to archive the program or to provide backup in case it is accidentally destroyed. The ultimate claim seems to be that anything you do in your home is your own business, so long as you don't try to sell the copied software to other people.

In truth, software theft is tolerated because it appears to be very hard to stop. It is believed that so much of it is going on today that the judicial system could not handle the volume of cases that would be involved with wholesale prosecution of offenders. How about discriminatory prosecution of those most guilty of commercial exploitation? Where illegal profits and large financial losses can be proved in specific cases, litigation seems to work. In any case, the economics of going to court and the difficulty in obtaining proof of loss are major considerations, and can be stumbling blocks to legal action.

In addition, our social system seems to find it difficult to successfully prosecute young individuals for civil or criminal crimes, who for all other purposes do not engage in unlawful acts other than occasionally making a copy of a computer game or a word processing package for a friend.

Maybe we tolerate the problem of software theft because under our present legal system we are not really prepared to do anything about it. Perhaps the answer lies elsewhere.

How Much Does It Really Cost?

The numbers themselves may be deceiving. What are a few million dollars, more or less, to the computer software industry? The answer: The loss is considerable. Consider, for instance, the overall impact upon large and small companies and individual entrepreneurs of being deprived of legitimate profits or even cost recovery of a growing number of their new software product offerings. What can happen to their incentive, as well as their ability, to stay in business?

The real cost of software piracy can be the devastation of a very important industry in the United States, and, as has happened in many other industries, added costs from white-collar crimes are simply passed on to customers in higher prices. Eventually, the price gets too high, fewer people buy the product, and then fewer companies enter and compete in the business. Then, foreign competition steps in.

To avoid crippling this important industry in the United States, we cannot afford to ignore this problem. However, if more civil and criminal action in our courts is not the answer, then what is?

What Can Be Done to Stop It?

A good approach would probably be to carefully distinguish commercial piracy and exploitation from the noncommercial acts of individuals in their homes. Laws are needed that would facilitate the successful prosecution of the heavy commercial abuser while dealing in a discriminating fashion with individuals. (Although there are those who claim the unethical personal computer owner or hobbyist is just as dangerous, if not more so.)

Everyone needs to take the matter of software piracy more seriously. Even the software companies and individuals being exploited seem to lack the necessary dedication to take effective action. Their main defense thus far seems to be the packaging and selling of software to users under licensing agreements as opposed to outright sales.

In particular, consider the industry's approach to providing access protection for removable media (i.e., floppy disks, cassette tapes, cartridges) upon which the software is *fixed* or reproduced.

Numerous companies have entered the market in the past several years with access control products designed to reduce software theft from removable media such as floppy disks. Many copy-protection schemes make use of nonstandard disk formats to make it difficult or even impossible for the casual user to copy a program.

Although no ultimate solution has been adopted by the software industry, most of the innovations seem to work with varying degrees of success. Antagonists to these inventions and products say that if the access protection systems can be compromised in any way, or if they are too costly or inconvenient, their use cannot be justified.

This is probably a defeatist attitude, which does not give the new protection systems a chance to work. Granted, if a protection system is so weak that the average home user or personal computer expert can override it, its protection value would be minimal. On the other hand, many innovative (but not always inexpensive or flexible) protection systems for microcomputer or personal computer software are available. Figure 5-1 is a brief overview of the main features of a number of these protection systems.

The fact that the software industry itself may not be taking these new protection systems seriously is, of course, part of the problem. As an example, a computer magazine article says: "Piracy is estimated to cost software developers millions of dollars in lost revenues, and efforts are under way to develop hardware-embedded protection for commercial programs. But there appears to be no demand for the products as yet" [FE 1984].*

A potential customer for software protection said in response that, in his opinion, "software vendors that do adopt the system (hardware-embedded protection) will be limiting their market, since software protected by that method will only run on what will initially be a few machines." The executive concluded with the opinion that "the only type of protection that is unbreakable is a hardware scheme" [FE 1984].

The answer to an important part of the software piracy problem, therefore, may be the incorporation of better protection mechanisms into new personal and home computers that will run software. But then, what about all those other millions of personal computers out there that have already been delivered and are also markets for new software? Obviously some compromises will have to be made. And some software may have to be withheld from markets that offer exploitation potential.

Another proposed solution to software piracy is that software companies will eventually raise their prices to compensate for revenue losses from

---

*Copyright © 1984 by C W Communications/Inc., Framingham, Mass. Reprinted from *Computerworld*.

Protection method	Hardware- and/or software-oriented	Protection method description	Compromise potential
Basic software protection	Software	Uses software to record areas of a legitimate disk differently from a normal diskette. Normal operating system routines are not able to read the disk, and most users are prevented from copying the software.	May be compromised by use of special software copy routines.
Combination hardware/software protection devices and systems	Hardware and software	Assures that each software license sold permits only one executing copy of the software package. Even if an unauthorized copy is made, it will run only on the computer that contained the special hardware/software protection device. Product "device" is installed either as a black panel slip-on or as a board requiring one memory I/O slot. Protection is initiated by a specially encoded software package that accompanies the hardware.	Effective protection against all but experienced hardware and software compromise efforts.
Physical imprint or "fingerprint" on floppy disk	Hardware and software	Special code is recorded in surface material of disk when the disk is inserted in drive. A special subroutine appended to the software packages searches for the fingerprint. If it can read the code, then the program can be run on the microcomputer. If not, it cannot be read.	Casual copying should be quite difficult. Special sophisticated equipment would be required to compromise the disk. Other users in same office or area can share code/key.
Electronic key devices	Hardware and software	A special code-generating device must be pointed at the CRT or monitor to run the software.	Physical compromise of key entry devices and user password sharing.

54

Method	Type	Description	Comments
Insertion of hidden passwords (and copyright notice)	Software	Hidden passwords and copyright notices can be inserted to prohibit listing or printing a program. Converts a program in ASCII form to a protected version, and saves a program on the same disk under a new name selected by the user.	May be compromised by an expert systems programmer. Insertion of copyright notice may be of little protection value unless the identification of the user and the events associated with the copying can be proved.
"Time bomb" protection	Software	Instructions included in software package to control the trial use of a program or its periodic license renewal.	Unauthorized modification or disarming of the time bomb instructions possible.
Computer hardware serial number encoding	Hardware	A serial number or special ID code is introduced into the computer hardware to control whether or not the machine can run a specific software package.	Possibility of transferring serial number or special ID into another computer.
Encryption	Hardware and/or software	Enciphers a stored program so symbol names for variables, labels, defined functions, and subroutines are deleted from the program listing.	Can be compromised by obtaining key or breaking encryption method.
Special duplication tape system	Software	Prevents duplication of programs stored on tape cartridges so they cannot be copied or run unless the original tape is also present.	Unauthorized copying of original tape.
Special software and instruction manuals	Documentation	Special instruction manual must be used to run the software.	The special instruction manual can be copied, but at added cost.

Figure 5-1 Protection methods for microcomputer or personal computer software.

piracy. This is a solution of limited value because what will happen if there are not enough customers who can afford the price of the software to assure its profitability? Even though we have seen many cases where white-collar crime and pilferage resulted in increased consumer costs without a disastrous economic consequence, there is no evidence that the software business will have the same experience.

The problem of software protection is also complicated by the way the present laws treat licensing agreements. The following is an example of this problem: "Aside from the ambiguity in its definition, the issue of software piracy is further confused by the software licenses implicitly accepted by those of us who buy microcomputer software. Those licenses typically stipulate that it is a violation of the license agreement to use the software on more than one machine, even if those machines are personally owned by the buyer and used by no one else. . . . It is apparent that the current copyright laws are not always relevant to computer software" [MA 1984].

In the meantime, software owners must seek competent legal advice to ensure that they are protected as fully as possible under existing trade-secret and copyright laws.

Summary

Gradually, new laws will be passed which will provide better protection for software owners and producers. However, for now and for some time in the future, we must continue to rely heavily upon the protection provided software owners by current laws and by the use of access protection technology and procedures, which are rapidly improving and which will offer excellent possibilities for the future.

Establishing a
System Security
Policy

COMPUTER SECURITY AWARENESS PROGRAM

PLANNING PHASES

LOGICAL ACCESS CONTROL PLAN

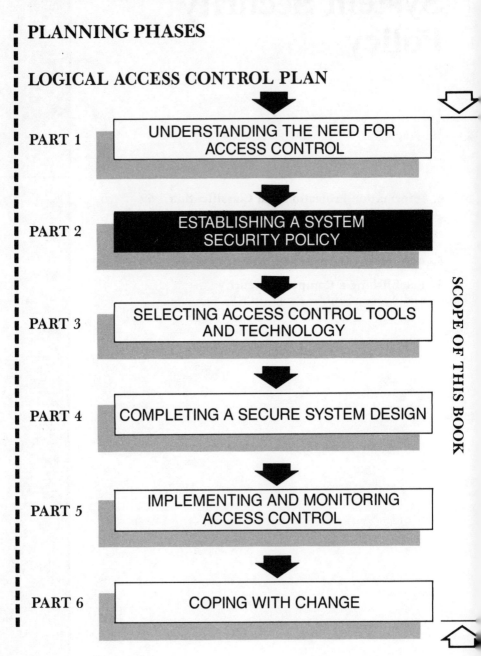

PART 1 — UNDERSTANDING THE NEED FOR ACCESS CONTROL

PART 2 — ESTABLISHING A SYSTEM SECURITY POLICY

PART 3 — SELECTING ACCESS CONTROL TOOLS AND TECHNOLOGY

PART 4 — COMPLETING A SECURE SYSTEM DESIGN

PART 5 — IMPLEMENTING AND MONITORING ACCESS CONTROL

PART 6 — COPING WITH CHANGE

SCOPE OF THIS BOOK

6. Information Protection and Classification

An *information classification activity* is usually the result of a careful analysis of an organization's data and its value—both to the enterprise and to others (i.e., competitors). While most large organizations and government agencies implement formal *data classification systems* (i.e., a written policy identifying the various classes of sensitive data and appropriate access authorization), smaller businesses and agencies tend to get along with rather informal information classification policies. Sometimes these policies are not even documented, but their existence is understood by employees.

Computers and data communications have greatly increased the need for a more formal approach to data classification by most organizations, including very small ones. An organization's data classification system provides the criteria and rules that help to establish the operating requirements for both its manual and automated access control system. Therefore, a careful study of information classification requirements in an organization will result in appropriate and effective access rules. In this chapter we will examine how this can be accomplished by addressing the following key questions:

- What information needs to be protected?
- How are information classification categories established?
- What are the important relationships between commercial and government or military data classification systems?
- How important are classification marking procedures to computer users?

What Information Needs to Be Protected?

Generally, it is good business to maximize profits and avoid giving the competition any unnecessary advantage. Information should not be divulged that could have a negative impact on the organization's operation. This is clearly a responsibility of management.

In addition, management guidance is required to avoid the pitfalls of too much security (overclassification) as well as too little security (underclassification). Management must recognize the value of all organizational data and set policy with regard to its protection. Some data is clearly of a sensitive nature, such as manufacturing and marketing data and financial plans and results. The protection of trade secrets should be a designated responsibility for both management and employees.

Other data, which is probably the bulk of an organization's information, may or may not be sensitive. Sometimes only the originator of the data will know if certain data is really sensitive. Under such conditions, management policy (i.e., a data classification policy) might specify that the particular person who originates the data should be the one to determine its level of classification or sensitivity.

A considerable amount of organizational data may appear to be of a relatively benign or nonsensitive nature. The tendency may be not to classify such data in order to avoid unnecessary expense or inconvenience to employees, customers, and others. Many organizations believe that this type of data management could in itself be a problem, because a lack of control of certain organizational data could lead to unexpected and perhaps harmful results.

To begin with, data that has not specifically been identified as available for full public release may not yet have been adequately screened. In addition, there is the question of *who* should give the data to an outsider. A well-developed data classification program would include policies and procedures to cover these requirements.

For instance, if the policy stated that all organizational data *except* that which has been specified as nonrestricted (because it has been published in public media or in advertisements) can be released only by authorized individuals, uncertainty in this area would be significantly reduced.

Another problem that a good data classification system will address is the difference between *data* and *information*. Up to this point the two words have not been differentiated in this book since common usage tends to allow for their interchangeability or equivalency. In this chapter, for example, the terms *data classification* and *information classification* are used interchangeably.

However, there can be considerable differences in sensitivity between purely raw data and information. *Raw data* implies that there has been little or no prior relating of the data to other data. *Information*, on the other hand, implies that as a result of some form of data reduction, structuring, analysis, or other conditioning, the data now represents some higher form of meaning or intelligence than before the particular data was processed or converted into information.

The classic example of the difference between data and information as often discussed in the intelligence community (both military and commercial) is how so much data or information which is released and published of a nonsensitive nature "suddenly" becomes sensitive because of its relationship to the whole. In other words, when enough unrestricted data is released, secret or proprietary information may be exposed through the process of association and analysis. Therefore, a good classification system will have carefully specified levels of sensitivity for all organizational data and a clear policy regarding who can classify, declassify, and release data and how this can be accomplished.

Legal Requirements

Many organizations, including both commercial enterprises and government agencies, are obligated or required by law or regulation to protect access to certain categories of data contained in their files or operational locations. Certain laws may even include the opposite requirement—the obligation to release certain data. In general, legislation and government regulations contain legal requirements that tell businesses and government agencies what data they must protect and what data they must release and the conditions and exceptions associated with protection and release.

The study of just a few pieces of legislation, such as the Security Exchange Act of 1934, the Fair Credit Reporting Act, the Privacy Act of 1974, the Bank Secrecy Act, or the Federal Foreign Corrupt Practices Act of 1977, will demonstrate the variety and potential of this legislation. Legislative or regulatory requirements (i.e., a legal requirement to protect or release data) have an impact on many aspects of life in the United States today. Furthermore, the criminal and civil penalties specified by such legislation should be sufficient to attract the attention of executives in both business and government.

What does all this have to do with computers and data communications systems? The answer is: A great deal! Pleading ignorance may result in only a minimal reduction in a fine or a sentence if the violation happens to be based upon a fifty-year-old law that applies to every information system relevant. The fact that the violator's system was only recently converted to a state-of-the-art computer and database management system will probably fall on deaf ears. Information protection classification and access control requirements should apply equally to both manual and automated information systems.

How Are Information Classification Categories Established?

The ideal data classification system would perfectly match protection and control features to data sensitivity requirements. Absolute perfection in this area is not about to be achieved, however, because of the extreme subjectivity of the problem (i.e., five different people might each classify differently a particular piece of data or information. Required for most organizations is a simplified procedure that will support the changes that need to be made continually to an information classification system.

One such recommended approach, called the *model protection program*, includes the following basic concepts:

- Information should be established as an asset which is the property of the organization and is not to be used or disclosed outside of the organization without prior management approval.

- Information which has not been specifically classified by organizational policy should be classified by the originator, as he/she should be best able to make the classification decision.

- Information should be disseminated within the organization on a need-to-know basis. [KO 1980]

This approach would directly involve every executive and employee of an organization in the data protection and classification program. A condition of initial employment should include the signing of a nondisclosure agreement by all new employees. This agreement and a clear explanation of the organization's data classification program plus a personal copy of the employee data classification manual would make every new employee aware of his or her responsibilities in this area.

Another part of the model protection program addresses the classification, or data sensitivity, labeling requirement. The recommendation is that sensitivity labeling, or classifying, include three major categories plus three subcategories. It is believed that by minimizing the number of different levels and classes of sensitive information, there will be less confusion in the process of making classification decisions.

The major classification categories include:

- *Restricted*: A subset of the valuable information belonging to an organization that is thought to have quantifiable value outside of the organization (i.e., to competitors).

- *Sensitive and/or confidential*: Consequences of its theft, misuse or improper disclosure, while significant to the organization, would certainly be far less serious . . . than *highly confidential* classified data.

- *Highly classified*: A small grouping of one to two percent of the information which is highly sensitive or confidential, and whose loss, misuse or improper disclosure would have a substantive negative impact on the organization. Most of this type of information is either time-sensitive or highly valuable technology. Typically, pre-announcement information concerning major reorganizations or personnel changes, acquisitions, divestitures, earnings and dividends, or information about long range plans, or high value proprietary processes would fall in this category. [KO 1980]

By the above definitions, restricted data might include up to 90 percent of an organization's information. Restricted data would also include both the categories of sensitive and/or confidential data and highly classified data. The sensitive and/or confidential category might comprise about 20 to 30 percent of the restricted data. Highly confidential data would probably constitute only 1 to 2 percent of the restricted data.

Most organizations that maintain data classification systems utilize the above three-part classification scheme with relatively minor variations. One variation is a subcategory for the sensitive and/or confidential category.

- *Business confidential*: For administrative and financial matters not related to employees.
- *Personal or personal and confidential*: For all administrative, financial, medical and other employee-related records.
- *Proprietary or technical confidential*: For trade secrets and technical information. [KO 1980]

It is believed that the main objective of this second set of categories is to establish special procedures in order to limit the distribution of information to certain groups of employees.

What Are the Important Relationships between Commercial and Government or Military Data Classification Systems?

Many organizations supplement their classification system with a concept referred to as *need to know*. In a way, all classification systems are based to some degree on this rather basic concept or premise: If you need certain information to do your job, then you should have access to it.

Major application of the basic need-to-know data classification concepts moved from U.S. Department of Defense agencies into U.S. industries as a result of their need to comply with defense contracts that involved classified military data.

To help industries meet their classified data protection requirements, the U.S. Department of Defense publishes the *Industrial Security Manual for Safeguarding Classified Information* [IN 1983]. This manual, often called the ISM, is a valuable source of information on good data classification and protection procedures generally required by defense contractors. This manual should be of assistance to any organization initiating a data classification system.

Included in the ISM are instructions on how to clear people who will be authorized to access sensitive government data and how the data itself should be classified and protected. The following definitions from the ISM are particularly appropriate to our discussion of classification systems:

- *Authorized persons*: Those persons who have a need-to-know for the classified information involved, and have been cleared for the receipt of such information.
- *Classified information*: Information or material that is (i) owned by, produced by or for, or under the control of the United States Government; (ii) determined . . . or prior orders to require protection against unauthorized disclosure; and (iii) so designated.

• *Need-to-know*: A determination made by the possessor of classified information that a prospective recipient, in the interest of national security, has a requirement for access to . . . , knowledge of, or possession of the classified information in order to perform tasks or services essential to the fulfillment of a classified contract or program approved by a User (Government) Agency. [IN 1983]

The ISM defines three primary classification designations for government data:

• *Confidential* is the designation that shall be applied to information or material the unauthorized disclosure of which reasonably could be expected to cause damage to national security.

• *Secret* is the description that shall be applied only to information or material the unauthorized disclosure of which reasonably could be expected to cause serious damage to national security.

• *Top secret* is the designation that shall be applied only to information or material the unauthorized disclosure of which reasonably could be expected to cause exceptionally grave damage to the national security. [IN 1983]

It is interesting to note the similarity between the data classification terminology used in both the commercial and government spheres:

COMMERCIAL	ISM
Restricted	Confidential
Sensitive/confidential	Secret
Highly classified	Top secret

The ISM use of the term *restricted* appears only where reference to nuclear or atomic weapons is made.

Need-to-know terminology in both industry and government applies to all categories of data and allows for numerous additional categories of data sensitivity. Most classification systems, therefore, allow for multiple levels of need to know for a particular individual, depending on his or her job or project.

Also, Section XIII of the ISM, "Security Requirements for ADP Systems," contains recommendations pertaining exclusively to the protection of automated information systems. This section describes many valuable procedures that can be used to protect access to heavily shared systems or systems that must operate under different levels or modes of security.

The manual relates the multilevel security problem to the need for security modes. It says that "the ADP security mode refers to authorized variations in the security environments and methods of operating ADP systems that handle classified information. The modes are primarily defined by the manner in which the basic access requirements for user personnel security clearance and need-to-know are implemented in an ADP system. The modes involve a varying mix of automated (i.e., hardware/software) and conventional (i.e., personnel, physical, administrative/procedural and, where appropriate, communications) security measures and techniques in discharging these basic access requirements" [IN 1983].

Altogether, the ISM lists three approved levels of processing or security modes:

1. *Dedicated security mode:* Operating in a dedicated security mode where all users with access to the system have both a security clearance and need to know for all classified information then contained in the system. . . .

2. *System high security mode:* Operating in a system high security mode where all users with access to the system shall have a security clearance for the highest classification and most restrictive type(s) of information then contained in the system, but at least some users do not have a need-to-know for all classified information then in the system. . . .

3. *Controlled security mode:* Operating in a controlled security mode where at least some users with access to the system have neither a security clearance nor a need-to-know for all classified information then contained in the system, in a manner that the cognizant security office or higher authority has determined will achieve and maintain the degree of security that is consistent with this manual. This mode provides a limited capability for the concurrent access to and utilization of the ADP system by users having different security clearance and need to know. [IN 1983]

In general, most commercial data processing users tend toward the third category of protection: the controlled security mode. Exceptions, however, do exist; for example, even strictly commercial organizations might run a program or operate on data that is so sensitive their system will be dedicated to solely one user or one program. Under these conditions all other users, including their own communications facilities, will be denied system access.

Obviously, there is a significant added cost for restricting system access as recommended by the ISM in order to enforce a system for data classification and related personnel clearance. Indeed, for primarily this reason the U.S. Department of Defense has spent tens of millions of dollars during the past fifteen years researching technological solutions to the problem of multilevel secure access (i.e., secure operating systems). This subject will be discussed in Part 3.

How Important Are Classification Marking Procedures to Computer Users?

A critical part of any classification system is the *marking*, or physical labeling, of the documents or media containing the sensitive data. The huge amount of paper output from computer printers plus the large number of electronic storage devices and media makes proper classification marking a real challenge. A good classification system must also include all data that can be viewed from a terminal, workstation, or personal computer.

Basic rules for classification marking are fairly simple, but are not always easy to implement and maintain. Without a reliable classification marking procedure, however, the entire system is faulty.

Hard-Copy Marking

There are many variations of the rules for marking or labeling classified documents or printouts in order to control their access. A good marking procedure will specify the following:

- Overall classification on the front cover, title page, first page, and back cover of a document
- Special warning notices, as required
- Special access markings, as required
- Marking of each portion to eliminate any doubt as to classification level
- Identification of all classified and unclassified data within the document
- Marking of every portion with its highest classification or appropriate mark if it is unclassified
- Marking of each portion immediately following its identification or designation number, if any

MAGNETIC MEDIA (fixed and removable)

- Removable machine-readable media should be kept in containers clearly labeled with the contents' classification and downgrading markings.
- Magnetic classification labels should be internally recorded at the beginning and end of each reel or disk (including each data file or program where multiple files or programs exist).

MISCELLANEOUS INPUT AND OUTPUT

- All punched cards, paper tape, or other encoded input and output media should have beginning and ending classification labels (i.e., first and last punched card).

VIDEO-SCREEN OUTPUT

- All data or files accessible from terminals, workstations, or personal computers must be internally labeled in such a way as to display on the user's screen the correct classification of the material being viewed.

Classification labeling or marking is an important, but often neglected, procedure. Correct and consistent classification marking is essential if individuals are to be held accountable for the security of the data that passes through their hands or before their eyes.

Summary

A comprehensive data classification program establishes the foundation for an effective computer security and access control activity. The coupling of personnel clearances and need-to-know requirements with a carefully designed data classification system produces the primary constraints needed to govern access to an information system. Computer user organizations that are willing to exert the effort will find that the implementation of their security policies and requirements inside the computer itself does not have to be a formidable task.

7. Risk Analysis and Technical Vulnerability Studies

The primary purpose of this chapter is to describe two of the more formidable tools that can be brought to bear on the problem of unauthorized computer system access. The two processes are called *risk analysis* and *technical vulnerability assessment*. In many articles and texts the terms are used interchangeably. For explanatory purposes, these subjects will be treated separately here in order to differentiate between the more formal (and less technical) activity of risk analysis and the more rigorous process of technical vulnerability assessment. Several other key topics will be included in this chapter in order to complete the discussion of risk management tools. Also included is a review of the following related topics:

- Comparison of risk analysis versus technical vulnerability assessment
- Benefits of risk analysis
- Benefits of technical vulnerability assessments
- Electronic data processing audits and internal control questionnaires
- Risk analysis and personal computers

Comparison of Risk Analysis versus Technical Vulnerability Assessments

A *risk analysis* is generally a team effort by inside or outside computer security consultants along with the help of computer system users. Its objective is to determine on a systematic basis the losses that might result from a computer abuse or crime, a natural disaster, or an accident. The study is a management tool designed to identify *generally* areas requiring improvements in security policies, administrative procedures, and/or technical safeguards. All manual and automated system input, output, and processes are surveyed when circumstances permit. Internal control weaknesses are given considerable attention.

A *technical vulnerability assessment* is a study by a team of computer software, hardware, and communications experts. The study group is often called a "tiger team." Their study objective is normally limited to exposing technical vulnerabilities or weaknesses in the design of specific hardware, software, and communications systems. Their study approach is not necessarily systematic, but may involve any form of devious or unorthodox (but possible) means that could be used by a culprit to break the system, circumvent built-in protection features, or even implant technical mechanisms in the system itself that would make a future compromise of the system easier.

Tiger teams attack the technical features of a system which most users have no access to or ability to modify. Users are therefore most vulnerable to an attack or compromise in this area because (1) they may not know the weakness exists, and (2) the correction may only be made by the system supplier for technical, economic, or legal reasons.

Tiger teams are usually formed by government agencies, academic institutions, or high-technology consulting firms. Some private organizations have implemented their own counterparts to a tiger team. The special team's objective may be to test or attempt to breach the security of internal application programs, databases, or data communication networks. Again, the approach would differ from a typical risk analysis by the nature of the unorthodox procedures used to prove weaknesses and by the significant amount of technical skill that may have to be applied to circumvent or break built-in system or internal controls.

Risk analyses, or risk studies, are more in tune with the normal management, control, and audit functions in an organization. Vulnerability assessment or tiger-team studies may, in fact, be desirable, but may only be affordable by substantially funded study groups. Ultimately, the results of both risk analysis surveys and tiger-team studies will be needed to achieve the highest degree of protection possible for a computer system or network.

Benefits of Risk Analysis

Beginning in the early 1970s, there has been an increasing interest in finding a reliable way to quantify the risks, or loss potential, of computer-oriented information systems. The motivation for this effort was the desire to discover with reasonable precision how much and where an organization might be exposed to loss or incapacitation as a result of its dependence upon one or more computer systems.

Proponents of a formal (i.e., quantitative) method of risk analysis claimed that better identification and quantification of potential computer security problems (including fraud, malicious attacks, and disaster recovery) would lead to improved risk avoidance and risk management decisions.

The appeal of this approach to management was significant, even if the results obtained left much to be desired. From a better definition of the problem it was hoped that more effective and efficient ways would be found to:

• Make system protection decisions
• Set security design and implementation priorities

- Justify expenditure of company funds and resources for computer security
- Measure progress toward planned objectives
- Delegate security authority and pinpoint related responsibility
- Enhance the security awareness and attitude of company personnel

Many businesses and government agencies joined in the study of computer systems risk analysis. Out of these efforts evolved a generalized procedure which thus far has demonstrated that computer systems risk analysis is a much more difficult problem that it was originally perceived to be. The classic approach to these risk-oriented studies does seem to produce recognizable benefits for those who perform them except for one significant weakness—the precision and reliability of study results.

Most approaches to computer risk analysis involve the following steps:

1. Identification of critical events which would cause great financial loss, incapacitation, or embarrassment to the organization or provide some form of advantage to a competitor

2. Estimation of the frequency or probability of the occurrence of events

3. Estimation of the quantitative significance of loss (i.e., U.S. dollars) for each time the event might occur

4. Calculation or estimation of the annual loss or impact that might result from the cumulative or occasional occurrence of each type of event

5. Identification of preventative or corrective measures that should eliminate or reduce the probability of a particular event's occurrence

6. Estimation of the cost of the preventative or corrective measure(s)

7. Calculation of the return on investment (ROI), payback, or cost benefit (if any) from the implementation of preventative or corrective measures

8. Establishment of a risk reduction policy, including an implementation plan and schedule based on priorities derived from an ROI or cost-benefit analysis

9. Securing of management approval (including funding) to proceed with risk reduction activities

10. Periodic review and update of the risk reduction program

Figures 7-1 to 7-3 are examples of the classic approach and mathematical procedures used by many companies and government agencies to initiate their computer risk analysis studies [LO 1979].

Alternatives

Unfortunately, formal (i.e., quantifiable) risk analysis is not the panacea of computer security that it was first declared to be. On the other hand, through trial and error, many organizations have developed their own variations of risk analysis and management by combining quantitative methods with sub-

E/Y = frequency of event
P = probability

Example:

Let P = 0 if practically never
     = 1 if once in 300 years
     = 2 if once in 30 years
     = 3 if once in 3 years
     = 4 if once in 100 days
     = 5 if once in 10 days
     = 6 if once per day
     = 7 if 10 times per day
     = 8 if 100 times per day

(If 3 years = 1000 days)

Figure 7-1 Probability of frequency estimation.

Example:

Let cost = 12 if loss is $3,333,333
       = 11 if loss is $1,000,000
       = 10 if loss is $ 333,333
       = 9 if loss is $ 100,000
       = 8 if loss is $ 33,333
       = 7 if loss is $ 10,000
       = 6 if loss is $ 3,333
       = 5 if loss is $ 1,000
       = 4 if loss is $ 333
       = 3 if loss is $ 100
       = 2 if loss is $ 33
       = 1 if loss is $ 10
       = 0 if loss is $ 3

L/E = loss per event

Figure 7-2 Estimate of order of magnitude.

Example:

L/E = expected loss per event
E/Y = expected frequency of event
L/Y = expected average loss per year

$$L/Y = (L/E)(E/Y)$$

Figure 7-3 Calculation of expected average loss per year.

jective observations. Their objective is to simplify the process and derive a more practical result from their computer risk studies.

Typically, the risk reduction conclusions of the more productive efforts have been based on *macro* (general) analysis versus *micro* (highly quantifiable or statistical) analysis.

The macro approach to risk analysis is a more practical procedure which attempts to produce better results by:

1. Concentrating risk study efforts in areas of obvious or previously experienced losses
2. Simplifying the study process through the use of more subjective criteria [i.e., loss defined in general and graduated terms such as catastrophies (major, minor, inconsequential)] versus complex mathematical procedures
3. Establishing a risk or loss prevention plan based on more subjective or clear-cut management priorities (i.e., business continuation, customer satisfaction, minimum denial of information system services)

Figures 7-4 to 7-8 are examples of the documentation and criteria that various computer organizations have used to implement a macro analysis or a simplified system risk study [LO 1979].

Risk analysis, or risk management, can be applied to any area or component of an information system. It can be applied to a personal computer as well as to a large-scale host computer and network environment. Obviously, the time it takes to perform the study, the complexity of study areas, and the cost and nature of the risk reduction plan will vary.

In addition, access control is only one of the many areas of vulnerability in information systems that might be studied. However, the focus of a study designed to evaluate the loss potential of unauthorized access to a computer or network should be essentially the same:

- Access control problems can be broken down into the main categories mentioned previously: identification, authentication, and authorization.
- The key physical or logical point of weakness for the system or network needs to be identified.
- Risk reduction policies, priorities, and implementation plans need to be approved by management.
- Some form of organizational or management activity is needed to implement and control risk reduction procedures and to report on any system access or protection violations. An example of the relationships in this risk reduction approach is outlined in Figure 7-9. The matrix for each computer system or network would vary depending upon such factors as size, configuration, number of users, geographic distribution, communications, applications, data sensitivity, and other equally important variables.

```
┌──────────────────────────────────────────────────────────┐
│                                            ┌─────────┐    │
│              Computer Security Analysis     │ Critical│    │
│                                            ├─────────┤    │
│                                            └─────────┘    │
│                                                          │
│   System name _____ System identification _____ │
│                                                          │
│   Description of system:                                 │
│                                                          │
│          ◄── Manual systems ──►◄──── Computer systems ──►│
│   ┌──────────┬────┬────┬────┬────┬────┬────┬────┐        │
│   Input from │    │    │    │    │    │    │    │        │
│   ├──────────┼────┼────┼────┼────┼────┼────┼────┤        │
│   Output to  │    │    │    │    │    │    │    │        │
│   └──────────┴────┴────┴────┴────┴────┴────┴────┘        │
│                                                          │
│   Effect of disruption of service:                       │
│                                                          │
│   Alternate method:                                      │
│                                                          │
│   Effect of loss or destruction of files:                │
│                                                          │
│                    Fire Power Earth Sabotage Fraud Error │
│   Probabilities of occurrence                            │
│   Recovery plan established                              │
│   Countermeasures taken                                  │
│                                                          │
│   Remarks and notes:                                     │
│                                                          │
└──────────────────────────────────────────────────────────┘
```

	Fire	Power	Earth	Sabotage	Fraud	Error
Probabilities of occurrence						
Recovery plan established						
Countermeasures taken						

	Cost of loss	
Type of loss	Files	Business
Permanent		
Temporary		

Figure 7-4 Computer security analysis form. **Objective:** *A simpler, less expensive procedure.* These computer users reported that they operated a medium-sized installation, and didn't have the work force to implement a "formal and extensive" risk analysis program. Their solution was to develop a simplified data gathering form which they felt short-cut a more expensive and time-consuming study.

Benefits of Technical Vulnerability Assessments

Most technical vulnerability studies of computer systems performed in the past have been extremely expensive and difficult to carry out, and have produced results of questionable value. In spite of these negative aspects, the overall benefits should outweigh the costs for the following reasons.

First, if the original system suppliers are told about inherent computer system design faults, eventually there will be major architectural improve-

Risk Impact Indexes

Major Systems Index

9-10	More than 60 programs or 100 worker-months of maintenance, or 10,000 computer hours annually, and updates a major master file and interfaces with another major system
7-8	35 to 60 programs or 20 to 100 worker-months of maintenance, or 1,000 to 10,000 computer hours annually, and updates a master file and interfaces with another system
5-6	10 to 34 programs or 10 to 20 worker-months of maintenance, or 250 to 5,000 computer hours annually
3-4	5 to 9 programs or 5 to 9 worker-months of maintenance, or 50 to 249 computer hours annually
≤ 2	Other system

Company Assets Index

9-10	Directly affects cash
8	Affects movement of assets
6-7	Indirectly affects movement of assets
≤ 5	Less effect on assets

Critical System Index

9-10	Necessary to maintain daily business
7-8	Necessary to maintain statutory requirements and monthly reporting
5-6	Necessary to maintain business
≤ 4	Not primary to business

Figure 7-5   Risk impact indexing system. **Objective:** *Shorten the risk analysis data gathering cycle and expedite evaluation of more critical computer applications.* This organization initially used the evaluation procedure published by the Institute of Internal Auditors in their "Systems Auditability and Control-Audit Practices" guide. They reported that they didn't have time, however, to compile all the required data, but determined that they could get by with three indexes and an overall summary. The indexes are referred to as the (1) major systems index, (2) company assets index, and (3) critical systems index.

ments in security systems. Second, computer users can be forewarned about inherent weaknesses and, where feasible, can seek alternative system solutions. Third, as a result of tiger-team studies, new and better ways to write system specifications and requirements, including security features, have been developed. In spite of the unorthodox (nonsystematic) approaches taken to prove the vulnerability of certain system designs, a set of classic principles of vulnerability has in fact evolved.

For example, the cumulative efforts of a number of tiger teams and other

Degree-of-Loss Matrix			
Hazard: ——— No. Type		Ratings	
Degree of loss	Manifestations	Loss	Frequency
A. Minor annoyance			
B. Major annoyance			
C. Minor loss recovery			
D. Major loss recovery			
E. Major interruption			
F. Severe disruption			
G. Major disaster			

Figure 7-6 Degree-of-loss form. **Objective:** *Modify standard risk analysis procedures to more clearly distinguish the severity of impact of different classes of hazards.* This organization developed an eight-point degree-of-loss index and a special form to permit a more quantitative review of information hazard systems.

organizations that have conducted computer security research have resulted in a comprehensive list of potential system vulnerabilities. These include the following:

- *Trojan horse attack*:   A process that involves tricking people or programs with legitimate access into doing things they ordinarily wouldn't do. Trojan horses (i.e., logic) may be put into an operating system by designers or even by technically skilled system users.

- *Trapdoor*:   Usually a mechanism placed into an operating system to allow a user program to perform a privileged (system) function. Includes the condition where a preinstalled code can allow a user program to "trick" the operating system into believing that the program should be allowed to perform a privileged function.

- *Spoofing*:   Actions that can be taken to mislead the system into performing an operation that appears normal but that actually results in unauthorized access.

- *Covert channel*:   A communications channel that allows a process to transfer information in a way that violates a system's security policy.

- *Logic bomb*:   A set of programming instructions entered without trace into a

```
Example

        Asset List              Value Points

    1. Operators manual            10
    2. System reference            50
       manuals
    3. Operational files          100
    4. Database file              250
    5. Program library            300
       .                            .
       .                            .
       .                            .



Note:
Sensitivity value factor plus backup factor may be used to cal-
late exposure points value per year
```

Figure 7-7 Sensitivity value scale. **Objective:** *Modify risk analysis procedure to permit an evaluation of risks that do not lend themselves to monetary measurement criteria such as events involving adverse social or political consequences.* This organization is experimenting with the coupling of conventional risk evaluation procedures with a unique sensitivity value, or point, scale in order to measure critical events which do not permit monetary assignments.

computer system to perform some function at a later time. May include the alteration or destruction of a computer operating system, application programs, or data files. Also referred to as a *time bomb*.

- *Impersonation*: Use of another person's (or process's) password or other identification to achieve unauthorized system or file access. Also referred to as *masquerading* or *aliasing*.

- *Piggybacking*: A condition where a computer user makes use of a computer terminal that has been made operational (i.e., via log-on) by a legitimate user who has left the terminal unattended.

- *Salami technique*: A covert and unauthorized process of taking small amounts of money from many sources by special rounding calculations. A fraud perpetrated by programming the remainders from an interest computation to be moved to an accessible account (of the culprit) instead of being legitimately distributed to authorized accounts.

- *Browsing*: An unauthorized and covert process designed to obtain information that may be left in some part of a computer system after the execution of a job. The illegal search for data residue within computer storage areas or media. Also called *scavenging*.

Major threats:	An event of catastrophic proportions that destroys the DP facility or renders it inoperable. Examples: fire, flood, earthquake, tornado, bombing, riot. Assumption is made that all attendant areas of the facility, such as the tape/disk library, are destroyed. Relocation to an alternate processing site is required. Only the material stored off-site is available for use.
Minor threats:	This category includes all the failures, errors, and mishaps encountered daily. While each occurrence may result in relatively short processing delay or minor distortion or loss of data, the cumulative cost of many occurrences can be significant. Examples: CPU failure, wrong tape or pack mounted, listings lost, air conditioning failure.

Security Exposure	**Possible Results of Security Failure**
1. **Data integrity**	Destruction or unauthorized modification of data, unintentional or deliberate.
2. **Data confidentiality**	Unauthorized disclosure of sensitive data.
3. **Operational reliability**	Undependable or inadequate processing: unavailability of processing. (Processing should be accurate, dependable, and timely.)
4. **Asset integrity**	Destruction or physical damage to buildings and equipment and supporting functions.

Note:
In general, the first three categories represent threats to data and processing. Asset integrity can most often be related to physical assets, for example, equipment, supplies, furniture, storage media.

Figure 7-8 Two-level threat classification system. **Objective:** *More clearly distinguish between major and minor threats and class of exposure present in an information system.* In the interest of simplifying the risk analysis procedure and at the same time to focus attention on the threats of potentially great severity, this very large computer user developed a unique two-level threat classification system. A major benefit of the procedure is that it highlights the very separate problem of minor threats so that they can be treated more adequately. It also helps to prevent multiple threat levels. In addition, this user divided potential security exposures into four categories.

- *Super zapping:* The unauthorized use of a computer program (instructions) designed to violate established computer access controls in order to modify, destroy, or obtain data illegally from a computer.
- *Wiretapping:* Unauthorized interception of communications through a direct connection with the intention of gaining access to transmitted data. If done indirectly, the process is called *eavesdropping.*

Location in system of identified risk

Risk identification	Terminal	Communications carrier	Communications processor	Host operating system	Database managment system	Other	Approved prevention or correction	Organization responsible for action
Identification risks:								
1.								
2.								
3.								
4.								
5.								
Authentication risks:			TO BE COMPLETED					
1.			AS THE RESULT					
2.			OF DOING A RISK					
3.			ANALYSIS STUDY					
4.								
5.								
Authorization risks:								
1.								
2.								
3.								
4.								
5.								

Figure 7-9   A structured approach to access control using risk analysis.

• *Contamination*:   The erroneous or deliberate alteration of data by modification in order to change the accuracy or integrity of the original data (or program). May also be referred to as a *computer virus*.

In many well-known security research projects, the tiger-team approach has been used to test the vulnerabilities of computer systems. The use of devious and unorthodox penetration techniques to test for computer access control weaknesses and design flaws is still practiced. Computer user organizations are learning to carry the approach one step further; they are testing for vulnerabilities in their application programs. It is not uncommon for management to advise its homegrown tiger team or computer security consultant that it is all right to "think like a thief."

Although many of the original tiger teams have now been disbanded, work in this area is still continuing. One organization that is well-equipped to do further research in this area is the U.S. Department of Defense Computer Security Center located at Fort George G. Meade, Maryland.

EDP Audits and Internal Control Questionnaires

Thus far in this chapter, we have discussed how risk analysis and technical vulnerability studies can be used to provide solutions to unauthorized access problems in computer systems and networks. Another process for discovering system weaknesses that has been in use a long time is called the *operations* or *management audit*. Properly carried out by professionally trained EDP auditors with the help of appropriately designed internal control questionnaires, system audits can and do reveal both administrative and technical weaknesses.

Computer system audits have a definite role in the creation of a secure information system. They can (and often do) reveal access control weaknesses. The management letters or reports that result from the EDP audit are an excellent source of systems security planning data. Together with the risk analysis and technical vulnerability study, management is given an array of useful tools with which to formulate a workable and efficient policy for total system access control.

Risk Analysis and Personal Computers

Before concluding this chapter, it is important to comment on the use and application of risk analysis and technical vulnerability studies to the new personal computer, workstation, and related microcomputer environments.

The analytical tools described above were developed initially to address the security problems of mainframe or host computers. The use of these tools has produced an array of benefits, not the least of which is a greater appreciation of the types of access control problems to be expected in a network or communications environment.

The difference today is that personal computers and workstations cannot be treated as ordinary terminals. For users they are a versatile and highly necessary information resource—whether they are connected to a host computer located elsewhere or are just stand-alone systems. However, the fact that the systems may be satellites to a larger system or network necessitates an evaluation of unauthorized access potential. The size of a system is not a reliable criterion of loss potential or data sensitivity. On the other hand, if a personal computer is being used as a stand-alone computer, a different and less complex approach may be sufficient to place security and access control risks into proper perspective.

With a personal computer the physical risks associated with unauthorized access may be significant, because a microcomputer located in a remote office or home will not be given the same physical protection that it would receive if it were located in a centralized data entry or data processing environment or in a large, busy office complex. However, justification for and creation of a secure environment for personal computers and professional or expert workstations are slow processes for the average home computer user. Without professional help or experience, risk analysis for personal and other microcomputers will be highly subjective with concomitant cost-justification problems, in contrast to risk analysis for larger systems managed with a significant amount of control provided by a professionally run centralized data processing function.

Summary

System risk management should include some form of risk analysis as the basis for planning and controlling system access. It is possible that for some information systems, a more difficult technical vulnerability assessment should also be made to identify problems, particularly architectural problems, outside the computer user's control. Professional EDP audits can also provide valuable access control requirements. Finally, in today's environment, the rapid increase in personal computers and expert or professional workstations will require, in many cases, more difficult and subjective access control and risk evaluation because of decentralized user authority and security and financial resources that are less than ideal.

Risk management is a never-ending activity. It is part of the price that must be paid for extremely rapid implementation of new information technologies.

8. Automating Information Security Policies

Information security policies relating to data classification and access rules must be automated because of the sheer volume of access control decisions that need to be made for most systems. Access control must be quick and efficient, both to please system users and to ensure that destructive nonauthorized activity is not taking place in the system.

In this chapter we will discuss the various approaches that can be taken to automate the information access control policies of an organization. A discussion of a total information security policy which would include physical protection, operations security, backup disaster recovery planning, and systems auditability is beyond the scope of this book.

The two most important subjects to be addressed in the planning of access control automation include:

- Impact of existing system constraints on access control, and
- Architectural improvements in system security features

Impact of Existing System Constraints on Access Control

One of the first questions an organization should ask when addressing the problem of computer security is: What access control protection does our present computer provide? Many computer systems today already offer users some form of access protection; however, many users do not take advantage of it. Why? One of the most likely answers is that many organizations are not prepared to use the security features of their existing systems because they haven't yet defined their company's information security policies and data access rules.

Granted, the automation of an organization's security policy, including the data classification and access permission systems, may be a demanding task. Eventually, however, most organizations will have to do it. And the company that has a workable manual or semiautomated system already in place may have a major competitive advantage.

Generally, the protection features built into existing computers consist of those designed into the hardware and software by the manufacturer. Honeywell's Multics computer is a prime example of this type of system. Specifically, through very specialized hardware and software architecture, users of Multics can specify the degree of access control or security protection they wish to have. In the case of Multics, its security capabilities were part of its initial design specifications.

Manufacturer's features can be better utilized and/or reinforced by:

- Supplementing the manufacturer's hardware and software protection with add-on hardware and software security features (i.e., internally implemented or acquired from an outside source)
- Creating security-related policies, programs, or procedures by users to reinforce their computer's security capabilities
- Enforcing the use of operational techniques or procedures (both manual and automated) that prevent circumvention of built-in computer access controls (i.e., the automated security features)

The first step to access control is to become familiar with the security features of your own system. (A discussion of security operating systems can be found in Part 3.)

There are many differences in the security features of the various brands of computers and even in computers built by the same manufacturer. The strengths and weaknesses of the various security features are described particularly well in a special report [FL 1981]. This report states that the primary areas of weakness or unauthorized access in the present-generation systems include:

1. Internal system data, by unauthorized persons via use of a system or application program, utility, or electronic device.
2. Computer software programs within the system, by unauthorized persons via use of a system or application program, utility, or electronic device.
3. Data external to the system, by unauthorized persons, whether destined to become input or output.
4. Computer software programs external to the system, regardless of media—cards, tapes, and others—by unauthorized persons.
5. Unauthorized use, modification, or destruction of computing equipment or supplies.
6. Unauthorized use of any computing services. [FL 1981]

This report describes the logic that a typical system uses to "allow only authorized persons to use the system, and reject all others":

1. User turns on a terminal or dials up computer.
2. System asks, "Who are you?"

3. User identifies self.

4. System checks user's identity for permission to use system.
   a. If true, proceed.
   b. If false, go to step 16.

5. System checks user against terminal for permission to use it.
   a. If true, proceed.
   b. If false, go to step 16.

6. System asks user, "What do you want to do?"

7. User replies, "I want to run program A."

8. System checks user's permission to use program A.
   a. If true, proceed.
   b. If false, go to step 16.

9. Program A is running; user wants to open and update file X. System checks user for file X permission.
   a. If true, proceed.
   b. If false, go to step 16.

10. System checks program A for file X use permission.
    a. If true, proceed.
    b. If false, go to step 16.

11. Program A is executing, updating file X.

12. Program is finished, and user wants to print file X on the terminal.

13. System checks file X permission to use this terminal.
    a. If true, proceed.
    b. If false, go to step 16.

14. File X prints on terminal.

15. Printing stops when finished. If user continues on system, security monitoring continues at step 6.

16. System prints on terminal, "Permission denied to use XXX. What do you want to do?" [FL 1981]

The ideal secure computer system would have at least two key system capabilities:

- A list of valid users, to examine when the user logs on system.
- A list of each user's preassigned permissions such as programs, data and any peripherals, hardware modules or communications links, games or other services. [FL 1981]

Architectural configuration of these security capabilities in a computer would probably take the form of an access control list (ACL). "The ACL could be held on a segment of the data base, or in the form of a permanent file, preferably on disk for quick access by the system. Input to definition of the ACL design and format could come from preliminary planning in categorizing different types of users" (see Figure 8-1) [FL 1981].

User permission category*

System facilities	Clerk (user)	Programmer	Operator	Supervisor	Data entry operator	System programmer	Security data system administrator	Student
Time sharing	X	X		X		X	X	X
Application A	X							
COBOL		X				X	X	X
Application B	X							
FORTRAN		X				X	X	X
Common database	UR						UR	
BASIC assembly language						X		
Dial-up terminal		X		X		X	X	X
Direct terminal	X		X			X	X	
Remote terminal						X	X	
File generation		X		X	X	X	X	X(S)
ACL file	UX						UX	
File X		RX				RX	UX	
File Y	R	RX				UX	UX	
Console			X					

*X = General execute permission
U = Update permission
R = Read permission
S = Special resource limitation for students

Figure 8-1 Access control matrix.

86

In actual practice, the access control problem in current-generation computer systems is handled in many different ways. The variations are considerable, both in the techniques (hardware and software) employed and in the degree of security obtained. It is critical, therefore, that each computer user organization make a careful analysis of its existing system capabilities. The findings will greatly influence the extent to which the organization's data classification and access control policies can be automated on existing hardware and software systems.

Architectural Improvements in System Security Features

There is a major difference between the consideration of an information access policy and its implementation. The complexity of computer hardware and software coupled with the constant striving for more user friendliness makes the implementation of a security policy an almost unattainable goal for some businesses. This is further complicated by the continual introduction of new technology into the marketplace.

Slowly but surely, through a heavy injection of capital into security research, major progress is being made by the federal government and a handful of computer manufacturers in the area of secure computer systems. One of the objectives of this research has been to find an easier way to enforce organizational security policies with regard to data access.

One of the solutions developed with the infusion of large amounts of funds from the Department of Defense (DOD) is called the *trusted computer*. A more technical treatment of this subject is included in Part 3 of this book. The trusted computer research and development activity is mentioned in this chapter because it offers a potentially easier and more secure way of implementing within the computer itself a company's security policies and clearance and classification systems.

The document that best describes the progress in this area is published by the U.S. Department of Defense Computer Security Center. The work described included the design of highly mathematically oriented secure computer models. These models or mathematical approaches were in turn converted into hardware and software solutions. This is a computer system concept that permits users to provide their own personnel clearance, data classification, and access rules and lets the computer control access from that point on [DE 1983].

The conversion of DOD data security and classification policies into computer logic is at this time approaching a successful stage of development. The time when commercial computer users can run their information system on one of the 100 secure computers on the DOD's yet-to-be-approved list is not too far away.

First, however, the data access rules of the security policy must be defined. According to this DOD document, a *security policy* is "the set of laws, rules, and practices that regulate how an organization manages, protects, and distributes sensitive information" [DE 1983].

In the case of the DOD, the Bell–La Padula model was used to produce a mathematically proved, secure computer concept.
More correctly, the Bell–La Padula model is

> a formal state transition model of computer security policy that describes a set of access control rules. In this formal model, the entities in a computer system are divided into abstract sets of subjects and objects. The notion of a secure state is defined and it is proven that each state transition preserves security by moving from secure state to secure state; thus, inductively proving that the system is secure. A system state is defined to be "secure" if the only permitted access modes of subjects [i.e., a person] to objects [i.e., data or system resources] are in accordance with a specific security policy. In order to determine whether or not a specific access mode is allowed, the clearance of a subject is compared to the classification of the object and a determination is made as to whether the subject is authorized for the specific access mode. [BE 1976]

As complicated as this sounds, the Bell–La Padula model permits the testing of a computer design to ensure that the system will only allow users with specific access rights to read or write data in the system. "Accesses permitted between subjects and objects are explicitly defined for the fundamental modes of access, including read-only access, read-write access, and write-only access" [BE 1976].

The importance of this DOD research to computer users is simply that computers will soon be introduced into the commercial market that can offer very high degrees of access control (i.e, security policy implementation). Users, however, cannot avoid the basic preparation required to use the new systems. This includes the implementation or, at minimum, the completion of the design of an adequate system for personnel clearance and data classification.

Summary

A high degree of access control is already possible for organizations that have established clear data classification and access rules that can utilize the security features of their present operating system. In addition, for many systems, users can buy or develop access control software packages to be added to their system to give them greater access protection.

Unfortunately, too few computer user organizations have developed their security policies and rules with enough precision to automate them, even if sufficient built-in hardware and software security features were originally available in their computer.

On the other hand, there is a point of view that present-day computers, particularly operating systems, do not contain the combination of security features necessary to make the automation of security policies and access controls worthwhile for many companies.

The answer to inadequate security technology (in operating systems) may soon be forthcoming as a result of DOD research and development in this area and commercial production of more secure computers.

Computer users, therefore, who want more security and access control protection need to formulate in the near future security policies and access rules that lend themselves to automation in the new system environments.

9. Establishing a Computer Security and Access Control Program

Poor management-employee communications can produce or increase information security problems. The introduction of technological solutions to information security risks is generally no substitute for cooperative employee behavior. The following aspects of information security are discussed in this chapter:

- Security management and organization
- Security awareness programs
- Security of microcomputers

Security Management and Organization

Larger business organizations and government agencies have gradually developed their own style of information security management during the past ten to fifteen years. Few organizations, however, have been able to set definitive management goals in the area of information security and actually achieve them. For the most part, security management, including access control, has been a very elusive target or at least one that has not lent itself to conventional management approaches such as planning, organizing, or controlling.

The main reasons for the fact that information systems abuse, including unauthorized access, is such a difficult management problem are as follows:

- The development of security technology has always lagged behind the production of newer, faster, less expensive, and more functional computers. In other words, management of the unauthorized access problem has been a no-win situation for many organizations regardless of how much effort and money has been expended.
- Computer abuse and unauthorized access are not problems that necessarily lend themselves to quantitative analysis.
- Computer security, including access control, has been a relatively low-priority problem until recently.

Appropriate management solutions to information security problems in general have therefore been very slow to evolve. Even today, the types of definitive data on which management likes to base decisions are grossly inadequate. Intuition, deductive reasoning, and legal or administrative regulations seem to influence management actions more than the few cold hard facts that are available.

In large organizations security management has evolved into a pattern of very similar steps:

1. The assignment of one or more employees or a committee to study the computer security problem in the organization

2. The application of some form of risk analysis, risk measurement, or other qualitative or quantitative tools to establish some feeling for the organization's loss potential from possible system abuses such as unauthorized access or denial of systems services

3. The creation of an overall management-approved policy of risk reduction, based upon a variety of risk management guidelines, procedures, or practices

4. The establishment of one or more technical groups or organizations with the charter to more clearly define specific information system risks, the possible solutions, and recommended actions by priority

5. The approval of funding and other resources that will be needed to implement changes to the information system for security purposes

For extremely large organizations with numerous computers, different geographic locations, and varied business interests and divisions, a centralized computer security staff is often created at the corporate level to perform steps 1, 2, and 3 and to provide assistance and oversee the implementation of steps 4 and 5 at the divisional level.

In support of the technical improvements and changes for enhancing computer and network security, many organizations in the United States have implemented various forms of security awareness programs at both the corporate and divisional levels to gain the support of their employees for the security of their information systems.

The objective of these computer security awareness programs has been to ensure that extremely important behavioral factors are not overlooked in favor of a high-technology approach to the solution of computer security problems.

Top management personnel have investigated the reasons behind computer abuse (i.e., people behavior) and have been very supportive of computer security awareness programs in their organizations. In many cases, they have initiated the requirements for such programs. They know as well as anyone that an employee who chooses not to protect or conceal his or her personal password to a sensitive file is capable of compromising almost any technical system security program or technical protection mechanism. The point is, of course, that employee confidence and trust cannot be taken for granted.

Security Awareness Programs

Many of the larger corporations in the United States have implemented an employee computer security awareness program. The following is an example of the activities that typically support such a project [CO 1981].

First, a security task force is established to study and develop security protocol recommendations. The goals of the security awareness program usually include:

- Accuracy and reliability of computerized data.
- Adequacy of protection of resources and data from anticipated threats or hazards.
- Operational reliability and performance of automated information processing and communication services. [CO 1981]

The task force often establishes a set of baseline requirements for application security and control. These may include:

- Organization responsibilities for specification and approval of application controls—that is, the role of I/S (Information System organization), user and auditor.
- Need for standard software development methodology and documentation.
- Appropriate and realistic segregation of responsibilities during the application life cycle.
- Information classification system to prioritize investment in security and control measures.
- Guidelines for approval and documentation of application software changes.
- Maintenance of appropriate audit trails, particularly for on-line transaction processing. [CO 1981]

The task force may develop a recommended list of responsibilities for each of the organization's computer security officers. The responsibilities might include the following:

- Manage the organization's (unit, division, etc.) information security function
- Assist with compliance to EDP audit standards and guidelines
- Assist with the implementation and adaptation of computer security policies, practices, and guidelines
- Monitor password and access control compliance
- Develop, test, and maintain a disaster recovery plan
- Facilitate and maintain a risk management program
- Continually monitor and test system security

- Conduct computer security training and awareness programs for company employees

Access Policy and Microcomputers

The best way to address and initiate organizational relationships with regard to personal computer and workstation security is first to determine the answers to the following questions:

- Is the system intended to be a stand-alone system? This assumes there are no present communications with or connection to a host computer or network.
- If not, is the system directly connected to a host computer with no outside communications capabilities? If not, it is assumed that the system is communications-oriented and can access other systems or can be accessed from an external source.

Stand-alone systems have unique access control problems of a physical rather than logical nature. In most organizations access control risks of stand-alone systems are managed through policies and procedures that pertain primarily to environmental, physical, or personnel protection.

The strength of this approach is that many highly complex and technical problems do not have to be dealt with. The primary weaknesses are that it is expensive and requires cooperative employee behavior. If the system is truly a sensitive one with a high loss potential, the costs of physical or environmental safeguards (e.g., locks, electronic surveillance systems) can probably be justified.

Insufficient internal control because of noncooperative employee behavior is probably not just a data processing department problem. This is because most systems referred to here will probably be located in user departments that do not report to data processing or in remote locations (including homes) where direct and centralized control is nearly impossible.

Unfortunately, the solutions to microcomputer security may be difficult. For example, in some instances, it might be dangerous to authorize their acquisition in the first place. Alternatives might be tougher employee compliance policies and more frequent operational audits of the system.

Managing access control to *microcomputers directly connected only to host computers* will be less difficult than if the microcomputer were connected to a system with outside communications capabilities. In such cases unauthorized access by outsiders via communication will be difficult—so long as the host itself does not have significant external communications facilities.

Successful application of special electronic switches and programmed input-output controls have been used where the host does have external communications capabilities. Examples of this can be found in the protection afforded many law enforcement and criminal justice agency terminals and microcomputers.

Microcomputers attached to host computers have significant access control risks similar to those of computers that utilize their own outside communications modem. Centralized management control is necessary here to protect both the host and the smaller user system.

Communications-oriented personal computers and workstations can have all the access control problems of a host computer capable of external communications, particularly if they maintain an on-line database and software system. The advantage of the personal computer might be that under many circumstances the personal computer can be turned off when not in use or communications disconnected when especially sensitive jobs are being performed.

Management control of the communications-oriented personal computer or workstation is important and in some cases imperative, depending on the sensitivity of *both* the microcomputer and any host it is normally associated with. Also, the possibility that an organization's personal computers may be used to compromise other network-connected systems must be met with clear and strict security policy enforcement. If access control and system security is to be achieved, then user friendliness must be a negotiated issue between management, the centralized data processing function, and the individual user.

Summary

In the final analysis, those who manage the network and the centralized host computers need control over their informational assets just as they need control over the expert or professional workstation or personal computer. If personal computer users do not appreciate this, they may be rudely awakened when, as time passes, they have to ask for and be cleared for more mainframe and centralized database access in order to perform more valuable functions on their microcomputers. Eventually, the need to share may make system control and security more palatable to the new users.

Selecting Access Control Tools and Technology

COMPUTER SECURITY AWARENESS PROGRAM

PLANNING PHASES

LOGICAL ACCESS CONTROL PLAN

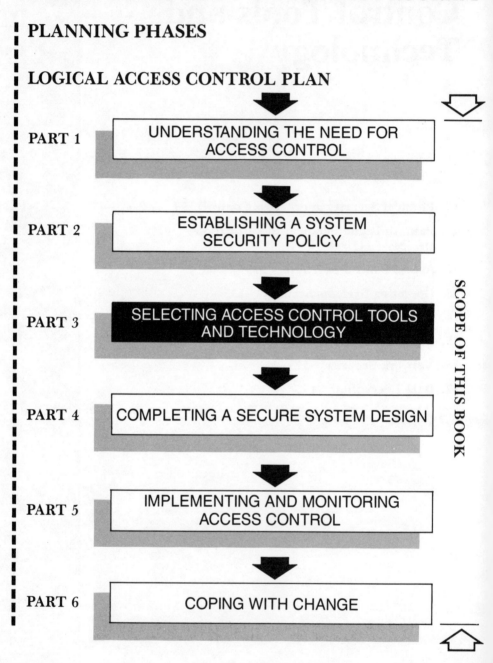

PART 1 — UNDERSTANDING THE NEED FOR ACCESS CONTROL

PART 2 — ESTABLISHING A SYSTEM SECURITY POLICY

PART 3 — SELECTING ACCESS CONTROL TOOLS AND TECHNOLOGY

PART 4 — COMPLETING A SECURE SYSTEM DESIGN

PART 5 — IMPLEMENTING AND MONITORING ACCESS CONTROL

PART 6 — COPING WITH CHANGE

SCOPE OF THIS BOOK

10. Physical Security and Access Control

Physical and logical access controls are normally interrelated and highly dependent upon each other. A breakdown or weakness in one can result in a compromise or vulnerability to the other. Physical access control is just as important as logical access control (i.e., hardware and software) because if both controls are not secure, the system is not secure.

Physical protection, therefore, cannot be a weak link if logical access control is to be achieved. A significant amount of money can be wasted on security if logical access safeguards are funded at the expense of, or in the absence of, physical security, and, of course, the reverse is equally true.

In this chapter, therefore, we will discuss how to select physical access controls that will be complementary to other system safeguards and supportive of total systems security. The following key issues will be addressed:

- Differences between physical access control and other physical security safeguards
- Value of the depth-of-protection approach to physical access control
- Available physical security technologies and products
- Security requirements for communications-oriented systems
- Optimization of physical access control selection
- Testing of physical access controls
- Justification of physical access control for remotely located personal computers and terminals

Differences between Physical Access Control and Other Physical Security Safeguards

Most organizations implement a high level of physical security safeguards and physical access control long before much attention is paid to logical access control. Expenditures for physical security are therefore often enormous, and safeguards are sometimes elaborate because physical security needs are usually easier to identify (and resolve) than logical security problems.

In addition, physical security usually includes both environmental protection as well as physical access. Safeguards designed to protect the system against losses from fire, explosions, natural disasters, power failure, and even from human destructiveness such as riots involve significant study and large expenditures, as do many of the physical controls and protection systems that might be implemented to provide backup or disaster recovery capabilities. These are important requirements, but are not within the scope of this book.

Physical access control requirements can be identified only by a systematic review of computer hardware, software, and communications facility vulnerabilities. Typically a systems approach to this review would work best because a thorough analysis will identify all areas that are vulnerable to unauthorized physical access (Figure 10-1), and they can then be dealt with systematically.

The results of a comprehensive review of all system components (physical

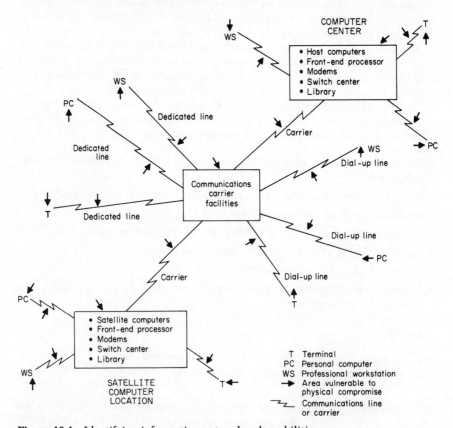

Figure 10-1 Identifying information network vulnerabilities.

as well as electronic and procedural) for loss potential from unauthorized access should produce an action plan that identifies physical access control needs and priorities. The cost and justification for implementation of such a plan might stem from a formalized risk analysis study if resources permit.

Recommended protection or prevention measures might range from hiring more guards to implementing a sophisticated electronic surveillance system or to a major redesign of the computer center and other areas.

Ideally, physical security and access control protection planning should start with the initial system design. This should include the construction or adaptation of a new or special building or office facilities for security enhancement. Early attention to architectural considerations can save substantial sums of money later for security-related changes.

The systems approach to identifying access control weaknesses can be implemented easily if checklists are used to ensure that no area of possible vulnerability is neglected. The typical checklist should include detailed questions designed to expose weaknesses or access protection needs in all physical, manual, and operational areas that relate to the information system. The general categories that should be reviewed with a detailed questionnaire might include:

- System site selection
- Computer center (building) access (including visible access)
- Computer room access
- Terminal areas
- Media library
- Equipment (i.e., hardware) protection
- Removable media protection, including floppy disks
- Supplies
- System document files
- Central communications facilities
- Distributed communications facilities
- Personal computers and workstations
- All on-line or communications-equipped satellite computers
- All backup facilities, including off-site vaults
- Customer engineering and maintenance facilities
- Satellite computer systems

Physical access control, therefore, is the protection of all computer-related and communications-related resources and facilities in which unauthorized access might result in any form of loss, modification, or destruction of data, interruption or denial of service to system users, or compromise of any logical access control.

The Depth-of-Protection Approach to Physical Security

Most advanced protection systems utilize some form of alarm system to protect sensitive or valuable property. These systems usually consist of three parts:

1. *Sensing devices*:   the process where an intrusion is detected
2. *Alarm control*:   the process that turns an alarm mechanism on or off
3. *Alarm signaling*:   the process where a responsible person is notified that an alarm detection system has been activated

The depth-of-protection approach to physical security is essentially the implementation of multiple levels of security to protect a computer facility or some component of an information system.

This approach proposes that at least three safeguards, or layers of defense, be established to protect a system from unauthorized access. They are normally classified as follows:

1. Perimeter or entryway protection
2. Area protection
3. Object protection

As shown in Figure 10-2, the perimeter defense might be a fence or the security afforded by doors and windows; the risk area protection might be controlled access to a room or vault; and the object (i.e., computer, terminal, magnetic file, report, communications line, CRT screen) protection might be through some form of electronic sensor or magnetic contact protecting the container (file, drawer, vault) that holds the object itself.

The tools or technologies used to provide the protection needed at all levels might be selected from a wide variety of possible sources (i.e., a guard, a magnetic contact and alarm, a card key, or electronic access control device). Most security or electronic surveillance devices are designed to safeguard one or more areas of potential vulnerability.

Available Security Technologies and Products

New highly sophisticated electronic security mechanisms and other devices are put on the market almost daily. Many of these products are as scientifically or technically advanced as the hardware and software that comprise the information system that needs protection. Special computers and communications facilities are often included in a total information security protection system.

Because the state of the art is so complex, expert and professional advice should be used in the selection of physical security mechanisms and systems.

Examples of available security protection devices and systems include:

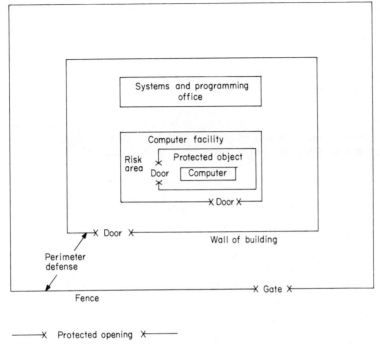

------X Protected opening X-------

Figure 10-2 Zone approach to physical security.

- *Magnetic contact devices*: (to protect doors and windows). Include related devices such as pressure mats and traps.
- *Photoelectric devices*: used for perimeter defense.
- *Modulated light*: uses a multibeam "wall of light" which reacts only to the light generated by its own source.
- *Vibration and audio detection*: used to monitor unauthorized physical access or penetration.
- *Closed-circuit television*: used to monitor sensitive areas from a central guard station.
- *Capacitance detection*: used to generate an alarm when an intruder approaches a sensitive area or object.
- *Motion detection*: uses ultrasonic or microwave energy to identify an intrusion when some form of movement creates a Doppler shift which is registered by the system.
- *Optical and infrared systems*: used to detect the heat generated by the body movement of an intruder.
- *Magnometers or metal detectors*: used to sense the unauthorized entry of dangerous metal objects into a sensitive area.

• *Electronic entry control devices*:   include card and key entry systems which control the opening and closing of doors and other accesses to sensitive areas. (There are many variations of these devices, such as those that require the input of special digits or codes into the entry system.)

In addition to the protection systems described above, there are numerous personal identification devices and systems that can be used in conjunction with physical access control devices. These also provide user identification information and/or logical access to computer resources such as programs, files, and communications facilities. (Personal positive identification procedures and devices will be discussed in the next chapter.)

Security Requirements for Communications-Oriented Systems

The physical security aspects of communications systems as opposed to logical compromises will be examined in this section. Hackers, as an example, initially have legal physical access to certain communications facilities. They allegedly break the law when they use their systems to gain illegal entry to other communications and computer facilities for the purpose of committing certain logical compromises.

On the other hand, it is generally agreed that the weakest physical link in many information systems is in the data communications area. One reason is that most systems seem to have been created with the notion that public communications carrier systems are inviolate. Even people who should know better have built (and are still building) information networks that rely on federal laws, government regulations, or the goodwill or ignorance of the general population for communications protection.

It has long been known that common carrier communications are extremely vulnerable to wiretaps and microwave interceptions at certain critical physical locations. Privately owned and local communications systems are not necessarily less vulnerable to physical compromise unless special measures are taken.

As shown in Figure 10-3, data communications vulnerabilities can be identified in at least four major areas:

1. Communications devices
2. Communication lines and switch systems within a building or complex of buildings
3. The cable from the nearest telephone pole to the building itself
4. Microwave and satellite systems

This list does not, of course, include all the possible locations or facilities where communications can be compromised. Even in facilities where large amounts of data are being transmitted, technology exists that can intercept

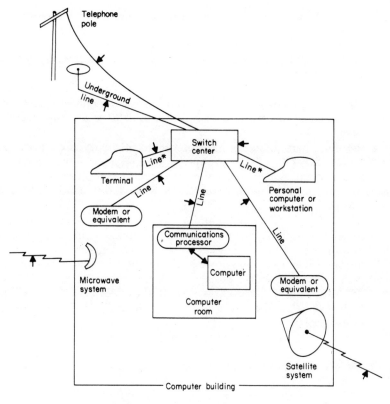

* Assumes connection to switch center (no shielded
  cables directly connected to communications processor)
→ Areas most vulnerable to compromise

Figure 10-3 Communications vulnerabilities.

and reduce certain classes of communications to an intelligent form, thus resulting in a system compromise.

Communications Devices

There are areas where a physical compromise can be made without an actual physical contact, and this possibility must be considered when communications vulnerabilities and safeguards are examined. For example, transmissions through a carrier (including internal transmission from one device to another) via electromagnetic radiation given off by electronic computers and communications devices are susceptible to unauthorized detection and recording. Even inexpensive recording devices and radio transmitters have been used to accomplish this compromise. A classic weakness that is often ne-glected is the unauthorized recording of signals generated by an unshielded terminal or personal computer in a nearby location.

Today computer and communications products to be purchased by the Department of Defense and other government agencies may require a *tempest rating*. This specification, which may even be classified for certain systems, defines the amount of allowable signal radiation a device may give off. Confor-mance to specifications may require special shielding or other technical enhancements.

For the most part, industry has not yet taken this type of threat very seriously. The threat does exist, however, and an organization's communica-tions devices should not be allowed to be *the* weak link, particularly when considerable money is being spent to tighten up all the other vulnerable areas in communications.

All communications devices, including terminals, personal computers, mo-dems, communications controllers, and concentrators (including carrier-supplied equipment), require physical protection from unauthorized access or use. Simple physical protection procedures and mechanisms, such as guards, locked doors, device locks (to table), keyboard locks, concealment, closed-circuit TV, etc., can all be used to protect these devices. The protection selected, however, should not be arbitrary but should be designed to accom-plish specific objectives.

Communications Lines and Switching Centers

Data communications users generally do not take enough interest in the protection either of communications facilities located on their own premises or of those located off their premises on public or common-carrier property.

The recent introduction of more advanced communications systems, such as private networks, satellite and microwave systems, local area networks, and PBX systems designed to integrate voice and data communications, make physical protection more imperative. The new equipment is not more vulnerable than the older telephone company-supplied systems, but much more sensitive data is being handled by these systems.

On the other hand, the fundamentals for providing physical protection for communications facilities have not changed particularly. As has already been discussed, the manual procedures and electronic surveillance and alarm systems needed to prevent intrusion into sensitive areas, including cable and telephone-line facilities, are more than adequate against all but the most sophisticated culprits. The improvements in wiretap detection and preven-tion equipment can thwart most intruders.

So, if the problem is not with security technology, where does it lie? The answer is in two parts: cost justification and the acquisition of an intimate knowledge of the physical components of the communications system and their specific locations.

For intimate knowledge of facilities, help should be sought from a local communications equipment technical service representative. Next, a complete inventory and layout of all communications-related facilities that are accessible to, or used by, the information system should be documented. With this information, it should be possible to design and implement an adequate protection system for on-premise communications facilities.

Generally, the five main areas of a typical communications system that will be investigated and which require protection include:

1. Relay node devices
2. Coupling devices (connect the source and destination devices to the interconnecting lines and trunks of the network
3. Distribution lines, trunks, and links (connect the different nodes of the communications network)
4. Switches
5. Source and destination devices (computers, terminals, etc.)

The following will also require investigation: satellite and microwave links; certain components of local area networks; and all host or terminal-oriented communications facilities, such as front-end communications processors, concentrators, and modem devices.

Some of the more specialized physical communications protection considerations include cable and device shielding (e.g., lead shielding, burying lines in concrete) and vacuum leak–detection equipment where sealed cables and facilities are used. Generally, standard off-the-shelf electronic (or other types of) surveillance systems will provide adequate protection for on-premise communications facilities. The use of encryption for the protection of communications will be discussed in Chapter 16.

Local Telephone Cables

Local telephone cables are one of the most vulnerable points in a communications network, because often all or most of the data flowing to and from a particular facility uses the wires in a cable. The problem of sorting out one company's communications from another's is avoided, making the job of data compromise considerably easier.

Numerous physical security devices and electronic surveillance systems can solve this problem. Depending on the vulnerability of the system, several levels of protection may have to be implemented to protect this weak area. In addition to surveillance and alarm devices, the system owners or users may wish to have underground cables installed and/or use encryption as the ultimate protective measure.

Microwave and Satellite Systems

The primary vulnerability of *microwave* communications (high-frequency signals passed through terrestrial relay stations) and *satellite* communications (ultrahigh-frequency signals relayed via a device orbiting the earth) is interception. The devices themselves require the same physical protection afforded other communications facilities. The solution to unauthorized access through message interception—encryption—will be discussed later.

Optimizing Physical Access Control Selection

There are many security devices and systems to choose from because so many new products are continually entering the market. Some security businesses specialize in the manufacture and distribution of one product or a small line of products, while other companies offer more of a full-service arrangement, including security system planning, maintenance, and, in some cases, even operation.

However, as mentioned earlier, there is no substitute for professional advice, including an outside independent security consultant. Security products are not inexpensive. Door entry systems may cost as little as $200 per door, or a sophisticated microprocessor system may cost as much as $2,000. An extremely sophisticated and technically advanced personal identification system can cost as much as $10,000 per installation or location.

In addition, there is a real need to protect *both* physical and logical accesses in an information system. As mentioned earlier, weaknesses in one area tend to result in vulnerabilities in the other. The objective of balancing both physical and logical security is primarily to avoid weak links and to increase the *penetration work factor*, which is the theoretical amount of effort or expense necessary to compromise a security mechanism such as a code.

A balanced security system (i.e., physical and logical areas) should result in the culprit or perpetrator expending the most effort and money possible to breach the system. A balanced security system should create the highest possible risk of detection for the person or persons attempting unauthorized access. It should also result in the lowest possible expenditure for total systems security to the organization. The balanced systems approach, in other words, should provide the most security for the least investment.

Testing Physical Access Controls

As a general rule, every security procedure, device, or system should be tested periodically for compliance with established standards or specifications. Unfortunately, after the installation, owners of security devices and systems tend to become complacent.

Security systems, both manual and automated, are not infallible. In addition, even when security devices are tied into centralized guard or alarm stations, periodic testing can reveal system inadequacies, areas that need changes, new facilities that need protection, and unexpected latent defects in the equipment.

The more sensitive the protected information system is, the more attention that must be given to test its security. An ideal program would include:

- Tests made to determine if the security system was properly installed
- Periodic tests to determine operational compliance with established standards and specifications
- Periodic tests to determine if any systems have been disabled or are being circumvented by employees or system users
- Periodic tests to determine if innovative methods can be or are being used to breach the security of the different protection systems requiring a reevaluation of existing security

As an example of how important periodic testing can be, an outside security consultant was hired by a large bank to review the physical security of the bank's new data center. The independent report revealed that:

- The new employee badge entry and identification system was not working properly because many data processing employees did not take the system seriously. They frequently left their badges at home, because they knew their managers would quickly authorize their entry into work and sensitive areas in order to maintain their productivity.
- The entry-area guard who examined the badges of arriving employees, vendors, and other guests could not see the closed-circuit TV monitor or sensitive hallways and areas while checking badges because of their inappropriate location.
- The expensive in-plant "mantrap" in the entryway that had been installed was disabled by the building supervisor because "it was a nuisance, and slowed down the entry and exit of personnel during the morning arrivals and afternoon departure time."
- The TV monitor screens located in the guard area displayed extremely poor images because they didn't comply with the original specifications, and certain hallways were not adequately lighted.

The bank had authorized its architect to spend approximately $200,000 for the security systems to be incorporated into the building during its construction. The architect contracted for the equipment directly from a single vendor. No other security expert was consulted.

As it turned out, the bank's data center was considerably less secure than was expected. Later, the bank had to contract for an entirely new security specification study and purchase and install completely new devices and systems—after competitive bidding.

Justification of Physical Access Control for Remotely Located Personal Computers and Terminals

The physical protection of personal computers and terminals in homes or remotely located offices is justifiable if for no other reason than the possibility of the theft of the entire system or even just part of it.

Unfortunately for many computer users and owners, the theft of their equipment may be the least of the damages or losses incurred. Many or maybe even most systems have valuable and possibly sensitive programs and data files attached to or stored in the vicinity of the hardware (i.e., in fixed or floppy disks). Because many individuals and companies have inadequate program and data backup and extremely sensitive data, the losses that might be sustained in the event of theft or destruction could be catastrophic.

When the computer or terminal belong to a viable business or organization as opposed to an individual, some measure of special physical security should be easily justifiable (including electronic surveillance and alarm systems). Adequate insurance coverage may or may not be obtainable but should be acquired as circumstances permit. In some cases, where considerable losses might be sustained as a result of theft or data compromise, a professional risk analysis study might be justified.

On the other hand, adequate security for systems located in homes or remote offices may simply be uneconomical or impractical or, in some cases, impossible. There are choices, however. Backup by physical removal and storage of floppy disk files off-site or dumping of files via communications to another system might be an adequate solution.

In addition, there are other solutions to the personal computer security problem, such as the use of portable systems or the implementation of logical file protection and destruction mechanisms.

It appears that remotely located personal computers and terminals are more vulnerable to abuse than are systems located in well-guarded areas with expensive electronic protection systems. However, creative thinking might produce solutions. How about concealment—the system no one knows about? Or, there is an even more total solution: A sensitive system that cannot be given adequate protection can be located away from the premises.

Summary

Computer systems require a balancing of physical and logical security because of their mutual dependence. Security must be looked at as a whole, to the extent that a "chain is no stronger than its weakest link." This applies to most computerized information systems and networks.

Typically, we have seen organizations spend far more on the physical and environmental security of their information system than on logical and communications security. Fortunately, people are developing a better understanding of why physical and logical computer security needs balancing and how security justification should proceed. It is also fortunate that, in the case of physical security, the tools needed for implementation either are presently available or will be soon.

11. Passwords and Personal Identification Devices

In this chapter we will cover the subject of computer user identification. The first line of defense in a shared computer environment (other than physical protection) is normally the user's personal password. Many organizations supplement passwords with various mechanical and electronic card-key systems. For even more identification security, other organizations are examining and testing new technologies that use some physical characteristics of a person to further confirm the personal positive identification of a system user.

The primary user identification subjects discussed in this chapter include:

- A formal approach to access control
- The importance of passwords
- Password system characteristics and selection
- Physical identification mechanisms
- Personal positive identification through characteristic matching

A Formal Approach to User Identification

Positive user identification is an essential part of access control systems. These systems usually have three major functions or objectives: identification, authentication, and authorization (Figure 11-1).

- *Identification* includes the initial and most basic user information such as a family name or a pseudonym that is used at log-on time to save time or computer memory. These primary IDs are normally public data.
- The password or secret code associated with the users' names or IDs is a primary mechanism used to confirm or *authenticate* that the persons logging on or desiring access to the computer or network are who they say they are.
- *Authorization* to access specific system resources such as files, programs, or specific devices is determined by a comparison of the users' IDs and passwords (and possibly other data) with a set of predetermined permissions to

111

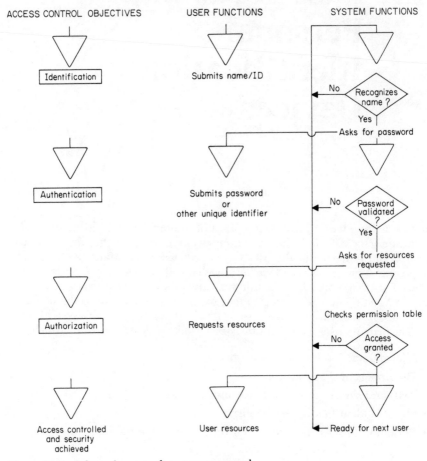

Figure 11-1 A formal approach to access control.

use the system that is normally always available to the system. The process that compares permission tables or rules with the users' IDs and passwords varies considerably from system to system. Also, the nature of access granted or the permissions handled by each computer system varies considerably. (For example, how much access should be given to a file, record, or field of data, and how much functionality, such as read, write, or execute instructions, should be given?)

There are three classes of mechanisms used to control a person's access to a system:

1. Something the user knows (e.g., password or other unique personal data)

2. Something the user possesses (e.g., physical key or magnetically encoded card key)

3. Something personal about the user (e.g., fingerprint, voiceprint, or signature)

The password is the most widely used identification and access control mechanism.

Password Importance

It is essential to place the importance of a password into the proper perspective. Consider the case where a single password may at some point in time be the only remaining safeguard between a penetration attempt and unauthorized access to a sensitive file or valuable system resource.

Granted, there are other security mechanisms that could be utilized to provide system access control. However, for reasons of convenience and cost, the password stands out as a key mechanism, if not *the* mechanism, used today to ensure that system users are really who they say they are.

In addition, even with an array of highly sophisticated electronic entry and surveillance mechanisms in place, all may be compromised by just one individual giving up his or her personal password either intentionally or accidentally.

Physical mechanisms, such as locks and magnetic card keys, can be compromised. Personal characteristic matching systems are still costly, inconvenient, and complex. It appears as if passwords will continue to be an important protection mechanism for system access control. It behooves us, therefore, to learn as much about passwords as we possibly can.

Password System Characteristics and Selection

Passwords used to provide access control for a computer or a network are generally divided into two categories: personal passwords and data or resource passwords. A *personal password* normally consists of a string of characters and/or digits used by an individual to gain access to a computer or other resources maintained in the system.

Ideally each individual entitled to use a system will have a unique password. Likewise only unique passwords would be assigned to a particular data set or system resource. Personal passwords should not be used as a data set or resource password.

A *data set* or *resource password* is used to authorize access to data and is known only to people who have similar authorization. A resource password allows shared access to a data file or systems resource.

Centralized Password Control

So, what happens when several people need to share numerous data and resources and all have unique passwords? The answer is that some form of relatively complex, centralized password control will probably be necessary in order to ensure that the system and its users are adequately protected. Sharing of individual passwords should not be allowed except in emergencies and then followed up with proper password regeneration and distribution.

Password Variations

There are in fact many password concepts in use today. Different passwords have been developed and used to:

- Increase the degree of protection provided
- Reduce system overhead and resource requirements
- Improve a system's response time
- Improve a system's convenience for users

The following are a few examples of the many password systems that can be found in use today:

- *User-generated passwords*
- *System-generated random passwords*
- *Once-only codes*:   the password is good for only one access. In this case the password is provided to the user directly from the system when he or she signs on, or a secret password list may be given from which the user extracts one password at a time.
- *Pass phrases*:   normally user-selected passwords thirty to eighty characters in length. Each pass phrase might be divided into 64 bits using a one-way encryption algorithm so the computer has only to store and compare 64 bits per pass phrase.
- *Limited-use passwords*:   a system that is somewhere between normal reusable passwords and once-only codes. *Limited* implies that the password may be used for only a prescribed number of times or until a given date.
- *Interactive question-and-answer sequence*:   requires that a list of questions and answers be previously recorded which because of their personal nature should be known only by the owner (i.e., system user) and the system itself.

In general, password protection in the past has been dependent on the extent to which system operators and users have followed a set of rather loosely assembled guidelines based more on experience than on scientific study. These guidelines include:

- Random derivation of the password
- Close control of its distribution if centrally administered

- An adequate password change policy rigorously administered
- Encryption of all computerized password files
- Concealment of all passwords that might have been displayed on a CRT or a teletypewriter device
- Use of a password in conjunction with some form of physical identification device, such as a magnetically encoded identification card or badge
- An administrative program designed to constantly remind employees or computer users to protect and not divulge their passwords

Password System Weaknesses

In spite of good intentions, many, if not most, password systems have not produced the degree of protection for which they were designed. Most of the failures result from the following:

- Accidentally divulged passwords by users
- Intentionally divulged passwords by users
- Easy passwords selected by users (so they won't forget)
- Passwords that are too short
- Inadequate password change procedure
- Password sharing required
- Overhead of adequate password change policy considered too high by management
- No random password generator in use
- Inadequate lost or forgotten password recovery procedure
- No formal password compromise incident report
- No backup or supplementary user ID and authentication system, such as use of magnetically encoded user ID cards
- Passwords easily compromised sometime during distribution from a centralized password management source
- Inadequate disconnect procedure when more than three incorrect password log-ons are attempted

Interactive Password Systems

Many users have attempted to introduce innovative procedures to make their password system work more effectively. One of the more interesting variations has been the addition of an interactive or *question-and-answer* password system. This system asks each user to establish a list of questions and responses that only he or she should know or remember (e.g., mother-in-law's maiden name). During the log-on, the access control system would be programmed to randomly select one or more of the questions and request an answer from the user.

The following are weaknesses in this additional password system which have resulted in its limited adoption:

- Forgotten exact answers
- Other people who know the user can give too many correct responses
- Research into the user's background can reveal response data
- System overhead is usually increased
- User friendliness of the system (i.e., convenience) is reduced

Call-Up and Answer-Back Protection

Further attempts to improve on the functions of user identification and authentication have resulted in interest in a protection concept called *call-up and answer-back*. This process is used to confirm a user's identity or authenticate a transaction by disconnecting the user before allowing access to system resources. The destination then manually or automatically calls back the preestablished phone number of the user who initially logged on and confirms that the user is an approved user, and the intended transaction can be validated.

Vendor-Supplied Passwords

The vulnerability of inadequately managed password and change systems was demonstrated quite vividly not long ago during one of the notorious hacker system intrusions. It was reported that hackers found certain systems particularly vulnerable to compromise because the standard manufacturer-supplied password that was delivered with the system to assist with initialization was never changed. The result was that this allegedly provided the hackers with particularly easy unauthorized access to those computers.

Password Guidelines and Standards

The lack of scientifically established guidelines or standards for computer password construction, utilization, and management has caused very uneven results in the use of password systems by both private industry and government. Arguments have raged for years with regard to proper password composition, length, lifetime, and best methods of distribution.

Probably one of the most important contributions toward good computer password development, use, and management will result from a study performed by the U.S. National Bureau of Standards [PA 1984].

The NBS password standard (draft 1984) recommends a 64-bit personal identification code. The ideal code, it suggests, should be derived from randomly selected passwords (six to eight characters long) and created from a set of sixty-two letters and digits. The NBS study further recommends that extremely sensitive passwords, if transmitted, be sent through networks that provide a secret key for encrypted communications between terminals or personal computers and host computers.

Theoretically, the implementation of password systems like that recommended by the NBS should take about one week of system designing, programming, and testing to install. The result would be a total password pool of 2.2×1014 possible combinations. It was estimated that it would take an average of seven years to compromise one password if attempts were made at a rate of one million tries per second.

The draft report generated from the NBS study also established the following list of ten factors and a minimum acceptable criteria for each to be considered in the design, implementation, and use of password systems.

1. Character length
2. Composition
3. Lifetime
4. Source
5. Ownership
6. Distribution
7. Storage
8. Entry
9. Transmission
10. Authentication frequency [PA 1984]

In Figure 11-2 is a brief summary of the minimum acceptable criteria for the ten factors depending on the level of defined security needed by a system (i.e., low, medium, or high).

All computer users and data processing organizations should carefully examine the drafted NBS guidelines in light of their own access control requirements and present password policies and practices. Most users and organizations will probably find inadequacies in their present password system.

Password System Controversies

As indicated earlier there has been and still is considerable controversy in most organizations with regard to the ideal password composition, length, lifetime, and distribution methods, to name only a few of the sensitive issues. Many of the debates focus on human factors or behavioral problems because of the increasing need in most organizations to enhance the user friendliness of their information systems in order to promote both system and user productivity.

For instance, what length must a password be to provide *enough* access control protection? Studies show that most people cannot correctly remember a password that is longer than seven characters. Even though longer

Factors that affect password security	Minimum acceptable criteria by protection level required in the system		
	Low	Medium	High
1. Character length	4–6	4–6	6–8
2. Composition	(0–9)	(A–Z) (a–3) (0–9)	Full character set
3. Lifetime	One year	Six months	One month
4. Source	User	System-generated and user-selected	Authentication system
5. Ownership	Per account (possibly shared)	Individual	Individual
6. Distribution	Unmarked envelope in U.S. mail	Terminal and special mailer	Registered mail, receipt required; personal delivery, affadavit required
7. Storage	Central computer on-line storage as plaintext	Encrypted passwords	Encrypted passwords
8. Entry	Nonprinting PIN-PAD	Nonprinting keyboard and masked-printing keyboard	Nonprinting keyboards
9. Transmission	Plaintext	Clear text	Encrypted communication with message numbering
10. Authentication frequency	Each transaction	Log in and after ten minutes of terminal inactivity	Log in and after five minutes of terminal inactivity

Figure 11-2 NBS guidelines for security password systems. (Data from *Passage Usage Standards*, National Bureau of Standards Pub. No. Draft, 1984.)

passwords may technically appear to be more secure, are they really? Consider the consequences if a typical user decides to write down the longer password and save it in some convenient place (e.g., taped to the side of the terminal).

What about password composition? Aside from the NBS guidelines, you will read expert opinions that say that easy-to-remember passwords don't get written down or compromised as much. Other experts insist that passwords that are difficult to pronounce (without vowels and with digits) are the only way to ensure protection.

Who should be the source of the password? Some experts will claim that if the password is supposed to be personal, then only the individual user should generate it. An equal number of security professionals conclude that a password generated by the system or security officer is in fact the best source.

How important is it to have passwords with more than five characters when five characters are the most people can easily remember? Then what about a four-character password? If five characters provide 45,535,424 possible combinations of usable passwords and four characters provide 1,336,336 possibilities, how much protection is really needed? The answer will depend on such factors as the number of employees or system users and the frequency of password changes.

There are a number of other system characteristics that should also be considered in the selection of password length. For systems available through dial-up networks, consideration has to be given to the increasing number of personal computers with communications capabilities that are being installed and the marked improvement in performance of those systems currently being sold.

In other words, a sensitive system with the above characteristics should have both a more sophisticated password system and possibly some significant architectural changes. For example, a dial-up feature for some parts of the system may not be acceptable unless communications and/or file encryption are required.

Also, secure password distribution problems are still not easily solvable. Consider for instance the question of whether passwords generated from a central management source in a large distributed system should be downloaded or distributed by courier. Everything from manual intervention and compromise to sophisticated communications wiretapping and interception may have to be considered. Maybe a form of mail system is a viable answer, and maybe it is not.

The above issues are raised to demonstrate the need to pay more attention to password systems and to point out that obvious answers will not necessarily be good solutions. The point is that the more you know about your system security needs, the better prepared you will be to select, implement, and maintain a password system that will balance cost, system convenience, and secure access control.

Physical Identification Mechanisms

Magnetic card and key entry systems (including cards that are not coded magnetically), first mentioned in Chapter 10, "Physical Access Control," are capable of controlling access to entryways or other openings to sensitive areas such as data centers, computer libraries, or terminal areas. The same technology is being used to upgrade logical computer system access control. This is done by supplementing password security with the addition of one more layer of protection: something that system users must have in their physical possession.

The main difference is in application of the device. These special identification and access control devices can be used to:

- Allow the possessor to unlock or make functional a personal or a host computer through a keyboard or a terminal

- Provide identification and a secret personal code to a local or remotely located computer for authentication purposes
- Provide another safeguard for reauthentication after log-on
- Provide a way to remotely verify, invalidate, cancel, or change the privileges extended to the cardholder

At the local level, the special identification card or device is used just like a simple key is used to unlock a keyboard. Keyboard locking systems have been around a long time and were designed primarily for local physical access protection and internal control purposes. In this case, the key itself, through possession, provided physical access to the system and a limited proof of identification.

The three main differences between an electronic card key (and similar devices) and a simple key are (1) secret information is normally encoded in the card, (2) device duplication or counterfeiting is usually more difficult, and (3) remote systems protection is extended through the communications network itself.

An excellent example of how card identification can be used to protect computer access is the typical system used by the banking industry to give customers access to automatic teller machines (ATMs). A customer carries a card which has identification and other related information such as account numbers magnetically encoded on it.

The insertion of an acceptable card into the card reader slot identifies a customer and initiates system activity. Most systems authenticate the cardholder's identification by requesting that a special remembered number—personal identification number (PIN)—also be inputted into the system through a keyboard that is integrated into the ATM. Customers can complete their transactions through the ATM terminal only after authentication is completed.

This, in essence, is how security experts and the companies producing the special card identification devices envision the addition of another layer of access control protection to information systems. There are significant variations in the card composition and coding technologies being offered, but most manufacturers tend to market reader systems that can operate in conjunction with a terminal or personal computer (a separate black box), or that can be integrated directly into the terminal or computer keyboard.

Encoding technologies include various magnetic-strip recording systems or the use of magnetic slugs imbedded into plastic cards. The magnetic slug systems offer more protection because the slugs cannot be altered without destroying the card.

Several new card identification and access control devices have also entered the market recently, which may provide another dimension of protection. These systems have some form of magnetic or optical memory device imbedded in plastic cards which can be used to store special user identification codes, passwords, or even encryption algorithms and variable data. Technological innovations, the "smart card," the "chip in the card," and optical systems offer such extensive memory capabilities that they can be used for numerous functional applications (e.g., bank balances, health data, scholastic achievement records, etc.) as well as for added system protection.

Special read-only memories and other patented protection features have been included in the design and construction of these cards to provide additional safeguards against card compromise or counterfeiting.

Another recent technological innovation which provides extra protection against card counterfeiting is holography. Master Card International has been issuing a new card featuring a *rainbow holograph*, or a three-dimensional image, with one number of the card embossed through it. Not only is the hologram difficult to counterfeit, but its placement over the last digit of the card makes it nearly impossible to alter.

Probably the most important restriction in the use of special card-oriented identification and access control systems is cost. Everything is expensive— from the card itself to the local reader device (usually attached or integrated into the keyboard) to the related systems logic design and programming. Local card reader terminals may range from several hundred to several thousand dollars apiece, depending on the technology and application. The decision to implement an advanced card identification and access control system depends on whether the considerable expense can be justified.

There are, however, some important advantages to a supplemental card identification system:

- It can add a layer of protection to systems access (something in possession)
- It can serve multiple purposes by protecting physical and logical access and fixed and variable data transactions
- It can serve both local and remote protection needs
- It can be controlled by a remotely located security administrator or access control software system (i.e., cards can be validated, cancelled, or altered via downloading of variable data or passwords)
- It can contain built-in self-destruct mechanisms to contend with tampering or counterfeit attempts

Overall, it would seem that there are advantages to the use of some form of special identification card system to supplement password protection. Larger organizations with more sensitive information and data communications systems might be better able to justify the expense of implementing card systems than smaller organizations or those with less sensitive systems. On the other hand, since there are many different card systems available, it is possible to find a system that offers the required level of protection at a justifiable cost.

Personal Positive Identification through Characteristic Matching

Systems of identification that are based on a comparison of one or more of a person's physical characteristics are frequently referred to as *biometric systems*. These systems can provide a third layer of access control protection by using a personal characteristic of a person to prove identity.

Biometric systems have been designed to satisfy both local and remote identification. A local system might use prerecorded characteristics stored in a magnetic card or a microprocessor. A remote identification system can authenticate the identity of an individual who is logging on a host computer from a distant terminal or personal computer by referring to prerecorded physical characteristics of the person located in an on-line storage device. Biometric systems on the market today can validate a person's identity by such physical characteristics as:

- Fingerprints
- Voiceprints
- Hand geometry
- Signatures and handwriting
- Palm prints
- Retinal patterns

These systems for positive personal identification are described as follows:

Fingerprints. Automatically compares the minutiae (relative positions of ridge endings and joins) of specific fingers placed on a scanning device by the person being identified. Primary difficulty is in obtaining a good registration, and cuts, blisters, and dirt may hinder a valid comparison. Most successful systems utilize optical scanning technology.

Voiceprints. Compares a person's voice pattern with an earlier recording. Most systems use quantification of the voice pattern and speed for comparison purposes. Rejection rates of legitimate users tend to be high because of voice variations caused by colds, laryngitis, and emotional stress.

Hand geometry. Compares the length and/or translucency of fingers laid on a special plate with a previous scan of the person's hand. These systems are quite reliable and have been available since 1968.

Signatures and handwriting. Compares differences in pressures and velocity to identify a person's handwriting with a previous recording. This type of identification system seems to have gained considerable public acceptance. The basic principle in this system is that people have a tendency to write or sign their names in a consistent and unique fashion. However, a valid comparison might be adversely influenced if a person had an injured hand or was under considerable stress.

Palm prints. Compares the unique pattern of a person's palm print with a prior registration, similar to automated fingerprint comparison technology.

Retinal patterns. Recognizes an individual by the blood vessel pattern of the eyes. A previously scanned image which has been converted from analog data to digital data is used to identify a particular person.

Most of these devices are highly technical and are, therefore, relatively expensive, particularly the remote sensing devices and characteristic readers.

From a practical standpoint, many of the characteristic matching systems do essentially what their manufacturers say they will do—under controlled conditions. The problem is that real-life environments do not provide controlled conditions. A physical injury, a temporary illness, a power failure, or any one of a number of unexpected situations can invalidate a biometric system identification.

Therefore, even though many systems succeed in recognizing systems access by an unauthorized person, many also reject legitimate computer users. The result is that very few of the characteristic matching systems are surviving the test of practical application.

On the other hand, security experts anticipate that biometric systems will improve in the near future. Besides advances in the basic technology, product costs are expected to decrease significantly. Hopefully, the final barrier to extensive biometric system utilization will also eventually be overcome—the user acceptance problem.

Any system that requires that people be fingerprinted, have their voices recorded, place their hands on an unusual looking contraption, or stare into some special device will not necessarily be well received. This problem, coupled with a high rejection rate for legitimate computer users and the general inconvenience of having to use still another device while trying to log on a system or initiate a transaction, means a probable slow takeoff for biometric access control systems.

Summary

To a large extent, systems access control is dependent on the success of an organization's personal password system. Funds spent for highly sophisticated physical and logical access control mechanisms are wasted if legitimate computer users accidentally or intentionally reveal their passwords to others.

On the other hand, new user identification and authentication systems are entering the marketplace with increasing frequency. Hopefully the costs of these new systems will decrease so they will be affordable.

Finally, important guidelines and standards are being developed for password systems and other personal identification and authentication devices. Future prospects, therefore, are looking better for systems that can *positively* identify a person at some remotely located personal computer or terminal who logs on the system and claims to be entitled to have access to a highly sensitive data file or program.

12. Access Control Software

The lack of security specifications during the design phase of most computer hardware and software development projects has resulted in an inadequate built-in access control capability for the majority of systems produced today. Manufacturers, software companies, and computer users have tried to overcome these deficiencies by implementing a variety of access control software packages that can be run "on top of," or "coresident" with, their computer's operating system.

Therefore, access control software, along with improvements in password protection schemes, physical communications security devices, and encryption, constitute the primary technical innovations or products being used to upgrade manufacturer-supplied hardware and operating systems software today. In this chapter we will discuss the more important characteristics of the presently available access control software products by addressing these four questions:

1. How do you know if you need special access control software in addition to the security presently provided in your system?

2. What are the more desirable features or options to look for in access control software?

3. How do you select a particular access control software package with a high degree of certainty that it will meet your needs?

4. What important benefits and problems have been reported by access control software users to date?

Identification of the Need for Access Control Software

In general, most access control software packages provide, to a greater or lesser degree, the logical protection for a computer system or a network in four main areas:

- User identification
- Authentication
- Authorization
- Security surveillance and reporting

Owners of a system which already has adequate protection in each of these areas probably cannot justify the additional expense of adding special access control software to the security already in place. Unfortunately, *adequate* security or access control is a gray area for many individual computer users and organizations. Most users base their justification for access control software on any of the following situations:

- Physical evidence that the system is being tampered with at the logical level in spite of existing safeguards
- Known deficiencies in any one or all of the four main areas of access protection previously described
- Completion of a formal risk analysis study of a system's access control vulnerabilities, including the scope of any loss potential
- Comparison of a system's access control capabilities with known accepted standards or guidelines, such as those contained in documents published or distributed by the DOD Director of Contract Administrator Services, the DOD Computer Security Center, or the National Bureau of Standards. Many nongovernment guidelines also exist, such as those published by the Institute of Internal Auditors, the American Institute of Certified Public Accountants, and professional associations, such as those that serve the banking industry
- Acquisition of access control software recommended and maintained by the organization's computer vendor(s)
- Acquisition of access control software recommended by a security consultant or by a representative of an access control software company

The justification for purchasing access control software for a sensitive system should not be exceedingly difficult where inadequacies or gross omissions exist in such areas as the following:

- User ID and password authentication
- Level of access control authorization
- Dial-up systems access control
- Reports of unauthorized systems access (or attempts)
- Facilities which limit the number of times an unauthorized (i.e., illegal ID or password) log-on attempt will be allowed before the user is disconnected
- Call-up and answer-back facilities in a dial-up network

Furthermore, even when justification for access control software does not lend itself to a simple quantification or cost-benefit analysis, in the absence of the above controls a direct management instruction to implement such a system would be in order.

Features of Access Control Software

It should not be surprising that the number and functionality of protection features offered in commercial access control software vary considerably. Reasons for this broad array of offerings relate to such market or user considerations as:

- The type of hardware and software architecture the package is designed to run on (i.e., virtual memory, disk operating system, type of communications facilities)
- Primary system functions such as time sharing or transaction processing
- The amount of system access overhead to be tolerated
- User response time requirements
- Existing installed access controls
- Number of system users
- Sensitivity of the system
- Type of access denial and alarm system needed

A complete access control software package should fulfill all four basic access control objectives: identification, authentication, authorization, and surveillance and reporting (Figure 12-1). Above all, access control software should be a major deterrent to system penetration; it should be a first line of defense against an unauthorized user or transaction. To accomplish this, the system should contain at a minimum the following three functions (Figure 12-2):

1. Prevention
2. Detection
3. Violation reporting

Conceptually, most access control systems protect access by one of three mechanisms:

- *Default principle or policy*: Access is not allowed without specific authorization.
- *Active request principle*: A file is not protected unless a specific request has been submitted for special safeguarding.

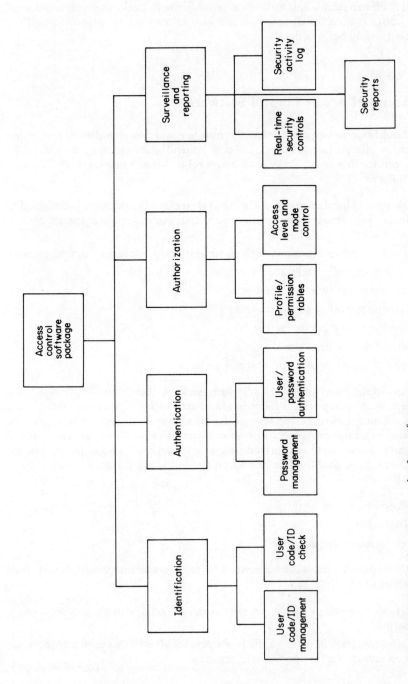

Figure 12-1 Typical access control software features.

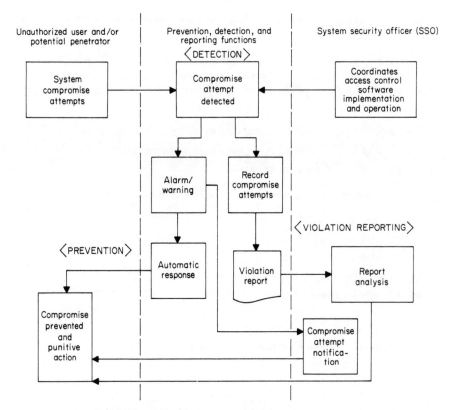

Figure 12-2 System functions of access control software.

- *Combination principle*:   Data and resources that are not sensitive can be made widely accessible; however, high-risk data and resources can still be designated inaccessible by default.

   Typically, most access control software packages include features that will provide the following (actual features would depend on the type of default system used and architectural considerations):

- Verification of log-on and passwords
- Restriction of access to sensitive data and resources by operator, day, time, and other protection criteria
- Protection of data and resources managed by the operating and file management systems, such as terminals, peripheral equipment, files, and programs
- Protection of data displays (output), data structures and fields, and other user-defined resources
- Enforcement of security requirements and monitoring usage of all defined resources

- Reporting of security violations immediately and preparation of access violation reports

The amount of security functionality and the number of special options provided in each of the major protection areas vary considerably from package to package. Some of the more significant differences between packages include:

- Scope of the password checking and management subsystem
- Number of levels of user access to resources provided
- System audit and logging capability

In addition, major differences are to be found in such operational areas as:

- Ease of installation
- Administrative controls
- Maintainability
- Documentation and training support
- Modification capability

Selection of Access Control Software

The selection of access control software may pose a problem. To begin with, there are very few access control packages available except for current-generation IBM computer systems. Many computers have only one or two independent software houses that offer special access control software that will supplement the built-in controls included in their systems. There are even fewer access control software packages to support minicomputers and personal computers. There are a few vendors in addition to IBM who do offer access control packages that are *unbundled* (i.e., sold separately from the computer hardware).

After confirming the need for better access control, the first option for many non-IBM computer users may be to evaluate the following possibilities:

- Design and program it yourself
- Have an outside consultant or software house produce it for you
- Find out if a major equipment supplier will develop it for you

The above analysis could take the form of a "make-buy" decision and might be the best thing to do even if you could purchase a commercially available system.

For example, a large county court administrative operation elected to have its national certified public accountant (CPA) firm design, program, and install its access control software. Results were particularly good because EDP consultants from the accounting firm had worked for the court on other assignments and were already familiar with the court's information security needs. A major benefit from having the consultant design the system to customize requirements was that only the access control features actually needed by the court administrative office and terminal users were implemented, resulting in no unnecessary system overhead.

The most important decision criteria with regard to which access control software package to acquire would include:

- Compatibility (with existing computer hardware and software)
- Functionality (meets protection requirements)
- Integrity (meets specifications)
- Efficiency (tolerable and minimum overhead)
- Ease of installation
- Ease of use (i.e., user friendliness)
- Cost
- Vendor technical support (trouble shooting, documentation, education, and maintenance)

The results of numerous comparative analysis studies of access control software packages that are vendor-compatible have been published in professional trade journals and in vendor sales literature for IBM. Most of the comparisons include the special unbundled access control software system offered by IBM called Resource Access Control Facility (RACF). One of the best comparative studies can be found in the September–October 1983 issue (volume 8, number 1) of *Data Processing & Communications Security* [CO 1983a]. Because of price changes, vendor enhancements, and the introduction of new products to the market, such studies, unfortunately, become obsolete soon after they are published.

Before making the final decision as to which access control package you need, you may wish to ask for product demonstrations and a list of referral customers or, better yet, participate in a hands-on test of the product. The hands-on test is a very good idea and might include the following testing procedures:

- Attempt to compromise the system functions.
- Attempt to access and modify (unauthorized) the access control software package itself and also any logs or reports generated by it.
- Try to interrupt the system by submitting error conditions.
- Try to crash the system and compromise the recovery procedure.
- Review all logs and security reports generated by the system to see if the system actually caught and documented all compromise attempts; also determine if all data specified to be on reports is actually printed.
- Monitor and review all system resource uses and response time degradation.

Reported User Benefits and Problems

Since several of the major access control software packages have been on the market for about ten years, there is a growing amount of customer testimony with regard to the benefits of these packages. Typical user experience includes the following strengths and weaknesses.

STRENGTHS

- Separates the ability to define and control system resources (i.e., resource ownership versus systems management)
- Allows and encourages the users themselves to decide how much protection they really need and can afford
- Promotes individual accountability
- Greatly enhances security accounting and auditability
- Systems generally easy to install
- Reliability and maintainability of systems generally excellent
- Systems easy to use, reasonably "friendly," and mostly invisible to users
- Requires minimum manual intervention and reduces work load of system security officer
- Helps to tie physical and logical security together
- Flexible and permits modification when necessary
- Use of software product does not require changes to operating system, stays upwardly compatible, and does not require reinstallation during operating system maintenance
- Keeps better track of systems accesses by providing a more realistic appraisal of level of access security that is maintained in the system

Not all the experiences have been positive however. The following are examples of major user concerns:

WEAKNESSES

- The access control software package itself could be compromised, giving everyone a false sense of security
- Very time-consuming installation because so many data sets and access levels had to be defined
- Still does not provide adequate security for dial-up systems
- Needs better on-line notification of attempted or suspected system penetration
- Security reports still need improvement
- Modification of package not as easy as claimed
- Still does not adequately protect against use of authorized passwords by unauthorized people

Since a particular access control software package is used in thousands of installations, most of the earlier bugs and inadequacies have been worked out. Possibly the only thing better than improvements in packaged access control software would be for computer manufacturers to build better access control features into all of their systems.

Summary

Access control software packages were first introduced to supplement the built-in access protection features of third- and fourth-generation computer systems. The variety of features available today (particularly IBM-compatible systems) make it possible for computer users to be very selective in their product choices.

Actual user experience indicates that the advantages and added protection provided by these systems far outweigh the disadvantages and additional costs. Once the need and cost benefits have been established, most organizations and computer users find that it is usually more economical and expeditious to acquire an existing software package from an outside vendor (when available) than to build the product themselves.

Eventually, when more powerful built-in access control features are provided in standard computer hardware and software, there will not be a need for a supplemental access control software package in order to achieve adequate system protection.

13. Operating Systems Security

In this chapter we will review the state of the art and discuss the importance of security features in operating systems. The chapter is divided into two sections. Section 1 addresses a few misconceptions that can cause the average computer users to misunderstand operating system security and access control, namely:

MISCONCEPTIONS

- Software for operating system security is independent of the hardware it runs on.
- Operating system security is the ultimate answer to trapdoors, Trojan horses, and attacks by system programmers.
- Secure operating systems are almost impossible to build.

Section 2 explores the background of several important questions associated with operating system security and access control:

QUESTIONS

- What is operating system security, and how does it affect access control?
- How did the requirement to share computer data resources trigger interest in secure operating systems?
- What are the primary security weaknesses found in most operating systems?
- Which security features should you look for in today's operating systems?

Section 1: Misconceptions

Misconception 1: Operating System Security Tends to be Independent of the Hardware the Software Runs On

This is a gross misconception since high levels of information systems security can only be achieved by user application programs, the operating system, and the computer hardware, all running in concert. Furthermore, it was discovered long ago that computer hardware *must* be used to assure the level of integrity and isolation needed to satisfy high-level security requirements. Operating system security is therefore very dependent on the hardware architecture that the software must run on.

Several important hardware mechanisms that can enhance the security of a system include:

- *Virtual addressing*:   A computer addressing scheme designed to control what parts of memory can be addressed and how. A very useful security mechanism because user access can be restricted to only those segments of memory currently in the user's mapping table.

- *Base and bounds*:   A protection mechanism that uses two hardware registers containing a base address and an offset limit. Protection is achieved by requiring that all memory addresses generated by a user fall within the limits specified by these registers. This mechanism is useful in protecting one user from the actions of another user, but does nothing to protect a user from his or her own mistakes.

- *Domain and rings*:   Mechanisms that divide memory into conceptual or logically concentric rings of increasing sensitivity. Protection is afforded by the control of user or subject access to the domain or ring.

On the other hand, it is difficult to separate user access control functionality from the logic embedded in the computer's operating system since it is the operating system that controls, assigns, allocates, and supervises all resources within the computer system. Memory, input-output (I/O) channels, peripheral units, data files, the master file index, and the central processing unit (CPU) are accessible to an application program only after appropriate dialogue (i.e., system calls) with the operating system. Should the operating system be tricked, subverted, controlled, or compromised by an application program, the confidentiality of information may be violated, regardless of whether the act of subversion was accidental or deliberate.

Misconception 2: Operating System Security Is the Ultimate Answer to Trapdoors, Trojan Horses, and Attacks by System Programmers

At best, this is an optimistic view of operating system security features. First, we need to consider the semantic difference between *operating system security* and a *secure operating system*.

Operating system security refers to the many internal programmed controls and technical features that may be built into an operating system to protect system users and resources from the consequences of unauthorized access.

A *secure operating system* refers to an operating system built with design objectives that include an architecture that precludes any form of system compromise. This includes protection against the compromise of any part of the operating system design itself (intentionally or unintentionally) and against attacks after the system has been installed in a user environment.

The question here is: If an operating system were designed and built to specifications, including certain mathematical proof of correctness (i.e., 100 percent security), would it be protected from compromises perpetrated through trapdoors, Trojan horses, or other extremely sophisticated technical manipulations?

Theoretically, this design objective for a secure operating system may be attainable. The utilization of an architecture called a *security kernel* prohibits errors and intentional instructions that might facilitate some future compromise. Most approaches to secure operating systems are based on a primary assumption that it is extremely important to restrict the number of control system access instructions to approximately 1,000. This set of highly sensitive, privileged instructions is the security kernel.

The question is: Can we ever be 100 percent certain that a probably secure computer architecture, once introduced into a typical people-oriented environment, will stay secure? The answer may be yes if we can completely trust the people who maintain the hardware and software and who are responsible for system security (i.e., the person in charge of the master keys or the systems security officer). Furthermore, we may still be unable to verify designs built to security kernel and similar specifications.

Ultimate security, or 100 percent security through technology, may be a goal for some computer users, but for the vast majority the solution will continue to be a balancing of risks and protection costs. And even when secure operating systems are implemented commercially, users will still be responsible for keeping their own systems uncontaminated.

Fortunately, the implementation of basic internal control principles such as separation of duties and responsibilities tends to work just as well in an automated systems environment as it does in a manual one.

Misconception 3: Secure Operating Systems Are Almost Impossible to Build

The position taken by the RISOS report [SE 1976] issued in April 1976 was as follows:

The ideal situation is one in which operating system security is a major design criterion. Even then, consideration must be given as to whether the design is correct, the design is correctly interpreted, and the interpretation is correctly implemented. Unfortunately, computer science has not advanced to the point where it is possible to *prove* that a sizable program has been correctly designed, interpreted, and implemented. It may well be that an incorrect design, an incorrect interpretation of that design, and an incorrect implementation may appear to provide a satisfactory operation system.

Considerable progress has been made since this report was issued. The major technical accomplishments will be discussed in Section 2 of this chapter.

The degree of protection obtainable in a secure operating system, therefore, depends on the extent to which the security kernel can be trusted. Its proof of correctness in design and implementation and its isolation or protection from compromise (besides its functionality) were considered by many to be extremely difficult to verify.

Actual experience (at a cost of millions of dollars) has demonstrated that security kernel–oriented operating systems are indeed feasible. And they have been built. (A more detailed description of the development of security kernel architecture will be presented in Section 2 of this chapter and in Chapter 14.)

Section 2: Operating System Security and Access Control

Question 1: What Is Operating System Security and How Does it Affect Access Control?

An *operating system* is an integrated set of computer programs that supervises and manages system resources in order to execute jobs or processes automatically. Primarily, an operating system controls and schedules system resources. User (subject) access to resources (objects such as data, programs, devices, etc.) is just one of many functions programmed into operating system software.

A critical aspect of an operating system is its *integrity*—the assurance that it will do everything it is supposed to do exactly right (i.e., according to its specifications). The problem is that the software can do everything exactly right and still be unable to prevent unauthorized access to data and system resources. There are at least four basic reasons for this:

1. Certain desirable security and access control features may not have been included in the operating system specifications in the first place.
2. Even though extensive security and access control mechanisms were included in the specifications, errors in design or implementation may have been made.
3. Testing for all possible conditions of unauthorized access that might occur was not done because of the size and complexity of the system, or as the result of an oversight.
4. Someone may have introduced a trapdoor or Trojan horse into the system during its development phase.

Therefore, even though access control is a primary function of the operating system, most commercial operating systems in use today are inadequately designed to fulfill this function. This is of paramount concern to users because their operating system is, for all practical purposes, the most important control mechanism in their computer system and, in many cases, the last line of defense against a dedicated compromiser.

Operating systems, along with hardware, provide logical access control security for the computer. In other words, logical access control protects hardware, software, and data from user-initiated actions that can be performed automatically once they are introduced into the system. Examples of this class of compromise might include:

- Subversion or bypassing of existing hardware or software controls to gain access to data or system resources
- Unauthorized use of system resources by compromising part of the operating system
- Intentional destruction or alteration of vital software
- Unauthorized access to user passwords or permission tables
- Intentional interruption of system processes, including denial of service to computer users

Since all operating systems employ some form of access control safeguards (if only to separate system users and programs to prevent accidental errors), what enables experts to say that one general-purpose computer is more secure than another?

The answer is that operating systems can be evaluated by the basic security criteria that was covered in earlier chapters:

- Identification capability
- Authentication capability
- Authorization capability

The more powerful the operating system controls are, the more secure the system is.

It is of interest to compare these criteria with those selected several years ago by a major computer manufacturer. The manufacturer assigned a task force made up of systems engineers to develop a set of security criteria that could be used in the design of a new operating system. The set of criteria arrived at for specification and test purposes included:

- Identification
- File protection
- Control integrity
- Resource control

The design team then utilized these criteria to add security features to the new operating systems that would otherwise not have been included. For example, the following safeguards were added to the operating system specification:

Identification. A password encryption scheme

File protection.   Levels of protection based on read, write, execute, and append modes and a security classification concept that established level-of-protection schemes

Control integrity.   A descriptor-driven access authorization mechanism

Resource control.   A set of special routines to control CPU, input-output device, and memory allocations

Specification of good security policies and access control mechanisms during the design phase of a new operating system is essential if the system is going to prevent unauthorized activity in the user environment. Users should also consider generating security specifications when preparing new computer proposal requests or when evaluating a new system. By prescribing security and access control criteria before selecting a new computer, users can avoid the costly mistakes made by others who purchased computers that were designed without internal security features.

Question 2: How Did the Requirement to Share Computer Data and Resources Trigger Interest in Secure Operating Systems?

With one major exception [HI 1975], security was not recognized during the 1960s as a function that needed to be built into operating systems. The design priority for second- and third-generation computers built in the 1960s and early 1970s was for basic operational requirements such as data processing and input-output control.

The primary movement that brought security to the attention of system developers was the great increase in computer resource sharing with the advent of systems that could perform multiprogramming, multiprocessing, memory mapping, and time sharing. Improvements in hardware and software technology caused the development of new system-use concepts to take advantage of the increased cost performance.

Most systems before this time operated for the benefit of one user at a time. Batch processing was the classic computer operating mode until the implementation of the new system-use concepts.

For all practical purposes, therefore, there were little or no shared access problems. The principal question of who to charge for computer time created a need for user identification that consisted of little more than an individual's name, organization or cost center, and job ID code. In addition, most user programs and files were not even loaded into card readers or tape handlers until it was time to run the job. Unauthorized access was, therefore, primarily a physical security problem.

With the great increase in computer resource sharing, on-line programs and files, and many new applications involving data communications, users became more concerned about who has access to the system and what they are doing.

Recognition of the access vulnerability of third-generation systems came too late for most computer vendors and users to do anything about the problem. Both the hardware and the operating systems that run on the hardware were, for the most part, designed with only the most rudimentary security features. Actually, operating systems were designed for maximum accessibility in order to make the new computers as easy as possible to use for the benefit of the many new users.

Operating system security was first examined by the Department of Defense (DOD), several of its contractors, and researchers at a number of U.S. universities. Their conclusions revealed an immediate need for more secure ways by which users could share computer resources with others.

The term most frequently applied to this requirement was *multilevel* security. Essentially, the Department of Defense agencies and their defense contractors desired more assurance that only people with proper clearances could gain access to classified data or sensitive computer resources.

In the absence of hardware and software architectures (with the notable exception of Honeywell's Multics [HO 1980] capable of supporting this need, DOD agencies and, subsequently, their contractors resorted to running sensitive or classified work one job at a time (i.e., uniprocessing) on machines capable of handling a large number of concurrent users. (Another alternative was to dedicate a system to top-secret users and data on one day and secret users and data on another day.) As a result huge amounts of federal (mostly DOD) funds were poured into research projects designed to produce new insights into how to build secure operating systems.

From the beginning, one secure systems concept attracted the most attention and was favored by computer security experts for its potential usefulness. The concept, called the *reference monitor* (Figure 13-1), was based on the

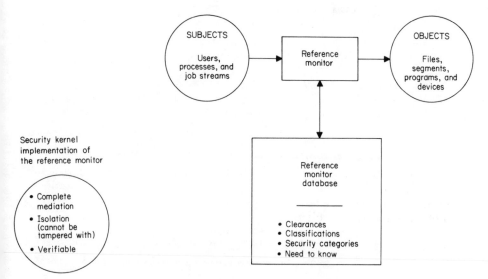

Figure 13-1 Reference monitor concept.

abstract modeling efforts of Butler Lampson [LA 1971]. The concept is a precisely defined internal access control mechanism with the internal security of the system as its primary goal.

A report [AN 1972] by a government consultant, James P. Anderson, described the new concept as a way of controlling multilevel access to data and other computer resources. The essential three design requirements are as follows:

1. The reference validation mechanism must be tamperproof.

2. The reference validation mechanism must always be invoked.

3. The reference validation mechanism must be small enough to be subject to analysis and tests, the completeness of which can be assured. [AN 1972]

The basic concept implies that multilevel secure computer systems can be based on controlled sharing. Implementation of the concept requires that "each subject of the system [system entities such as a user or program which can access system resources] and each object [system entities such as data, programs, peripheral devices, and main memory] must be identified and interrelated according to their authorized accessibility" [AN 1972].

One problem with the reference monitor approach was that it required a developer to start with a totally new operating system (and probably hardware) design. In essence, the reference monitor principles needed to be built into a security kernel (Figure 13-2).

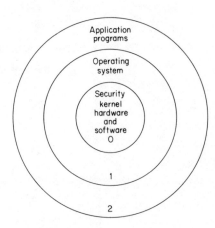

0 = Highest privilege or most secure
1 = Less privileged and secure than kernel,
    but more secure than applications or user programs
2 = Least privilege and lowest security (user programs)

Figure 13-2   Security kernel concept.

Most current general-purpose operating systems are quite vulnerable. As a result, many vendors and computer users have tried to "patch" security into their existing operating systems rather than start a new operating system project with security and access control as a high-priority design criteria. This is one reason why there is an increasing interest in access control software packages that can be run with existing operating systems.

Another problem with the reference monitor concept is that early attempts to reproduce it in actual hardware and software met with only minimal success, primarily because of unexpectedly high overhead and/or system performance degradation.

However, with the introduction of one computer (Honeywell's SCOMP) [BE 1983a] that has met the reference monitor specifications and the new DOD Computer Security Center's A1 evaluation criteria, success with the reference monitor concept does not seem too far away. Nevertheless, because of concerns about performance degradation, cost, language, and system software tools, government agencies and industrial computer manufacturers are being conservative in their use of this concept. The result is that other design concepts for secure operating systems are under consideration.

Question 3: What Are the Primary Weaknesses Found in Most Operating Systems?

In the late 1960s and early 1970s, it was realized that most commercial operating systems lacked real security and access control. Although expert system designers and experienced computer users could identify some of the vulnerabilities of a particular computer, a clear picture of the classic weaknesses of most computers was not readily available.

Progress was made as the result of several definitive studies financed mostly by the federal government or performed by the Department of Defense. The studies included:

- The Computer Security Planning Study by James P. Anderson & Co. (for the DOD/USAF)
- The RISOS Project (for the DOD/ARPA)
- The Joint Technical Support Activity (for the DOD/WWMCS)

The Anderson report. It is interesting to note how clearly some of the major system vulnerabilities were pointed out in this early study. The following are a few key quotations from the Anderson report [AN 1972]:

Another major problem is the fact that there are growing pressures to interlink separate but related computer systems into increasingly complex networks. The principal problem seen here is that the security dangers of such interlinking are masked by the apparently "safe" interaction directly between computer systems.

This was an extremely perceptive observation, because this was and still is a major weakness in most systems: the implementation of architectures that rely on the integrity and "trustworthiness" of the other computers or networks to which they happen to be connected.

The interactive resource-sharing systems also provide economical centralization of programs and especially data online to an application that permits them to be accessed upon demand from any terminal attached to the system. This factor, plus the nature of time-sharing itself which provides for two or more programs to be resident simultaneously in primary storage, erodes the separation principle that had been the keystone to security practice in the past. Further, it replaces manual, easily visible controls with reliance upon logical and intangible program controls to keep separate data and programs belonging to different users.

At first glance, the problems of providing privacy and security in resource-shared systems seem ridiculously simple. Since it is a generally accepted requirement that the executive (operating system) for resource-shared systems and other users must be protected from "buggy" programs, it follows that any of the various time-shared systems are "security." Unfortunately, this is not the case.

The essence of the multilevel security technical problem becomes clear when the fact that programs of users with different clearances and data of different classifications share primary storage simultaneously in resource-sharing systems that rely on an operating system program to maintain their separation. Furthermore, the situation is aggravated when the user of a resource-sharing system, to a greater or lesser degree, must program the system to accomplish his works.

It is generally true that contemporary systems provide limited protection against *accidental* violation of their operating systems; it is equally true that virtually none of them provide any protection against deliberate attempts to penetrate the nominal security controls provided. It is the possibility of deliberate penetration by a user that we call malicious threat.

The technical issue of multilevel computer security is concerned with the concept of malicious threat. By this we recognize that the nature of shared use multilevel computer systems presents to a malicious user a unique opportunity for attempting to subvert through programming the *mechanism* upon which security depends (i.e., the control of the computer vested in the operating system).

Underlying most current users' problems is the fact that contemporary commercially available hardware and operating systems do not provide adequate support for computer security. While some limited protection is supplied in the form of memory protection controls, master and slave modes, and privileged instructions, experienced programmers have had little difficulty in penetrating off-the-shelf systems and retrieving desired data items.

In contemporary systems, the attacker attempts to find design or implementation flaws that will give him supervisory control of the system. With supervisory control, he is then able to exercise parts of the operating system to access unauthorized classified data and return it to his own program in a way not anticipated by the operating system designers. Alternatively, he can either add to or temporarily replace parts of the operating system to give his program access and reference privileges not authorized to him. He may direct his attention specifically to the file containing the list of authorized users of a system [frequently containing the password(s) associated with each user]. In any case, the attacker is able to reference any data or programs in the system.

A contemporary system provides a limited form of reference validation in the form of the memory protect scheme for the system. These schemes are designed to isolate the running programs from other programs and the operating system, and in general, work well enough on most systems. Because the schemes are so simple . . . they are generally applied to user programs only. The operating system, because it needs to reference all of the real memory on a system in exercising its control functions, most frequently runs with the memory protect suspended (i.e., in a supervisory or control state, where no checking of a reference is done) or with the memory protect set to enable the executive to refer to any memory without restriction. . . . While it would be desirable to confine references from the centralized service functions of an operating system to those parts of memory allocated to the user making the request, there is no convenient way on most machines to do so. Compounding this condition is the fact that many of the service functions made available to user programs are also used by the operating system in exercising its control of the system. In most systems it is not possible for a called service function to determine the identity of the caller and thereby 'interpret' the validity of the parameters or the service requested.

In conventional two-state machines, unrestricted addressing and privilege for executing I/O operations and setting memory bounds registers are associated with the supervisory state. Thus, the two-state machine is forced to enter supervisory state to provide the needed addressing capability, even to perform services not requiring privileged instructions, but requiring a capability to refer to data or instructions in the caller's workspace. Because of the all or nothing approach to memory protection, and because the simple bounds register technique forces programs and data to be bound together in contiguous locations, there is no convenient way to localize the referencing capability of an operating system service function.

The limited reference control provided by the memory protect schemes on most contemporary systems thus leads to monolithic, totally privileged executives with an unrestricted capability to reference any part of main or auxiliary storage. Because of the total privilege and unrestricted referencing capability of the executive, it is necessary for all parts of the executive to be designed and implemented correctly in order to assure that a system is proof against an attack by a malicious user. The sheer size of contemporary operating systems (on the order of 10,000+ instructions) and their complexity makes it virtually impossible to validate the static design and implementation of the system. When the dynamic behavior of the system is contemplated as well, there is no practical way to validate that all of the possible control paths of the operating system in execution produce correct, error-free results.

Because nearly all of the contemporary operating systems have so much of their code running in supervisory state, there are a large number of places a malicious user can attempt to attack a system. The primary points of attack include the I/O interface and the various system supplied service functions.

The attacks are possible because the operating system/hardware architectures tend to promote a monolithic totally privileged executive with unrestricted capability to reference any main or auxiliary memory locations. While it would be possible to design a more modular executive, the present design approaches (on contemporary hardware) provide the most efficient operation of the executive. A more structured operating system could be achieved on contemporary systems only by providing software controls (at considerable penalties in operating efficiency) to restrict references by the operating system. These conditions coupled with flaws or misconceptions in the design, and the fact that the operating systems *were not designed to be secure*, provide a malicious user with any number of opportunities to subvert the operating system itself. [AN 1972]

The RISOS project.   The RISOS project [CO 1973] was funded by the Advanced Research Projects Agency of the Department of Defense and was performed under the auspices of the (then) U.S. Energy Research Development Administration at the Lawrence Livermore Laboratory in Berkeley, California. The project was of considerable importance because it was one of the first systematic efforts to analyze a group of commercial operating systems for security and access control vulnerabilities.

Specifically, four operating systems were evaluated in detail:

1. IBM's CS/MVT for the 360/370 series
2. Honeywell's GCOS III
3. Univac EXEC-8
4. Control Data Corporation's SCOPE 3.4

A large part of the RISOS project was devoted to the comparison of similar supervisory calls because, from the standpoint of operating system security, it was believed that this was the most logical area from which attempts would be made to gain control of the system.

Two of the most important publications as a result of the study were a "Taxonomy of Integrity Flaws" and a "Detailed Description of Operating System Security Flaws."

Integrity was defined as "the state that exists when there is a complete assurance that under all conditions a system works as intended." Integrity flaws can result in security flaws. "When an individual (or group) becomes aware of a flaw, an active potential to violate installation integrity is achieved." The operating system is listed as only one class of integrity flaws. "Thus, an operating system flaw is any condition that would permit a user (or his programs) to cause the operating system to cease reliable and secure operation" [CO 1973].

One of the most important benefits of the RISOS project was that a set of tools and analytical processes was developed that could be used to compare the security strengths (or weaknesses) of different operating systems.

The Joint Technical Support Activity.   Probably no computer system and network yet developed has been subjected to as much security vulnerability testing as the Honeywell series 6000/Level 66 GCOS III operating system, sometimes called WWMCCS-GCOS.

The computers were acquired as the primary mainframe of the DOD's worldwide military command and control system. Most of the vulnerability testing of the hardware, software, and communications facilities associated with the network was carried out by a special task force of computer experts working for the commander of the Joint Technical Support Activity (JTSA) task force.

The testing was of an extremely rigorous nature and resulted in the development of new insight into why certain computer architectures and processes are more secure than others. The result of the testing was the systematic elimination or reduction of discovered weaknesses or vulnerabilities. In order to meet DOD standards, an operating system was created that in some ways was distinctly different from the standard commercial GCOS.

Besides the elimination of vulnerabilities, a second accomplishment of the JTSA task force was the development of an extremely useful test report format that was used to document operating system access control and security problems. The document, called the "ADP Incident Report," included the following data input parameters:

- Report ID number
- Severity (of problem)
- Point of contact
- Phone number (network)
- Date
- Address (location)
- Date and time of incident
- Total time down
- System ID
- Operating system release/version
- Program ID
- Nature of activity
- Suspected problem type
- Description of incident
- Hardware components
- Corrective action taken
- Assistance required

- By date (needed)
- Supporting documentation
- Security classification

A major benefit of these three government-sponsored computer research projects was the dissemination of knowledge to people and organizations both inside and outside the federal government on how to build more secure computers.

Recently, a new generation of more secure hardware and operating systems has replaced those first subjected to rigorous analysis and comparison. The situation today is that government and industry apparently have learned enough about computer vulnerabilities from the early studies to focus new research efforts on ways to design more secure systems.

Question 4: Which Security Features Should You Look for in Today's Operating Systems?

All large general-purpose computer operating systems today offer less than verifiable security. Fortunately, most commercial and government computer users are looking for operating systems that have only enough access control and other security mechanisms to protect their information at an affordable price. In other words, users want an operating system that permits them to balance risks with costs of protection.

There are computers and operating systems available which, if used properly and given adequate physical protection, can provide thousands of computer users with a sufficient level of security. *Sufficient level of security* means that the protection provided by an operating system only needs to meet the realistically determined security requirements of an organization. An overly secure system would be overkill for most computer users.

So, how do you evaluate the security features of a particular operating system in the absence of standards, certification data, or adequate guidelines? The answer is that you must understand your own system security needs and enough about the computer operating system you are considering in order to make an informed decision.

Since most commercial and personal computer users have not yet developed a mathematical model of their own security policies, the results of advanced research in this area will do them little good at this time. The result is that most users, after documenting their basic requirements, will have to painstakingly read the manuals and specifications published by computer manufacturers. This literature can often provide valuable insight into just how much security a particular operating system provides.

The following is an example of the published security features of one present-day operating system—Honeywell's Multics (Multiplexed Information and Computer Service). Considerably more detailed information can be acquired by a thorough reading of manufacturer-supplied systems literature, independent reviews printed in professional journals, and technical security evaluation reports published by federal government agencies.

Multics has been considered for review here because more data has been published about the security features of this system than about any other presently available commercial computer system.

Multics.   One of the most noteworthy statements made about Honeywell's Multics was printed in a report [KA 1973] published by the U.S. Air Force:

> The report concludes that Multics as implemented today is not certifiably secure and cannot be used in an open use multi-level system. However, the Multics security design principles are significantly better than other contemporary systems. Thus, Multics as implemented today, can be used in a benign Secret/Top Secret environment. In addition, Multics forms a base from which a certifiably secure open use multi-level system can be developed.

One of the most unusual things about Multics is that a computer architecture developed in 1964 has been able to stand the test of time in the area of access control and security. Almost every independent evaluation of the system has come to the same conclusion: The inclusion of security requirements in its original specification and the subsequent building-in of its protection mechanism into the heart of its operating system produced an extremely secure computer.

Multics was originally designed as a prototype of a computer utility. It was developed with two seemingly incompatible purposes in mind: "to facilitate sharing of programs and data and to protect them from misuse" [MU 1982]. Honeywell literature contends that the Multics security features do make a considerable amount of controlled sharing possible.

The following description (and Figures 13-3 to 13-10) [MU 1982] of the Multics protection mechanisms has been reproduced here with the permission of Honeywell Information Systems Division.

MULTICS SECURITY APPROACH

> On Multics, as on many systems, the first line of defense is a set of tables which lists users and their access rights to data. These tables are scanned by the operating system on each user's reference to a block of data. In theory this is a simple and unbreachable defense. In practice it is often very vulnerable, for three reasons:
>
> 1. The hardware architecture may contain exploitable behavior (or misbehavior). For example, the hardware implementation may offer opportunities for trapdoors, which can be opened under specific conditions.
>
> 2. The software utilization of the table look-up mechanisms may contain exploitable errors.
>
> 3. The table mechanism may be completely circumvented by implementation errors in the system's operating software.
>
> Operating systems are prone to error because they are composed of many complex computer programs and, because they are repeatedly altered to extend the functions available to the user and patched to correct the prob-

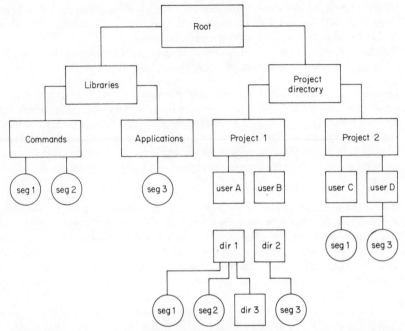

Figure 13-3   Storage system hierarchy. Each segment in the storage system has a unique path name or search strategy which lists, in turn, each of the directories under which it is located and its name, which is always unique among the segment names stored in the last directory in the sequence. The path name for seg2 in this example is *Root>libraries>commands>seg2*. Access control information for each segment is stored with the information about its location in the directory containing the segment. Thus the access information must be scanned when the storage system locates the segment for the user.

lems discovered in the software extensions. The complexity of the system makes it impossible to predict all of the effects of a proposed change with any degree of accuracy, so the effectiveness of the security mechanisms tends to decrease as the number of changes and patches increases. . . .

When Multics was developed, an attempt was made to design a system, including security mechanisms, which could grow without system reorganization. The designers recognized that it would be impossible, at the design stage, to anticipate all the problems which could crop up when the software was written. Therefore, if problems arose as a module of the system was implemented, it was redesigned, a process which served to reduce the convolution and complexity of the final software system. In addition, provision was made to allow functions to be added to the system as subsystems rather than as modifications of the operating system itself. For example, many programs which normally run under the GCOS operating system (General Comprehensive Operating Supervisor, Honeywell's

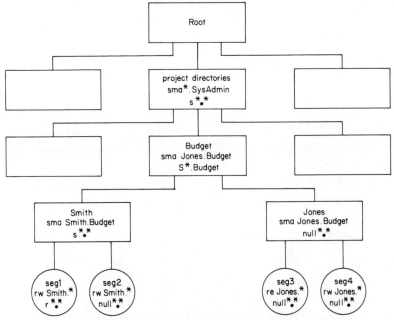

Figure 13-4 Access control lists (ACLs). The ACLs enforce a security policy based on the concept of (nonexclusive) "ownership." Each segment has an access control list which gives the access modes allowed users and groups of users. The ACLs are stored in the directory containing the segment, and the directories themselves have ACLs, which are stored in the next highest directory. Because of the hierarchical nature of the storage system, users with access to high-level directories can force access to subordinate segments by altering, in turn, the ACLs of all the containing directories and that of the segment itself. Thus, in the example, a system administrator with modify access to the project directory could obtain access to one of the segments belonging to Jones, even if Jones had written an ACL for the segment denying him access. In effect, therefore, everyone with modify access to a containing directory "owns" a segment in the sense that they control it. While modify access to directories close to the root is limited to a few system administrators, the power this confers on them constitutes a security risk.

operating system for its DPS/6, DPS/7 and DPS/8 small-, medium- and large-scale computers) also run unmodified in Multics in a GCOS-compatible subsystem. As a result of these and other design decisions, Multics has fewer exploitable software errors than other systems.

Before concluding the discussion of Multics, it is interesting to note the similarity in protection mechanisms employed by Honeywell's SCOMP (Secure Communications Processor) computer and those in Multics. One important difference, however, is the utilization of kernel technology in SCOMP and its subsequent approval by the DOD Computer Security Center for an A1 verified design certification. Multics in 1985 received a DOD Computer Security Center B2 certification.

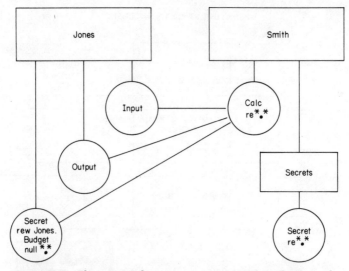

Figure 13-5 The access information monitor (AIM) mechanism. The AIM mechanism of access control is more restrictive than the ACL mechanism. The AIM rules, which define access rights on the basis of the match between a segment's classification and a user's clearance, ensure that information cannot flow from a higher to a lower clearance level, even if the ACLs on the segment containing the information would allow this. As a result, AIM blocks attempts to obtain data illicitly by means of "Trojan horse" code. A Trojan horse program is a program which serves some useful function and is therefore likely to be used by a wide variety of users, but which also contains undocumented code which uses the access rights of the user who has called the program to obtain information for the program's author. For example, it might copy segments to which the user has access but the author does not into segments beneath the author's directory. Since AIM does not permit information to be read or written to a lower clearance level or across categories, it effectively blocks this kind of attack on data security.

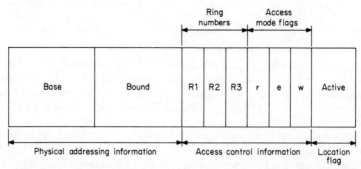

Figure 13-6 The segment descriptor word (SDW). The SDW contains fields for the physical address of the segment in main memory and for access control information. There will be several SDWs for a segment if several users are referring to it; the access control fields in these SDWs will have different settings.

152

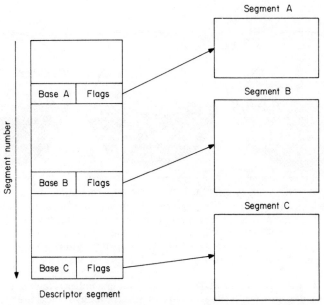

Figure 13-7 Referencing the SDW. No user ever has direct access to a segment in the Multics storage system. The user actually references the SDW for the segment, which leads to the physical address of the segment, and is stored in a special segment the system creates for each user when he or she logs in, called the descriptor segment. As a result of this arrangement, every reference to a segment is mediated by the hardware. The hardware examines the SDW on every reference by every computer instruction to a segment to determine its address and checks at the same time to see that the settings of the access fields in the SDW allow access.

Typical library segment   Typical operating system segment   Typical user segment

Figure 13-8 The ring numbers, ACL, and AIM. The ring numbers, the ACL, and AIM classifications all define access to segments. Each mechanism defines potential access, and a user's effective access is that permitted by all three. The ordered set of three ring numbers associated with each segment defines four access brackets. A user has read, write, or execute access to a segment only if his or her current ring number is within the appropriate ring bracket. There is, however, a special case; if a user attempts to transfer to a segment (to execute it) and is not within the execute bracket, but is within the call bracket, execute access is granted and the user's ring number is temporarily changed to the highest ring number in the segment's execute bracket. Typical user segments have wide write and read brackets and execute brackets, including rings to which most users have access. (The execute bracket is defined by the difference between the write and read brackets, and therefore, if these cover similar ranges, it cannot cover a wide range of rings.) Typical library segments have small write brackets to limit the circumstances under which users can modify them, but large read and, therefore, large execute brackets, because they must be read or executed by many users under a wide variety of circumstances. Typical operating system segments have small read, write, and execute brackets and null call brackets. A few, however, have large call brackets. These make the others accessible to a wide variety of users, but accessible only under carefully controlled circumstances.

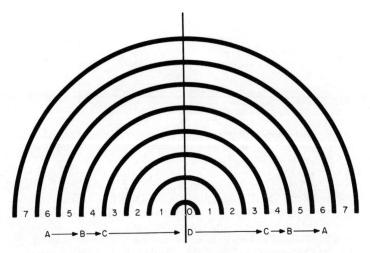

Figure 13-9 The call bracket. The call bracket defined by the ring numbers associated with each segment can be used to restrict the sequence in which a user process can execute segments and, therefore, in effect, the programs a user can write. In this example, the user's process, located at first in ring 6, references in turn segments A, B, C, and D, with ring numbers [6, 6, 6], [4, 4, 6], [2, 5, 6], and [0, 0, 4]. When the process calls segment B, its ring number changes to 4, the highest and only ring number in segment B's execute bracket. When it calls segment C from B, its ring number remains the same, but when it calls D from C, its ring number changes temporarily to 0. Because of the ring numbers on these segments, the user process cannot pass from segment A directly to segment D. It must pass through segment B, called a gate, because it has a nonnull call bracket, to reach segment D. The ACL and AIM settings on gates can be used to control access to inner ring programs and data, making it much easier to protect them from misuse. This structure also protects data in outer rings from misuse by a process temporarily executing with ring 0 privileges since it is generally not possible to read or write outer ring segments from ring 0. Note also that the user's current ring number reverts to its original value when a called segment has finished executing. In the example, the ring number would revert first to 4, after segment D had finished executing, and then to 6, after segment B had finished executing; the privilege conferred by the call is conferred temporarily.

155

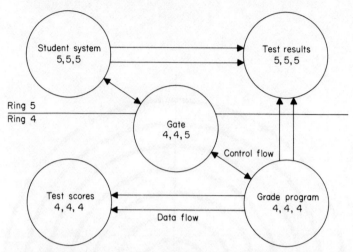

Figure 13-10 The ring structure. The ring structure is used to set up protected user subsystems, in addition to protecting operating systems segments. For example, a teacher could restrict students to ring 5 but allow them access to a gate into ring 4. When the students finished homework problems, they would call the gate segment, which would examine their work, entering a grade on their behalf in another segment in ring 4. Since they would have no access to the grade segment except through this particular gate, they would not be able to examine or modify the grades.

Summary

The importance of security protection afforded by computer operating systems is growing as computer users become more dependent on their systems. Also, protection requirements are increasing as users implement systems that encourage more data and resource sharing.

However, operating systems security mechanisms, including those employed in computers under consideration for certified verification, are not the final answer to system security. Although they will provide a critical element in total system security, they still add only one more layer to total systems protection. On the other hand, the combination of operating systems security and other controls such as physical security, good password management, and encryption can produce even higher levels of total system protection.

14. Trusted Computer Systems

There is little doubt that future operating systems will be considerably more secure than present commercial systems. The knowledge that has been gained during the past fifteen years is leading to a new generation of computers that will be significantly more secure from an architectural point of view than the systems produced between 1980 to 1985.

In addition to other breakthroughs, the two technological advances that may influence new directions in secure operating systems are:

- Security kernel designs
- Trusted computer evolution

Security Kernel Designs

The basic approach to security kernel architecture includes the implementation of the reference monitor mechanisms described in Chapter 13. While the kernel (through hardware and software) provides the protection needed, the reference monitor implementation provides the procedure whereby every reference to information or every change to authorization must go through the security kernel.

In other words, the security kernel provides the control as to what software shall be trusted to provide system security. The kernel solution is to severely restrict the code that must be "trusted" to a small operating system (the kernel), thereby achieving an extraordinary degree of internal computer security and access control.

This can be accomplished as long as the three basic conditions or assumptions of the reference monitor are met:

- *Completeness*: All accesses to information must be funneled through the kernel.
- *Isolation*: The kernel itself must be protected from all forms of unauthorized access or tampering.

• *Verifiability*:   The kernel must be small and simple enough to be submitted to a verification procedure to confirm that the kernel meets design specifications.

Evidence that the security kernel concept could in fact be implemented in a computer architecture was first successfully demonstrated in 1974 by Mitre Corporation on a PDP-11/45 [SC 1975]. The completed security kernel software systems consisted of less than twenty primitive subroutines (sets of coded instructions) and contained less than 1,000 coded language statements.

The development of a security kernel normally includes four important elements:

1. *A mathematical model* defines the rules for demonstrating that system security is preserved. An example of the rules [BE 1973] that are usually used for this purpose are:

   • *Simple security*:   Prohibits users from obtaining information they are not authorized to see.

   • *Property*:   Prohibits a program operating on behalf of a computer user from lowering the classification of data.

2. *Formal specification* can be used to bridge the gap between a mathematical model and the implementation of a kernel, through a set of hierarchical specifications.

3. *HOL (high-order language) code and implementation* includes the coded representation of the security kernel which can be verified for correctness.

4. *Kernel implementation* demonstrates that the security kernel software is the same as its HOL representation and that the hardware architecture meets specifications and is also correct.

One of the most important attributes of the security kernel approach is its mathematical basis and dependability. The fact that at least one commercial computer architecture (Honeywell's SCOMP [BE 1983]) has achieved the security kernel specification has also been encouraging.

Technological Breakthroughs

The problem of security kernel acceptance is twofold:

1. The overhead of the kernel (i.e., system performance degradation) has caused potential buyers to be cautious.
2. There is a question of kernel verifiability. Experts are questioning the adequacy and integrity of the verification tools (the software and mathematics) that are needed to certify the system.

In addition, there are computer scientists and security experts who contend that as hardware prices decline and performance improves, other security and access control architectural concepts will become just as attractive as the security kernel and, in some cases, will not have the accompanying overhead. One approach is to provide separate systems or resources for users that would otherwise have to share the same computer. Another approach recommends more extensive application of cryptography. Security kernel critics claim that limitations such as complex verification requirements and the limitation on the number of access control instructions will be diminished, if not eliminated, with anticipated technological advances.

Trusted Computer Evolution

The term *trusted computers* was derived from the concepts and objectives advanced by various DOD-sponsored computer security projects [DE 1983]. Technically, the basic constructs of a trusted computer include two of the mechanisms already described in this chapter: implementations of the reference monitor and the security kernel.

The trusted computer concept is more than a secure computer specification. It is the ongoing research and development efforts of the DOD in the area of secure computers converted into a set of evaluation criteria. It includes the program and rationale used by the DOD to convince commercial computer manufacturers that there is a market (other than the government) for secure systems. The trusted computer concept is also the communication of these findings and conclusions to computer users to convince them that they should seriously consider acquiring state-of-the-art computer security products to reduce their present system vulnerabilities.

It is quite likely that the trusted computer effort will have a significant long-range impact on the design and availability of secure operating systems, access control packages, network security devices, and related hardware-software products.

Historically, the beginning of this effort began in October 1967 when "a task force was assembled under the auspices of the Defense Science Board to address computer security safeguards that protect classified information in remote-access, resource-sharing computer systems." That task force report and several subsequent and related ones helped to establish a "uniform DOD (computer security) policy, security requirements, administrative controls, and technical measures to protect classified information processed by DOD computer systems."

Subsequently, other government organizations, including the Air Force, the Advanced Research Projects Agency, and other agencies, performed extremely important research assignments that supported and carried forward the earlier work in information systems security.

In 1977, the DOD established the Computer Security Initiative to become the focal point for its efforts into secure computing systems. In addition, the National Bureau of Standards and several government contractors, including the Mitre Corporation, performed valuable research on security for computer evaluation criteria. The trusted computer system evaluation criteria as first published by the Computer Security Initiative was a result of these combined efforts.

In 1981 the DOD Computer Security Center was established to "staff and expand on the work started by the DOD Computer Security Initiative."

One example of how the DOD trusted computer concept and evaluation criteria were derived from earlier research is the following set of recommendations which were the result of an NBS-sponsored Controlled Accessibility Workshop and which were discussed at the Third Seminar on the DOD Computer Security Initiative [JE 1980]:

- Control mechanisms should be formal and always invoked, never bypassed for efficiency or other rationalized reasons.
- The design must accommodate evaluation and easy system maintenance.
- The principle of "least privilege" should be applied to system operation.
- The computer system vendor will have the ultimate responsibility for delivering systems that can be operated securely.
- Product acceptance will require application of certification techniques.

According to a report prepared by Mitre Corporation [NI 1979] for the DOD: "Trusted computer systems are operating systems (including the underlying hardware base) capable of preventing users from accessing more information than that to which they are authorized."

The report said that a prerequisite to determining that a system might in fact be trusted would be the development of a set of criteria against which a secure system could be evaluated. The protection-related factors that might be used in the evaluation were referred to as follows:

- *Policies*: Provide the access rules under which the system is expected to operate.
- *Mechanisms*: Provide the foundation for policy enforcements.
- *Assurances*: Offer evidence that the mechanisms operate correctly. [NI 1979]

The Trusted Computer Base

According to a DOD report [DE 1983], "the heart of a trusted computer system is the trusted computing base (TCB) which contains all of the elements of the system responsible for supporting the security policy and supporting the isolation of objects (code and data) on which the protection is based."

The TCB can refer to reference validation mechanisms other than a security kernel, such as a front-end security filter or the entire trusted computer system. Most important, however, is the requirement that the TCB "must be of sufficiently simple organization and complexity to be subjected to analysis and tests, the completeness of which can be assured."

Evaluation Criteria

According to the DOD Computer Security Center, which is now operated by the National Security Agency (NSA), the computer security evaluation criteria were developed for primarily three reasons:

- To provide users with a metric with which to evaluate the degree of trust that can be placed in computer systems for the secure processing of classified and other sensitive information.
- To provide guidance to manufacturers as to what security features to build into their new and planned, commercial products in order to provide widely available systems that satisfy trust requirements for sensitive applications.
- To provide a basis for specifying security requirements in acquisition specifications. [DE 1983]

Essentially, the report on evaluation criteria for the DOD trusted computer systems is a document that classifies computer operating systems into four general hierarchical divisions of trustworthiness from "minimal" to "verified protection" (Figure 14-1).

For computer systems with built-in controls, the evaluation focuses on the essential design characteristics of the system being evaluated. A comparison is made between the architecture, its security criteria, and known trusted system design methodologies.

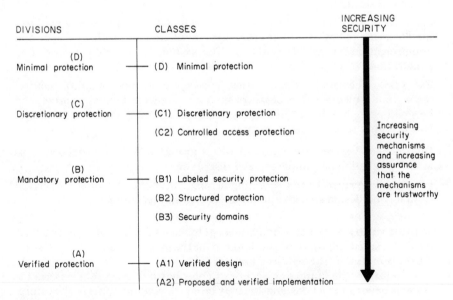

Figure 14-1 Trusted computer system evaluation criteria.

For systems with built-in controls such as access control software, the evaluation focuses primarily on policy requirement specifications as compared to system compliance and effectiveness.

The following is a brief summary of the evaluation criteria divisions and classes [DE 1983]:

DIVISION D: Minimal Protection

CLASS D: Minimal Protection—Reserved for those systems that have been evaluated but that fail to meet the requirements for a higher evaluation class.

DIVISION C: Discretionary Protection (need-to-know)

CLASS C1:   Discretionary Security Protection—"The Trusted Computing Base (TCB) of a class C1 system nominally satisfies the discretionary security requirements by providing separation of users and data."

CLASS C2:   Controlled Access Protection—"A more finely grained discretionary access control than C1."

DIVISION B: Mandatory Protection—Systems must carry the notion of a TCB, utilizing sensitivity labels with major data structures; and developer must provide the security model on which the TCB is based, furnish a specification of the TCB, and demonstrate that the reference monitor concept has been implemented.

CLASS B1:   Labeled Security Protection—"An informal statement of the security policy model, data labeling, and mandatory access over named subjects and objects must be present. The capability must exist for accurately labeling exported information."

CLASS B2:   Structured Protection—"A clearly defined and documented formal security policy model . . . TCB structured into protection-critical and non-protection-critical elements. . . . The system is relatively resistant to penetration."

CLASS B3:   Security Domains—Must "satisfy the reference monitor requirements that it mediate all accesses of subjects to objects, be tamperproof, and be small enough to be subjected to security policy enforcement. . . . The system is highly resistant to penetration."

DIVISION A: Verified Protection—Utilizes formal verification procedures to assure protection of mandatory and discretionary controls.

CLASS A1:   Verified Design—Distinguishing feature is "the analysis derived from formal design specification and verification techniques."

In all seven classes listed above (except for Class D), each succeeding class must also satisfy all the features required for the preceding class (i.e., Class B1 must also meet all the requirements for C2).

In addition, the Computer Security Center has indicated that criteria for systems beyond the A1 designation may be developed sometime in the future. For reference, one of the best sources of information with regard to trusted computer design alternatives and future expectations are the *Proceedings* of the past five IEEE Security and Privacy Symposiums [PR 1984].

Summary

The initial experience of the DOD/NSA Computer Security Center with its commercial trusted computer evaluation program seems to be that the special evaluation and testing needed to produce formal certification of such systems will take longer than was originally anticipated. This may or may not present a problem. As long as government agencies and businesses do not have to comply with specific security criteria when they buy new computer products, their total information-automation progress will not be impeded. If a policy of meeting the criteria should become mandatory sometime in the future, then the certification program may have to be expedited.

Progress in the field of computer security certification is being made slowly. However, major benefits from the trusted computer program will still occur as computer users become more knowledgeable in how to specify their security requirements and how to match available products to them.

15. Database Security

This chapter discusses the importance of database security and integrity. When a database management system (DBMS) is used to organize and coordinate a database, complete reliance on an operating system for security is not the best procedure. Instead this situation is an opportunity to generate one more layer of access control protection for most commercial information systems—through the DBMS.

Users of smaller or special-purpose systems, including personal computers, who cannot afford or do not require a DBMS, will have to rely on physical security and the access control provided by its operating and file management system for database protection. Either way, large or small, with or without DBMS or communications capabilities, every database should be given a special security review.

Since this chapter focuses on systems that do have database management systems, the following important questions will be answered for the benefit of information system users and designers:

- How does database design affect security?
- What are the primary weaknesses of the DBMS?
- How do most DBMSs provide access control?
- What can database users and designers do to improve on the protection afforded by their DBMS?

In addition, three other important subjects will be covered in this chapter:

- Database recovery and integrity
- The problem of statistical inference
- The security role of the database administrator (DBA)

How Does Database Design Affect Security?

In the early days of data processing, when almost all user's data was on removable magnetic tapes or card disks, security problems associated with unauthorized access, manipulation, or destruction were primarily of a physical nature. However, with the advent of fixed and removable disk systems, random access processing, and remote computer access (via communications), security considerations began to increase.

Part of the new database trend was toward more highly structured data files that could be shared. Design objectives were directed toward coordination of data files for the benefit of a multiple number of users. New database handling concepts were developed to permit the following:

- Placement of all relevant data in one file in a consistent and standard format
- Elimination of redundant or duplicate data and files and related processing
- Implementation of more selective and powerful data access and retrieval mechanisms (i.e., hardware and software)
- Creation of more responsive data access systems that assured users would get more timely data faster than ever before
- Update of data files via off-line batch or on a continuing on-line basis
- Implementation of all the above objectives in a way that would optimize use of the latest generation of hardware and software from the standpoint of both economy and efficiency

The result was the birth of a concept we call *database management*. Practically speaking, the database is everything (i.e., data and programs) that is now stored both on and off (i.e., removable media) the computer system. In a stricter sense, the *database* is the centralized collection of nonduplicated data to be shared by one or more computer users or applications. A *database system* (DBS) would include the whole database, the data query software, file structures, and all related data management functions. The term *database management system* normally refers to the software that coordinates and controls such functions as data organization, storage, and retrieval.

Associated with a DBMS is a function called *database administration* which is controlled by a *database administrator* (DBA). According to a special National Bureau of Standards report [MU 1976],

> The Data Base Administrator (DBA) function consists of the person or persons with the responsibility of maintaining the integrity of the data base and for its efficient organization. The DBA is also responsible for defining the rules and data descriptions for its use. The function is not to be confused with the Data Base Manager which is the software and hardware of the DBMS; and which is commonly thought of as *being* the DBMS. In the larger sense, however, it is generally agreed that a DBMS is not complete or viable without the central control functions of the DBA.

Of paramount importance to the DBMS are the following entities:

1. The data manipulation language (DML)
2. The data definition language (DDL)

3. The data dictionary/directory (DD/D)
4. The database administrator (DBA)

The actual structuring of the database itself is important since the structure has a major impact upon application programming and overall system performance from both a technical and a user's point of view. It also significantly affects system security.

At the most basic level, there are two major categories of database structures. These are nonrelational and relational. The essential difference is that the case of *nonrelational databases*, data in a file is logically and mathematically independent of data appearing in another file. Since there is no implied relationship between the data, the structure is called *nonrelational*.

A *relational database* by itself is a series of flat files with relationships between them. For example, two sequential files with a relationship defined by a common *set mechanism field* (i.e., the same social security number in each) would be a relational database. A relational structure can be controlled by what is called a *set mechanism*. A set mechanism establishes a logical relationship between records and becomes the basis upon which system data structures are built.

Most file structures in current general-purpose DBMSs are essentially nonrelational. The primary file organization methodologies in use today are sequential, random, and indexed. Of course, some file structures incorporate a combination of these structures, such as indexed sequential.

Another extremely important element of modern database systems is the schema-subschema concept. The *schema* (Figure 15-1) is the totally defined description of all the data elements that comprise the database, whereas a *subschema* contains only those data elements that would be required by a specific application program or set of programs. The subschema concept can be an extremely important facet of the security of a database because it is one of the few mechanisms that can prevent unauthorized data access.

As shown in Figure 15-1, there can be one schema, and there can be any number of subschemas within that schema. The subschema is a "view" into the database which is represented by the schema. The concept of view (Figure 15-2) is also important to the design of a secure database software system and to the security of the database itself. A *view* is a particular set of subschemas (i.e., data) that a user legally and logically requires to perform a job.

Thus the design of a DBMS can be extremely critical to the security of an information system. From a computer user's standpoint, it is important to recognize that there are major differences between the DBMSs offered by different computer vendors and independent software houses. Some are considerably more secure than others, particularly ones that offer significant access control over subschemas and views.

Unfortunately, once committed to a particular computer, users normally cannot greatly influence the design of the vendor-supplied DBMS. They can, however, decide on other system design constraints that could greatly enhance the information access control protection of their systems.

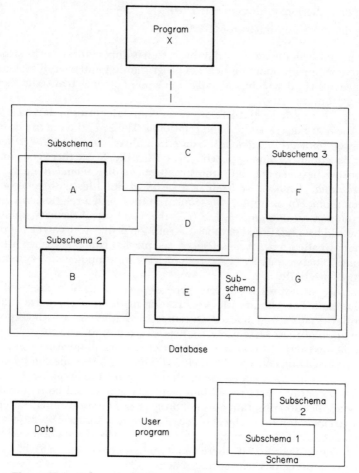

Figure 15-1   Schema-subschema concept.

What Are the Primary Weaknesses of the DBMS?

In most databases, storage of a user's data is like having all the user's "eggs in one large basket." In other words, a DBMS-managed database is essentially a multilevel-multiuser data storage system with all the potential weaknesses one might expect from a system designed for extensive user sharing without a primary emphasis on security.

To appreciate why this is the case, consider that the typical DBMS runs on top of the computer operating system and normally uses the operating system's input-output facilities for all data transfer to and from on-line storage. In many DBMSs, once a user's password has been authenticated and access permissions checked by the operating system access control facility, the user

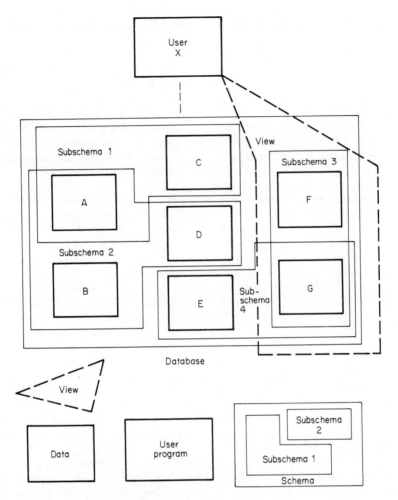

Figure 15-2 View concept.

may be given access to the database that resides within his or her prescribed view or data authorization profile (unless the resources have been explicitly secured).

In addition, even where the DBMS itself provides control over access levels, the end use of the data that is legitimately read cannot be controlled. Thus, most DBMSs do not provide sufficient multilevel access control unless special architectural safeguards have been installed. Part of this problem is that most operating system access control mechanisms only guard the "container" that the data is in, as opposed to the access to the data itself.

In addition, the access control safeguards imposed on a DBMS (other than those included with the operating system) usually add system overhead so that computer and DBMS software vendors have tended to minimize the problem. (This is not true of all systems and vendors, as will be discussed later in this chapter.) One study [WO 1974] reported that data access with user verification which did not depend upon data content was approximately 22 to 32 percent less efficient than access without this protection; access control overhead which included data content criteria was estimated to run as high as 187 percent of the original overhead.

Most computer systems use a file management system to execute all file storage input and output regardless of whether a DBMS is included in the architecture. Since these systems are usually designed to handle and optimize user authentication and authorization overhead prior to file management input-output, the duplication or insertion of additional access controls in the DBMS has been done very cautiously.

To begin with, most computer vendors provided DBMS security by taking advantage of user controllability through the schema-subschema and view concepts. Through intricate mapping (schema-subschema) of how much of the database could be accessed (viewed) by a user and the implementation of logical access locks, most DBMSs tend to provide a semblance of security at the database level. Access granularity, or degree of access control at the file, record, field, and data element level and for read, write, and execute permission, has been more of a problem for some DBMSs. The need, therefore, is for improved context- and content-dependent security to satisfy the multilevel security requirement of the database. In addition, since most system users will require only read privileges, operating systems capable of guarding access mode will still fall short of providing adequate database security.

There are also problems with database management systems that use tables to generate both user and resource profiles. These tables often maintain the relationship between authorized passwords, transactions, commands, databases, and programs, as well as between both logical and physical terminal identification. Unfortunately, these systems seldom relate user security to data categories. Users must therefore utilize a form of stratification in order to assign authorization permissions to system resources. Operative elements are transactions. Activities are associated with security levels, with the result that a user, once permitted access, may do nothing or everything. This occurs because once a security definition is associated with specific access categories or departments in the database, the user is allowed to access everything or nothing depending on his or her authorization profile.

How Do Most DBMSs Provide Access Control?

The security concepts that may be used by DBMSs to control access are similar to those already discussed in the previous two chapters: identification, authentication, authorization, and audit-security violation logs. A primary difference between how the DBMS handles these security functions compared to how the operating system handles them is mostly related to the organization of the databases themselves. Specifically, the more effective DBMS security mechanisms attempt to control access through reference to such database structures as view—schema-subschema systems and through specially designed lock and key mechanisms.

The actual implementation of access control features in a DBMS can occur in several areas. Specifically, the mechanisms can be introduced in the data definition language (DDL), such as in a CODASYL-oriented system, or in the query language [i.e., IBM's Query by Example (QBE)].

Data Description Language in Access Control

Although there are important variations in DBMSs, the typical system includes data descriptions in the same computer program as the instructions that access data.

The main function of the data definition language is to allow system designers to provide to the DBMS the structure, format, logical contents, and access rules of the user's file systems. The proper use of the DDL can have significant security implications. For example, access control codes or passwords for read and write operations on a particular file system can be specified through the DDL for some DBMSs. At least one system utilizes a special subschema DDL for accessing the database. Also, on some systems, the DDL can be used as a vehicle to place access locks on databases, files, records, and individual data elements.

Query Language Access Control

Query software programs provide a convenient mechanism for users to create references to a database. The user normally employs a special high-level language associated with the query system in order to express a data request. The execution of the request by the query software usually takes the form of a translation into points of access in the database and the subsequent return or response (or display) to the user of the selected data elements.

Query systems and languages can play a large part in invoking database access controls. For example, on the IBM System R, the query language SEQUEL can be used to define views. In this system, a view may be a subset of a relation, an encapsulation of information in a relation, or a joining of data in two or more relations. Access rights can be granted to views as opposed to being delivered to the original relation. This application of views results in a form of both content and context access control.

A Different Approach: DM-IV/I-D-S/II

Honeywell's approach to database control and security is significantly different, but unusually effective. Database management for its large-scale computer line includes two products called DM-IV and I-D-S/II. The DM-IV environment is entirely database-oriented. Within this database environment, DM-IV performs the data management functions. These include the translation of the DDL of the schema and subschema and the support of the DML through the DM-IV database control system. It also makes maximum use of standard Honeywell GCOS facilities, such as the GCOS file management supervisor (FMS) and the languages supported under GCOS, including various query languages.

In the case of DM-IV, privacy locks are implemented at multiple levels [SE 1979]. The first level involves applying privacy locks at the schema level (i.e., locks are defined by the database administrator). The DBA can apply locks on the following:

- *Lock file*
- *Copy instruction*:   to prevent validation of an unauthorized subschema
- *Display instruction*:   to suppress the listing of all prohibited references to that subschema
- *Alter instruction*:   to restrict the use of the schema file for restructuring and retranslation of the schema

The second level of privacy locks that may be invoked in Honeywell's DM-IV is at the subschema level:

- The first, or basic, *lock* would be the physical omission of sensitive or unauthorized data from the subschema in the first place.
- A *privacy key*, the value of the *copy lock*, can supply the key for the copy lock.
- A *diagnostic key* is supplied that contains the value of the display lock put into the schema.
- An *invoking lock* can be applied at the subschema level to prevent a user of the schema from even compiling a program if he or she doesn't have access to the key to the invoking lock.
- *Privacy locks* can also be applied to the data manipulation language verbs (within the source language) that permit users of the database to execute instructions.

One of the most important security features of Honeywell's DM-IV is that locks on data can be applied all the way down to the data element level. Even a field within a record can have a privacy lock placed on it.

Another important aspect of Honeywell's DM-IV system is its data dictionary capability. The *data dictionary* tells the database administrator which subschemas have been validated against the schema and which users can access the database. The data dictionary can also be used to provide the DBA with the names of all the users who have had access to any data element in the database and what type of access they were permitted. DM-IV also provides two different levels of encryption description for additional database security.

What Can Database Designers and Users Do to Improve on the Protection Afforded by the DBMS?

Probably the best advice that can be given to database users is not to assume anything with regard to the security of their databases. The same advice applies to organizations and management. Your database is one of your most valuable assets. Database management systems, no matter what their source or design, must be evaluated for adequacy in the light of each user's security and access control requirements.

As far as DBMS security is concerned, there are three important considerations:

• Selection of the right DBMS
• Security considerations during implementation
• Security considerations during operation

Selection of the Right DBMS

Depending on the model and manufacturer of the computer you have, you may not have a choice with regard to your DBMS selection. This is why some of the more advanced security approaches [GR 1984] [BO 1980] to DBMSs advocate the acceptance of off-the-shelf DBMSs the way they are and suggest that special access control or security mechanisms be implemented between the DBMS and the operating system (i.e., *integrity locks* and *back-ender security kernels*). Such mechanisms, however, are not likely to appear as commercial products for some time. The application of a back-ender security kernel (Figure 15-3) does seem promising, however, since systems already exist that can do this job.

Meanwhile, it might be wise to consider one expert's [DA 1981] suggested characteristics for a secure database management system:

• Access mode protection (including read, write, destroy, and modify protection)
• Data inference and manipulation protection
• Flexible security mechanisms (i.e., user-friendly)
• Minimal performance degradation (i.e., by invoking security)
• No reduction in system accessibility
• No great expansion of stored data
• Reasonable cost

These features should be regarded as minimal requirements for DBMS security. In addition, the following characteristics should also be given consideration:

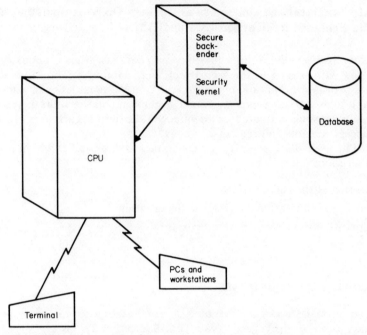

Figure 15-3   Proposed database protection solution: A secure back-ender.

- Relational versus nonrelational data structure capability (relational tends to permit finer access control granularity)
- Schema-subschema mechanisms
- Security capabilities included in the DBMS data query or data manipulation language, data definition language, data dictionary, and database administration system
- Any data encryption options
- The degree to which the access control protection features of the computer operating system complement and supplement those of the DBMS

The mating of the operating system and the DBMS is critical. For example, one group of authorities [FE 1981] recommends that an operating system, to adequately support a DBMS, should include the following security features:

- DBMS and user program protection against unauthorized modification
- Data memory protection
- Database access protection from outside the DBMS
- Input-output performance integrity
- DBMS user authentication mechanism

Finally, if possible, before a final selection is made, it would be wise to submit each prospective DBMS to a sufficient number and variety of tests to determine if the system access control and security mechanisms operate as represented, and to determine that the overall integrity of the DBMS is beyond question.

Security Considerations during Implementation

Of all the advice given with regard to practical ways to protect a database, probably the most salient is: Use the database organization and structure to protect itself—particularly where view and schema-subschema mechanisms can be invoked by the DBMS.

Essentially, it is extremely important during the implementation phase of a DBMS that the data description language and the data dictionary capabilities be used to define, separate, and distribute sensitive data in such a way as to optimize the security of the data and to prevent unauthorized access. In other words, don't make it easy for an unauthorized person to access your data.

Also, during the implementation phase, extra attention should be given to system privacy lock capabilities to ensure their proper use with regard to access control. In addition, certain data encryption options may be more easily initiated at this time.

Finally, special care should be given to prevention of unauthorized access to DBMS software and documentation. Start-up might present an excellent opportunity for someone interested in the insertion of a trapdoor or Trojan horse code into vulnerable parts of the system.

Security Considerations during Operation

Attention to database security must be a continuous and never-ending process. Addition of new data files, changes in information sensitivity, new system users, the permanent disengagement of old system users, updates to the DBMS, operating system modifications, and purging of old data files all involve certain major and minor security considerations. The constant physical and logical security of all DBMSs and operating system software is also of primary concern, as is proper management and protection of personal passwords, data passwords, encryption keys, and logical locks and keys.

Degaussing, or elimination of all magnetic data residue on both on-line and off-line media, is another database security consideration. Even unauthorized access to or modifications of database audit logs (and software) needs to be guarded against. Also, the logs themselves need to be regularly examined for information identifying all accesses and, in particular, suspicious accesses to highly sensitive data.

To protect against unauthorized modification of the database, it can occasionally be dumped and recreated later using the dump and audit log. Only modifications on the audit log should appear in the regenerated database.

Although some systems can perform these functions automatically, the procedure will be effective only against unauthorized data retrieval or modification, not against unauthorized program modification. Other procedures will have to be used to protect programs, such as documenting all changes and periodically checking program lengths. If the DBMS is acquired from an outside vendor, new copies may be acquired to check against unauthorized local program modification.

In addition, unauthorized software modifications may be detected by running the database software and related application programs against a special test database.

Other Major Database Security Considerations

Database Recovery and Integrity

The need for elaborate and reliable database recovery procedures and overall DBMS integrity is well covered in current literature [FE 1981]. The basic implications are that the damage caused by inaccurate information can be even worse than damage caused by a security compromise. Fortunately, the mechanisms that can be used to provide database integrity can also support the regeneration of a database that has been intentionally violated or even physically destroyed (assuming adequate off-site backup).

There are available mechanisms to handle crises such as integrity violations, concurrency deadlocks, and system crashes. Part of the DBA's responsibility should be to ascertain the operability and integrity of the controls themselves, including recovery logs, database backup procedures, and concurrency control locks.

The Problem of Statistical Inference

Depending on the type of database and its sensitivity , information security compromises that result from some form of statistically related inference can be costly. Violation of privacy legislation, compromise of national security information, and theft of valuable commercial data can all be accomplished through sophisticated statistical procedures and the exploitation of information regarding the characteristics of the database itself.

The problem as described by many expert analysts [MI 1980] is that because of the power of most DBMSs and related statistical DBMSs (or other statistical software packages), it is possible for a legitimate system user to access data from a system which, when submitted to special statistical procedures or correlation studies, can result in an information compromise not considered by the system designers or users and, therefore, not defended against.

Some experts [CL 1983] [DE 1982] believe that the problem could be solved by the use of certain security mechanisms (including the possible use of cryptography). Claybrook approaches the problem through the application of views, whereas Denning, Schlorer, and Wehrle believe that solutions are possible with the application of techniques that include:

- Restricting user queries
- Adding noise to data
- Monitoring all data requests to identify successive compromise attempts

The Security Role of the Database Administrator (DBA)

The DBA position is normally held by one or more technical experts who assist with database design and creation and the operation of DBMSs. Functionally, DBA is often referred to as *database administration* and includes the responsibility of maintaining the integrity of the database and assuring its efficient organization. The function also includes the definition of DBA rules and data descriptions. In lieu of another full-time system security officer, the database administrator(s) may be responsible for coordinating the design, implementation, operation, and violation reporting of all matters pertaining to database security and access control.

Overall, there are four major classes of DBA access control and security responsibilities:

- Separation of duties
- Database access controls
- Database operation controls
- Application control

Separation of duties. Database administration should include the separation of the major functions that influence DBMS design, implementation, operation, and audit. Those functions would normally include systems analysis and design, applications programming, operations, and database administration. The separation of database administration functions from the other information system departments constitutes an important internal control.

Database access control. Primary functions in this area that should be managed or controlled by the DBA include:

- Access to the DBMS library by utility programs
- Review of the operating system and DBMS logs
- Prevention of unauthorized access to the database when it is not under the control of the DBMS software
- Control of DBMS software maintenance
- Separation of the live database from the system during program testing
- Management of encryption system security if implemented as part of DBMS access control

Database operation controls. DBA responsibilities in this area should include:

- Approval of all modifications to DBMS software
- Approval and logging of all changes to the DBMS library
- Occasional review of the DBMS library to determine that no unauthorized modifications have occurred
- Review of all planned program operation activity against actual runs

Application controls. Certain DBA system protection responsibilities relate to application controls. These include:

- Restriction of certain data manipulation language (DML) call verbs when necessary
- Review of action taken following identification of a DBMS error condition
- Review of application program documentation to ascertain impact of new programs
- Specification or review of DBMS program test criteria and actual test results
- Recommendations review, and testing of database backup and disaster recovery capabilities

Summary

There is convincing evidence that the protection of access to a computer database cannot be left primarily to the operating system, particularly where the system includes a database management system (DBMS). Although DBMS access control mechanisms do provide another level of data security for the systems, they are still imperfect.

The problem is that in the trade-off of access control overhead versus operational efficiency, efficiency usually wins. The end result is that computer users, with the help of their database administrator, need to learn how to use the basic data organizational structures of the DBMS itself (particularly the view–schema-subschema mechanism) to provide adequate security for their data.

16. Network Security

Most of the progress that has been made during the past two decades in data communications and network applications has been a result of the continued advancement of computer technology. The benefits of allowing more people to share access to computer resources through a private communication-line interface or a dial-up connection have increased significantly. Communications facilities have become so integrated into each total information system that central computers, as well as minicomputers and personal computers, are not necessarily dominant factors in any given system. Instead, we are now seeing more *total information-communications systems*. In these systems, management must properly utilize, control, and protect all system resources, including the databases (wherever they happen to be) and the system communications facilities.

Access control of the communications facilities or network (i.e., physically separated computers connected by a telecommunications channel or carrier) has become an extremely complex and challenging problem. Probably nowhere else in the area of computer security and access control is the problem of balancing system resources, user convenience, and information security more difficult. For most computer managers and users, the job of system access control requires constant vigilance. In this chapter we hope to make this job a little easier by providing answers to these two major questions:

- What are the characteristics of networks that make them vulnerable to abuse?
- What are the most important tools that can be used to reduce network vulnerabilities?

What Are the Characteristics of Networks That Make Them Vulnerable to Abuse?

Information system networks come in all sizes and shapes with variable components. Security problems can occur almost anywhere in a network. The following topic structure should help the reader focus more clearly on all the elements of networks and network designs that might contribute to their vulnerability:

- Network perspectives
- Open networks defined
- Closed networks defined
- Open network security standards
- Local area networks
- Common carrier facilities

Network Perspectives

Communication is no longer simply a component, link, or functionality in an information system. It has become to a large extent the "glue" that holds the whole information system together. The classic (nondistributed) view of a data communications network (Figure 16-1) places the computer, database, and front-end processor in the central position of control in the network. Attention to security or access control protection is concentrated on either side of the host computer. In other words, access control itself is regarded primarily as a centralized function.

New network designs and structures, such as those included in the International Standards Organization (ISO) open system interconnection (OSI) reference model (Figure 16-2), produce an inverted perspective with regard to architectures and access control. As a result of the tremendous increase in the distribution and connectability of system services, security and control also need to be distributed (Figure 16-3). This conclusion is particularly applicable to systems that can be connected to the outside world through a telecommunications or network common carrier capability.

All systems, however, will not necessarily utilize these powerful new communications standards and related technologies. We undoubtedly will see the need for private or relatively closed-type data communications architectures such as an organization might implement within its own building or complex of buildings. In these systems which have no outside connectability, of course, communications, as well as data and system sharing, will be considerably restricted. On the other hand, there are certain obvious security advantages (i.e., no remotely located intruders).

Networks therefore can be divided into two broad categories: *open* systems and *closed* systems. Security requirements will be considerably different for each category.

Open Networks Defined

An *open network* is defined as an information system that includes physically dispersed computers connected by communications media which can be ac-

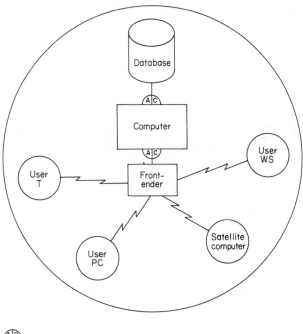

AC/AC Access control

T   Terminal

PC Personal computer

WS Workstation

Figure 16-1 Centralized information management.

cessed from computers connected to another network (i.e., through dial-up or dedicated lines). In the case of networks that conform to OSI standards, open networks permit connection to systems that run on equipment supplied by other manufacturers.

All computer networks, whether open or closed, are susceptible to similar types of abuses. The primary difference is that open network vulnerabilities are considered more dangerous and complex because the network provides an opportunity for an outsider to compromise the system. Closed networks, by definition, are accessible only to insiders or authorized personnel in the facilities that house the system elements. Externally located communications elements such as public carrier facilities (i.e., telephone lines) are especially vulnerable to compromise, including physical threats.

Primary network threats or vulnerabilities include:

- Impersonation
- Misrouting
- Unauthorized access
- Interception

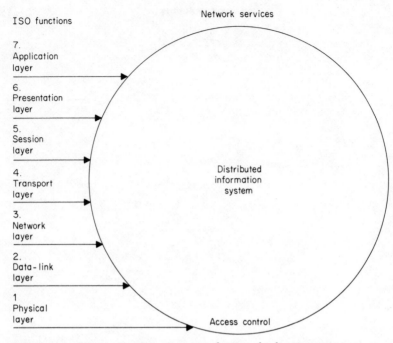

Figure 16-2 International Organization for Standardization open system interconnection reference model.

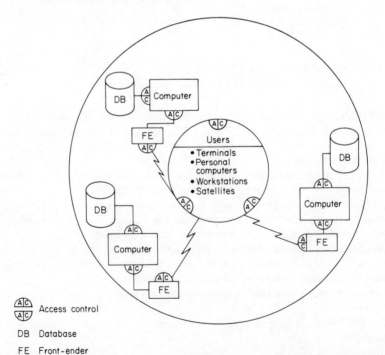

Figure 16-3 An inverted perspective: Distributed information management.

Closed Networks Defined

As mentioned earlier, the *closed network* has two important security advantages over the open network: (1) it is not connected to an outside system, and therefore none of the communications system elements are exposed to potential compromise in public areas, and (2) there is no potential for an outsider to compromise the system through a connected external communications network.

At this point you should ask: But where do I find this class of network? The answer is that it is not found in very many locations.

Such systems, built on a private internal communications network, would obviously have limited communications functionality because they do not have outside connections.

Do such systems exist and do they provide valuable functions? The answer is yes. Even these systems, however, often have some outside network connectability under controlled conditions. For example, they may utilize special communication switching systems that, through electronic or hardware switches, protect the sensitive part of the internal network.

A classic example of the use of these devices is provided by the relationship between local law enforcement agencies and the Federal Bureau of Investigation (FBI). The FBI objected when local law enforcement information systems ran on shared computer and communications facilities while simultaneously being connected to the bureau's National Crime Information Center (NCIC) system located in Washington, D.C. After special communication switches or processors were installed, non-law enforcement terminals, and, in some cases, data processors could be locked out of the sensitive law enforcement network.

But, then, could the new systems with outside connectability to NCIC be compromised? The answer, of course, was that compromise was possible even though dedicated communications lines were used in the network. The result was that extremely sensitive data probably was not communicated through this network unless encrypted, and computers that held even more sensitive intelligence files were switch-protected or physically isolated (i.e., disconnected) from the rest of the system.

The completely closed system, therefore, is more the exception than the rule. The point is that closed systems can be installed, but reasonable alternatives are possible in the design of partially closed systems.

Open Network Security Standards

In an open systems architecture such as that of OSI or those implemented by various computer manufacturers [e.g., Honeywell's distributed systems architecture (DSA) or IBM's systems network architecture (SNA)], network access control can be achieved by carefully defining security requirements, specifications, and solutions for each layer of protection:

• Application

- Presentation
- Session
- Transport
- Network
- Data link
- Physical

The *application layer* is the end-user application, where the equipment "talks" to system users. It is the most essential function in the network because it provides services directly to the end user.

The *presentation layer* prepares the information for the application such as in the remapping of the data format from one device to another.

The *session layer* establishes the communications connection between two network nodes and usually includes identification and authentication functionalities.

The *transport layer* provides a common interface to the communications network. It translates requirements from higher layers into a protocol that can be used by the network and performs numerous other functions such as logical transmission route selection, error detection and correction, and reestablishment of connections in the event of a network failure.

The *network layer* establishes the logical transmission path through a switched network (i.e., assuming alternative media or paths exist).

The *data link layer* performs the network accounting and traffic control functions that are required to move data through an electrical connection. This includes formatting data into character strings acceptable to different communications protocols, such as IBM's bisynchronous communications or ISO's high-level data link control (HDLC).

HDLC is the recommended standard in the frame-level portion of the Consultative Committee for International Telephone and Telegraph (CCITT) standard for the operation of a large packet-switching network called X.25. *Packet switching* is one of the three accepted ways to route messages from a sender or origin to a receiver or destination (i.e., message switching, packet switching, and time-division circuit switching). Packet switching involves the transmission of a string of characters (i.e., part or all of a message) in a block of data that usually includes addressing and routing information. Data packets can be transmitted independently through a network because they contain their own addressing and routing information. In *message switching*, a complete message is transmitted continuously until received at its destination. *Time-division circuit switching* utilizes separate signal and data channels to increase transmissions throughput.

The *physical layer* is the description of the physical and electrical connections in the network.

As of the writing of this book, the ISO draft recommendation on security [WO 1983] states: "Within the OSI framework, the only known method of protection must be the encryption of data on the physical links. (Techniques such as physically securing a line, or use of fiber optic links, are not within the OSI framework.)"

Encryption for all seven OSI layers can be accomplished through the physical links. For instance, the ISO recommends that encryption should be implemented at the transport layer level or higher in order to facilitate end-to-end encryption.

The ISO report also observes that "a primary objective of data communications security is to make the cost of obtaining or modifying the data greater than the value of obtaining or modifying that data."

The report suggests that there are three main categories of security features that relate to the basic OSI reference model. These are called [WO 1983]:

- Basic features [i.e., those within the state of the art]
- Desirable features [i.e., may or may not be within the state of the art]
- Important features that are outside the present scope of OSI security [i.e., outside the reference model or the state of the art]

BASIC FEATURES

Are generally applicable to all layers but may not be necessary or appropriate at all layers. . . . The basic features are the protection of connection-oriented data transfer with regard to:

- Confidentiality
- Integrity
- Authentication
- Protection against traffic analysis
- Protection against deliberate denial of service
- Security audit
- Compartmentalization

DESIRABLE FEATURES

- Signature service—protection against repudiation or forgery [i.e., denial of transaction or a counterfeit one]
- Network security access control
- Protection of connectionless data transfer
- Selective field protection [protection of only parts of a message]
- Protection against covert and unauthorized overt information channels
- Protection against traffic analysis (e.g., deriving information relative to the number and duration of connections, message format characteristics, origin-destination identities and traffic patterns)

The report also suggests that traffic analysis compromise may be avoided by such techniques as "header encryption, padding and dummy traffic insertion."

FEATURES OUTSIDE PRESENT SCOPE

- Physical security
- User authentication (i.e., advanced technologies)
- Security within end systems (i.e., operating systems)
- Audit record review for security purposes
- Electronic radiation emanation protection
- Trojan horse protection

Local Area Networks

Local area networks (LANs) may introduce unexpected vulnerabilities into an information system. The first LAN users rushed into implementation of their LANs without much consideration for access control security. After all, were not the problems of the open network (e.g., outside connectability) eliminated?

Unfortunately, the answer was no. People soon realized that the power of their LANs would be severely restricted if they did not allow for voice-data integration on their new digital private branch exchange (PBX), and thus the LAN (and the connected personal computers, hosts, and databases) would be vulnerable to anyone smart enough to dial in to an unprotected LAN.

In addition, LANs come in three basic architectural forms (Figure 16-4). The three topologies are called *star*, *bus*, and *ring*. Information is usually transmitted in a *packet*. LAN security problems, even if the LAN is primarily a closed system (as defined in this book, not by ISO), are many and varied.

If implemented on a facility that uses a "listen before you talk" communication scheme, all nodes may be receiving all information until the packet is delivered. This is certainly not conducive to internal security.

In addition, LAN users often download databases into their local or departmental system from other hosts. Unless special controls are introduced, such databases, if retransmitted back to the original host, may now contain contaminated data.

Electronic mail may also present a problem in the LAN. There is the possibility of interception of sensitive mail, and messages temporarily stored in a "mailbox" so they may be retrieved later may be compromised. These are potential problems for the database of any on-line word processing system.

Internal LAN functions, such as file servers, also can be compromised either by unauthorized use to obtain sensitive data or by the manipulation of the code or logic in the file server itself.

The possibility of serious physical compromises in a LAN should not be overlooked. For example, it is not difficult to wiretap a LAN to intercept sensitive data, since a connection to the LAN can be made without any interruption of transmission. This is particularly true of the LAN coaxial cable, because it does not have to be turned off in order to connect another node to the network.

Another potential LAN security problem is that physical access to LAN

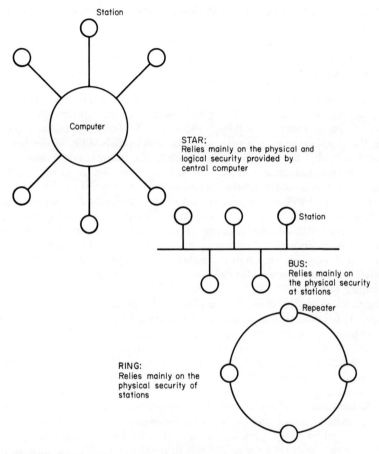

Figure 16-4 Local area network (LAN) topologies.

nodes, including terminals, personal computers, and workstations, becomes more difficult to control as they are distributed to remote locations.

LAN security problems resulting from outside network connectability have already been discussed. However, it might be wise to mention the potential compromises that can result if employees are allowed to connect to the company LAN from their homes. The potential threat to security should not be overlooked in assessing the assumed benefits of increased productivity or improved programming skills.

A final but important point is that it is possible to provide a fair measure of security for the LAN without the use of encryption [FA 1983]. One approach involves the use of separate cables to provide for security level separation. Another approach uses a broad-band mode of operation. This is similar to community antenna television (CATV) technology. One cable can provide approximately fifty channels of information. By adjusting the LAN interface units to channels associated with specific clearances, security or channel isolation can be achieved.

Common Carrier Facilities

Frequently we read that a hacker's penetration of some organization's computer system was executed through a common carrier communications system. The impression often left by the news article is that somewhere along the line, the common carrier's own security was breached or, at the least, the system provided some form of assistance to the unauthorized user.

The issues that arise out of these experiences are important and need examination. First of all, a *common carrier* is a commercial vendor of lines and other telecommunications media and of switch facilities that provide for interconnection of various types of transmission devices. Data networks operated in the United States by organizations that acquire basic transmission facilities from common carriers such as AT&T and GTE, add value to the service (i.e., error detection or special sharing capabilities), and then sell the service are called *value added networks* (VANs). Tymnet and Telenet are good examples of VANs.

Regardless of who provides the service, if it results in a network designed primarily for data transmission and for sharing by many users from different organizations, the system is called a *public data network* (PDN).

Carriers or media can include dial-up, dedicated, or private lines. Other forms of transmission might include satellite or microwave. These facilities are usually located in public areas and are available by simply dialing into a system via a telephone number.

The first step in abuse of such a system by an unauthorized user might be the attempt to avoid paying for a long-distance call. The abuse might be compounded by not paying for the use of some form of computing service. Although the initial log-on might not in itself be an illegal transaction, the attempt to impersonate a legitimate user to avoid charges probably would be.

Normally, common carrier security or access control on behalf of its customers does not include much more than providing basic system integrity and physical security of carrier property and hiring honest employees. Other security measures may be possible under special circumstances (e.g., wiretaps and interception).

It was once thought that a primary safeguard against unauthorized access to these systems was to have unlisted telephone numbers for carriers and customers. Unfortunately, hackers and others have cracked this safeguard, and today thousands of unlisted telephone numbers of computer facilities are available through the numerous hacker-maintained electronic bulletin boards.

Most experts agree that the primary defenses against an outsider compromise of a computer system through a common carrier or data network facility are, first, the security afforded by the customer's password system and, second, the implementation of a suitable encryption system.

Experts also point out that a system that is *too* user-friendly or too lenient is extremely vulnerable. A prime example of this was the Advanced Research Projects Agency Network (ARPANET) of the Department of Defense. At one time there were an estimated 50,000 users of ARPANET connected to approximately 300 host computers on this government-administered data network. The system was distinguished from other more secure DOD computers by the fact that it allowed dial-up access, and many of the host computers were located on college campuses.

The result, of course, was that the network became a prime target for computer hacker penetrations. Although the DOD claimed that no threats to national security resulted from ARPANET break-ins, the decision was made to divide it into two separate networks: Milnet, which contains all military-sensitive hosts, and R&Dnet, which contains less sensitive academic-type research data.

Government security experts say that the long-haul networks will be the most vulnerable part of Milnet because the communications facilities cannot be adequately secured under all conditions. Emphasis, therefore, will be more on controlling computer users and protecting host nodes than on safeguarding the data network itself.

What Are the Most Important Tools That Can Be Used to Reduce Network Vulnerabilities?

Most of the administrative, physical, and technical access control mechanisms that can be used to protect networks have already been discussed in previous chapters. In order to identify the specific security mechanisms that are needed to prevent a network compromise, an adequate network vulnerability classification system and a process for relating available security procedures and mechanisms to a particular security requirement must be developed. The following sections include recommendations for developing such a system.

Network Security Classification and Protection

Networks require three major classes of protection mechanisms:

- Host access control
- Communications carrier security
- Node security (excluding primary hosts only)

Host access control.   Network access control mechanisms must perform the three primary functions covered in earlier chapters:

- Identification
- Authentication
- Authorization

In communications systems, access objects might include:

- System nodes
- Mailboxes (workstations)
- Workstation processes
- Databases

Network access rights might be governed by such factors as:

- Systems environment
- Individual authorization
- Job or project
- Information classification system

Communications carrier security. In addition to the physical security of facilities and shielding, the primary security mechanism used to protect data during transmission is cryptography. Encryption will be mentioned here only with regard to opportunities for its application. Encryption mechanisms and techniques will be discussed in Chapter 17.

Encryption opportunities exist whenever communication is required between two or more nodes in a network. (Database encryption is normally associated with central processor and DBMS security functionalities.) Numerous cryptographic schemes that use both hardware and software are available. The selection of the right encryption and key management system for a particular network application will depend upon such variables as:

- Data sensitivity
- Encryption system costs
- Network performance requirements
- Carrier specifications (e.g., type of lines and transfer rates)
- Node exposure (physical and logical)
- Key management and distribution requirements
- System overhead tolerances
- Carrier vulnerabilities
- Trustworthiness of front-enders and host computers
- User convenience and friendliness requirements

Node security protection. Node security has the same problems as the physical and logical security of network elements, including terminals, personal computers, and satellite systems. Other communications devices that are included in the description of network nodes also need physical and logical access protection.

The following communications facilities will require protection from unauthorized physical access, modification, or other forms of compromise:

- Satellite processors
- Personal computers and workstations
- Front-end processor
- Terminal
- Concentrators
- Communication links
- Switching centers

Primary Network Protection Mechanisms

The selection of the proper network protection tools will depend on the variables discussed earlier in this chapter (i.e., sensitivity, cost, and performance requirements). Many protection mechanisms may operate independently. There are, however, three general principles or constraints that should be imposed in order to maximize total systems security:

1. Selection and implementation of network protection mechanisms should complement other system protection in order to enhance total security (i.e., fill voids).
2. Implementation of network protection mechanisms should not result in the compromise or degradation of other system security features.
3. Selection of system protection mechanisms should provide multiple layers or levels of security in order to minimize the potential of successful system penetration and compromise.

Summary

The important network protection concepts and mechanisms that can be used to identify and contain potential system threats are many and varied. Overall, the possibility of the simultaneous development of more powerful and more secure networks looks promising.

On the other hand, we must recognize that the present thrust toward more functionality and responsiveness in information networks will also produce more security problems. The solution proposed in this chapter is to rigorously balance efficient system resource sharing and user convenience with system security safeguards.

17. Data Encryption

An organization can control the security of network facilities on its physical property to the extent that it chooses. Actual implementation of the security will depend on the organization's knowledge of its requirements and its willingness to expend resources.

Many networks, however, utilize communications facilities provided by telephone companies and other carriers that are outside their decision-making domain. These facilities, including the media such as telephone lines and microwave and satellite systems, are vulnerable to wiretapping and other forms of data interception. Therefore, common carrier communications are considered to be the most vulnerable part of the typical information network.

The accepted state-of-the-art solution to this major communications problem is cryptography. Although not in general use today because of cost and technical and administrative complexities, the future for cryptography looks extremely promising. Major advances in the past decade have included the development of standards to assure secrecy and integrity, cost-performance improvements in hardware and software to make economic justification easier, and the distribution of more educational material to further the understanding and acceptance of modern cryptographic methods.

Since a better solution to the problem of network security is not yet available, the application of cryptography to network security problems is increasing.

Crytpography is a complex subject which requires considerable study of underlying mathematics to comprehend differences in implementation and application of alternative systems. Its treatment in this chapter will be relatively brief and will include the following topics:

- Important cryptographic concepts and applications
- Link encryption
- End-to-end encryption
- Data encryption standard (DES)
- Key management
- Public key systems

- Electronic signatures
- File encryption

Important Cryptographic Concepts and Applications

Cryptographic Concepts

Cryptography involves the transformation of ordinary understandable information (*plaintext*) into information that cannot be understood (*ciphertext*) except by some inverse transformation. The process of transforming the ciphertext back into plaintext is called *decryption*. The original transformation of the plaintext into a secret message is call *encryption* (Figure 17-1).

Ciphers are the product of the transformation of individual characters or letters into secret information. Ciphers are formed by transposition or substitution procedures. *Transposition* is the simple rearrangement of original characters from the plaintext. *Substitution ciphers*, on the other hand, substitute new characters for the original plaintext ones.

A combination of transposition and substitution is called a *product cipher*. A cipher normally includes an algorithm and a key. The *algorithm* describes the transformation process that will be used to encrypt the plaintext, while the *key* furnishes the parameters needed by the transformation. The algorithm may be extremely simple or complex. It can be published publicly and yet not result in a message compromise. The key, on the other hand, must be kept secret in most systems by its legitimate owners in order to protect encrypted information.

The process of compromising an encrypted message or cipher is called *cryptanalysis*. The cost (i.e., resources and time) required to break an encrypted message or cipher is called the *work factor*.

Ciphers are either symmetric or asymmetric. Asymmetric ciphers are considered more secure because the encryption algorithm and/or key is not the same as the decryption algorithm and/or key and, therefore, cannot be derived from each other. Normally, only the key in the system must be changed to provide message secrecy. Most crypto systems today, however, use symmetric-type ciphers. This includes the National Bureau of Standard's data encryption standard (DES).

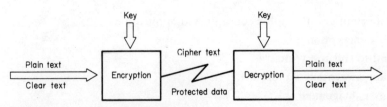

Figure 17-1 Basic crypotographic concept.

Cryptographic Applications

There are many opportunities to utilize cryptography to prevent the compromise of sensitive data. No one knows how much illegal wiretapping and data interception is actually occurring. However, law enforcement agencies assure us that there is a considerable amount of illegal data access occurring daily, and it is increasing significantly on an annual basis.

"Data tapping," or eavesdropping, is often extraordinarily easy and inexpensive to accomplish. Most of the required equipment can be purchased legally and is in plentiful supply. These items include impedance-matching devices, line amplifiers, recorders, miniature transmitters, modems, and computer terminals. In addition, wiretapping and bugging components are available, packaged in what appear to be standard telephone system components. The physical vulnerability of most office switch centers and junction boxes was discussed in a previous chapter.

Wiretapping implies a direct connection to some telecommunications component or system. Message or data-stream interception, however, does not require a direct connection; only the proper recorder and antenna are required to intercept data on a microwave or satellite link. Telephone lines are vulnerable to listening devices that can record electrical impulses. The resulting vulnerability of the common carrier part of the typical network can be significant. Encryption for most organizations, therefore, will be the most practical, cost-justifiable means to control this threat.

It is important to note that the technology required to encrypt data transmitted through a communications carrier has, of course, been available for a long time. However, as traffic rates have increased, along with more elaborate encryption algorithms, special devices have been designed that permit encryption-decryption at speeds that allow the use of cryptography in the latest high-speed computer-oriented networks. (However, a trade-off of some performance for security will almost always be necessary.)

Data encryption is the restructuring of the bit stream entering a device designed to perform cryptography. Most encryption devices are designed to be connected directly into the network between standard network components such as a terminal and a modem. Other cryptographic systems involve the integration of capabilities into a standard device such as a front-ender, a modem, or a terminal. From the time it has been encrypted until decryption takes place at some destination or relay mode, the bit stream is in ciphertext and, therefore, theoretically secure from any compromise as a result of a wiretap or an interception. Different cryptographic systems offer different levels of protection. For instance, the amount of protection provided by link encryption will be different from that of end-to-end encryption.

Link Encryption

Modern link encryption systems perform in a manner that is usually invisible to system users through the installation of devices at modem interfaces [SY

1976]. As shown in Figure 17-2, the plaintext bit stream entering the encryptor is reproduced at the exit from the decryptor. The result is that synchronization, delimiting, and control characters will be recognized by the receiving station.

Link encryption does have a major weakness, however. Even though it may function adequately to protect against wiretapping, it does not provide adequate safeguards against a misrouted message by a message switch. Message switches in the network must be able to decrypt and reencrypt messages with the key used at the next destination. The result is that a message could be misrouted to a destination that could decrypt it into plaintext.

As shown in Figure 17-3, an encrypted message sent from sender A using key 1 would be reencrypted by the message switch using key 2 instead of key 3, if the message were accidentally routed to receiver B instead of to receiver C as intended.

End-to-End Encryption

The primary advantage of end-to-end encryption is that only the originating location or source of a message and its legitimate receiver at the destination can encrypt and decrypt messages, unlike the case of link encryption (Figure 17-4). End-to-end encryption may be sent through networks of any type (private or public) that use circuit switching, message switching, or packet switching.

Since message headers may contain sensitive source and destination information (i.e., for traffic analysis), a countermeasure would be to superimpose link encryption onto an end-to-end encryption system (Figure 17-5). The result in this case would be that the message for a period of time would be double-encrypted. From a practical standpoint, the encryption devices at the source and destination would not be redundant as long as different keys are used at the proper time.

Data Encryption Standard (DES)

In 1977, the National Bureau of Standards (NBS) adopted and published a standard encryption methodology called the *data encryption standard* to provide for the protection of sensitive data. The DES was originally developed by

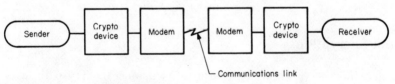

Figure 17-2   Link encryption.

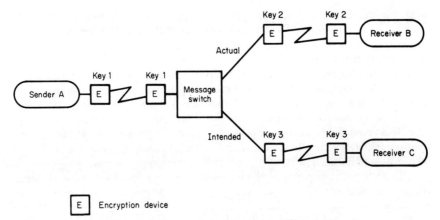

E   Encryption device

Figure 17-3 Link encryption vulnerability: A misrouted message.

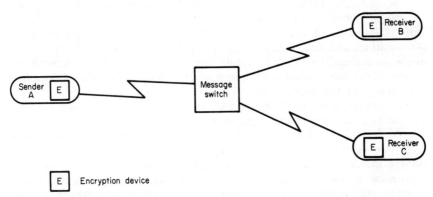

E   Encryption device

Figure 17-4 End-to-end encryption.

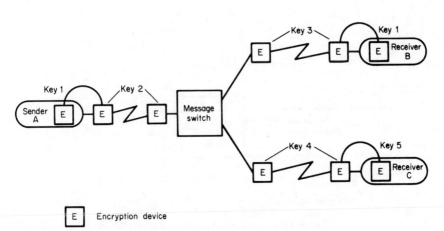

E   Encryption device

Figure 17-5 Combination line and end-to-end encryption.

IBM, which agreed to grant nonexclusive, royalty-free licenses under its patents to make, use, and sell apparatus which comply with the standard. Today the DES is the most popular cipher, primarily because it is treated as a federal information processing standard (FIPS).

One of the original objectives of the NBS was to specify a standard cryptographic algorithm whereby vendors of encryption devices and systems could provide equipment compatible with each other, while providing an adequate level of protection for most commercial, nonmilitary information systems. The DES is available at this time in various encryption devices. The devices contain DES logic in electronic chips manufactured by such companies as Motorola and Fairchild.

Although not as popular as the hardware-oriented cryptographic systems, the DES is also available in software which can be run on host computers or front-enders. Compared to the use of hardware devices, the software approach is relatively limited because of speed limitations, overhead, and key protection vulnerabilities.

Essentially, the DES algorithm is a recirculating block product cipher with 64 data bits input and output and 56 active key bits plus 8 parity bits. On the basis of the recirculating block cipher, plaintext bytes go through numerous permutations and transformations until encrypted (Figure 17-6). Hardware implementations, according to one authority, "are expected to perform the 64 bit encryption/decryption in the range of 5 to 200 microseconds, depending upon the technology used" [SY 1977].

How secure is the DES? There are those who say the DES is not secure enough because technologically advanced computers can be used to help decode a message. Most authorities, however, concluded that the DES is secure enough for most commercial and nonmilitary governmental applications. For example, one authority [BE 1983] says: "A total of 2^{56} different encryption keys is possible. If a determined penetrator had a computer that could try one encryption key possibility every microsecond, 2283 years would be required to try all possible combinations. Assuming that, on the average,

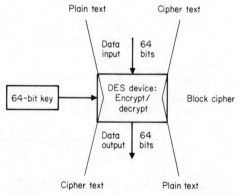

Figure 17-6 Data encryption standard (DES) algorithm: Recirculating block cipher.

the correct key is discovered halfway through the process, 1141 years will be required."*

Key Management

The security and integrity of the keys used to encrypt and decrypt information are of as much concern to organizations that employ cryptography as are the algorithms and devices used. Inadequate key security can result in the compromise of otherwise secure cryptographic systems. Unfortunately, many organizations fail to understand the rigor and discipline necessary to generate, distribute, and maintain key security. The problem is similar to that associated with passwords, except that a number of very effective special-purpose devices are available to assist encryption key distribution, and encryption keys tend to be more highly regarded and controlled. In either case, compromise of passwords or cryptographic keys can be extremely dangerous. It is also dangerous for system users to assume that because their systems employ cryptography, they are more secure than they would be without it. This attitude can create problems that might otherwise be avoided.

There are basically two different classes of key encryption systems: *secret* key and *public* key. The security of secret keys is obviously one of the most critical aspects of cryptographic systems. Public key systems, discussed below, utilize both secret (i.e., private) keys and public keys (i.e., those which may or may not be published, depending on the type of cryptographic system used and its application).

Ordinarily, secret cryptographic keys can be distributed using such services as:

- First-class mail
- Special courier
- A telecommunications carrier

Mail and couriers each have clear advantages and disadvantages. Mail is slow and inexpensive and provides only limited security. Couriers are faster than mail, usually more expensive, but offer a much higher level of security. Transmission via a communications carrier that employs encryption to transmit encrypted keys can be extremely fast. Costs can vary considerably. The security that this method provides, on the other hand, is well worth the expense.

One approach to key management and distribution is the use of link encryption. In this case, each user or network node is furnished with a key to be used to communicate with another specific network user. When a particular node receives a message, it is decrypted, reencrypted, and routed to the next appro-

---

*Hal B. Becker, *Information Integrity*, McGraw-Hill, New York, 1983. Reprinted with permission of McGraw-Hill.

priate node. The message is subsequently received by the correct receiving node. This key distribution system can work quite well in delivering secret keys to multiple users. The main problem in using link encryption for this application is the important need for physical and personnel security at each node in the network.

Another key distribution system utilizes end-to-end encryption to deliver keys to users, and this system is more secure than using link encryption. The concept is that each network user is given a key that enables him or her to communicate with a key distribution center (KDC). The KDC and each node share a master key. When users wish to communicate (using cryptography) with other users, they must first contact the KDC (the key server), which provides the appropriate keys for the various users. Since the keys are used only temporarily, the security of encrypted communications is significantly improved.

In addition to the possibility of downloading the keys as described above, four other key loading mechanisms might be considered (depending, of course, on the cryptographic devices in use):

• *Manual switches*:   Rotary or thumbwheel switches can be set manually at each encryption device located at the end of a link.

• *Plug-in modules*:   A device containing a read-only memory (ROM) can be used to directly insert a key into an encryption device without any individual knowing what the key is.

• *Magnetic stripe*:   A card with the key encoded on a magnetic stripe can be inserted into the encryption device to load the key—again without the key being visible or known to any individual.

• *Processor interfaces*:   After keys are derived in a CPU (via a special key-generation program), they can be loaded directly into an on-line encryption device (or a communications front-ender if it has cryptographic capabilities).

Public Key Systems

One of the big advantages of the public key encryption concept is that problems associated with key distribution in conventional cryptographic systems can be eliminated. In public key systems, it is not necessary to distribute keys so that only authorized users receive them. It is possible to actually publish the public keys so that anyone can have access to them. This is accomplished by the use of a special cryptographic system using an asymmetric cipher that was first introduced by Diffie and Hellman in 1976 [DI 1976].

The essence of the public key concept is that each user is given an encryption and a decryption algorithm. A trapdoor, or one-way function, makes computation quite easy in one direction, but an inverse computation requires private or secret trapdoor information.

Implementation involves giving users two keys, one for encryption and one for decryption. Typically the decryption key is a secret key, whereas the encryption key can be public. The result is that a user (with a public key) wishing to communicate with another user (with a private key) can do so with the assurance that only the intended receiver (the one with the private key) can decrypt the message. Knowing one key in this cryptographic system does not help someone to obtain the other key.

But how does the receiver of the encrypted message know who really sent the message? Who was the real originator or source of the message? The answer is that the public key concept makes it possible to attach "signatures" to the messages.

Electronic Signatures

Signatures are possible using the public key encryption concept because encryption-decryption keys can be used in either order. A message can be encrypted with a private key and decrypted with a public key, or the procedure can be reversed.

For instance, assume that a user encrypts a message first with a private decryption key and then encrypts the product with another user's (the intended receiver) public encryption key. The second user, after receiving the double-encrypted message, first decrypts the message using his or her own private decryption key. If this is followed by a second decryption process using the sender's public encryption key, the message will be produced in plaintext. A signature has been created as part of the message because only the original sender can produce an encrypted message that generates plaintext when his or her public encryption key is used to decrypt it.

Other cryptographic systems employing public key–type mechanisms have been developed to solve the problem of signatures on electronic messages. These systems all focus on the need to authenticate encrypted messages. The importance of these systems is that the signature will prove that the message was really sent by the purported sender and that the message could not have been transmitted by someone else. In addition, and most importantly, the sender cannot claim that he or she did not send the signed message, just as the receiver cannot modify its contents.

The legal implications of these communications system capabilities should not be underestimated. For example, the billions of dollars of fund transactions that are transferred daily between financial institutions can now be efficiently authenticated using one of the new electronic signature systems.

File Encryption

It would seem that file encryption should be part of computer host and database protection. This is not altogether true because personal computers, satellite computers, and even front-enders also maintain databases that may be extremely sensitive and vulnerable to compromise.

The use of encryption in data storage areas is not new. There are fewer applications of cryptography to databases than of encryption to communications, however, for the simple reason that very few systems employ host-oriented cryptography.

The reasons for and against database encryption are important, however, and should be considered whenever sensitive data resides in a database. The obvious benefit is that encrypted files add another layer of protection to the system. This could be particularly important for personal computer and satellite system users, since they probably are not afforded the same access control protection that a host computer provides to its own directly connected databases. In the host system, encrypted files are generally more secure from both intentional and accidental compromises.

Encryption of very sensitive databases is still not an easy decision even when the encrypting software is readily available and can be easily introduced into the system. Some of the many problems are as follows:

- Encryption overhead, particularly for software-managed encryption, is often intolerable. Excessive activity can accentuate the problem.
- Data sharing means sharing of keys—a significant problem in itself. Both data and keys suffer from overexposure.
- Lost keys or destroyed keys can make a file worthless or at least result in major inconvenience.
- Encrypted data first must be converted into plaintext before processing can occur. During processing in most systems, sensitive data may be vulnerable to compromise.

There are a number of excellent theories on how encrypted files can be protected during access and processing. However, implementation of these ideas into workable systems does not appear to be a high-priority requirement today.

On the other hand, file encryption through software has been accomplished in many computer systems. Both the DES and public key concepts have been applied to file encryption with a high degree of success for implemented projects.

Solutions to the file encryption feasibility or justification problem will occur in four areas: (1) when the cost-benefit analysis is favorable, only the most sensitive files will be encrypted; (2) development of hardware-oriented cryptography will significantly reduce overhead; (3) as the overall cost performance of systems improves, software file-managed encryption will be easier to justify; and (4) keeping encrypted files architecturally separate from nonencrypted files will minimize overhead and related processing vulnerabilities.

Summary

There are excellent cryptographic solutions to today's information network security problems. Encryption should be able to satisfy the most sensitive data transmission security problems of the most technically advanced systems. The tools currently available are extremely versatile and dependable.

The numerous implementations of the DES in modern cryptographic devices, and the latest encryption concepts such as public key and electronic signature systems, for instance, offer adequate security for most potential users.

Finally, it is becoming increasingly clear that organizations with networks that depend on common carrier facilities should evaluate more thoroughly their security needs in this area, and the sooner the better.

Completing a Secure System Design

PART 4

COMPUTER SECURITY AWARENESS PROGRAM

PLANNING PHASES

LOGICAL ACCESS CONTROL PLAN

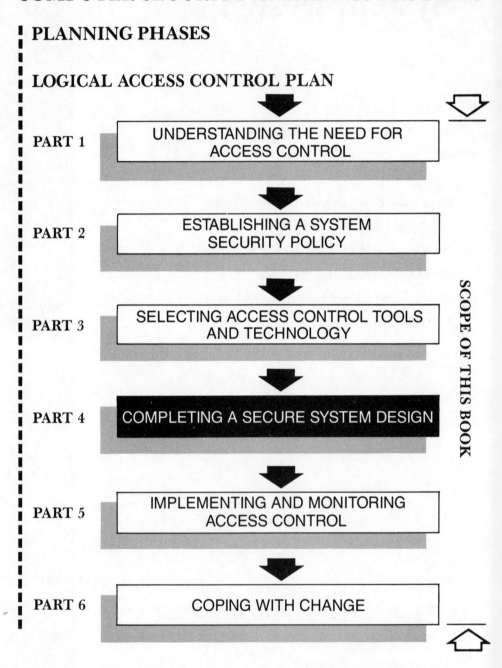

PART 1 — UNDERSTANDING THE NEED FOR ACCESS CONTROL

PART 2 — ESTABLISHING A SYSTEM SECURITY POLICY

PART 3 — SELECTING ACCESS CONTROL TOOLS AND TECHNOLOGY

PART 4 — COMPLETING A SECURE SYSTEM DESIGN

PART 5 — IMPLEMENTING AND MONITORING ACCESS CONTROL

PART 6 — COPING WITH CHANGE

SCOPE OF THIS BOOK

18. Access Control Specifications

Access control requirements need to be translated into functional specifications. Unfortunately, many organizations skip this step in their hurry to solve their information system security problems.

Failure to treat security specifications with the same respect accorded a major hardware or software acquisition is a serious oversight. Why this happens so often is not clearly understood. Most probably, security does not have a high enough priority. Whatever the reasons, the solution is rather simple: Utilize the same discipline and procedures that you would if you were going to make a decision regarding an important new computer application or a new major computer hardware acquisition. Ideally, access control requirements should be part of every new application or hardware or software decision.

This chapter will discuss how to develop a set of access control specifications by addressing the following questions:

- Who should write access control specifications?
- How should access control specifications be organized?
- How should access control requirements be identified?
- Which access control mechanisms require selection by specification?

Who Should Write Access Control Specifications?

Information access control specifications should reflect management policy. How the specification is generated and who generates it are important. The organization's executives should be informed of the project so they can support it with dedication and review the results carefully.

Past experience has shown that good specifications can be best developed by one of the following groups:

- A computer security task force made up of systems experts, users, auditors, and security professionals

- Data processing management with the help of appropriate internal and external consultants
- The organization's systems security officer with the help of systems security experts, users, and appropriate managers
- Outside consultants who are well qualified and who can work closely with all the internal people who can provide assistance

How Should Access Control Specifications Be Organized?

Each access control specification should address a specific security requirement. The written specification should be a clear description of the proposed solution to a potential security problem. Where possible, quantitative information should be provided to cover such factors as performance, reliability, maintainability, and test procedures.

For best results, access control specifications should be associated with the acquisition of major system components. For instance in the case of a computer request for proposal (RFP), the security specification that describes a required *authorization mechanism* should be included with the operating system specification.

Independent specifications, such as for an access control software package or an encryption system, are normally stand-alone documents. This class of specifications should include adequate interface or connectability data to ensure system compatibility.

The format or organization of an access control specification should be essentially the same as for any other technical product or service requirement. The following is a suggested format:

PART I. SCOPE: Provides a summary of the specification and identifies the product (or service) and its relation to other information system components.

PART II. APPLICABLE STANDARDS AND DOCUMENTS: References key standards [e.g., data encryption standard (DES)] or significant guideline documents.

PART III. FUNCTIONAL DESCRIPTION: Explains what the product must do and includes cost-performance data. The following information should be included in this section:

- System functions
- Product functions
- Performance levels
- Configuration and compatibility requirements
- Underwriter Laboratory and related standards
- Power requirements
- Physical aspects

- Restrictions
- Nonstandard design requirements
- Error recovery and restart

PART IV. TESTABILITY AND MAINTAINABILITY: The following information should be contained in this part of the specification:

- Conformance to testability guidelines
- Installation requirements
- Deinstallation requirements
- Maintenance requirements
- Test and diagnostic objectives
- Error logging and reporting
- Reliability specifications
- Documentation

Cost data is often included with performance requirements in formal specifications. Cost requirements or limits, when known, should be included somewhere in the specification for completeness and to minimize unacceptable vendor responses.

The content or comprehensiveness of a particular specification will vary depending on the complexity of the security requirement and the existence of some standard or document which can be referenced for more specific data. For example, a specification for a magnetic tape degausser (a device that eliminates latent magnetic images) might simply state: "Any device that complies with the National Security Agency's list of approved magnetic tape degaussing devices will meet this specification." On the other hand, the specification for an access control software package or a call-up and answer-back system might require considerably more detail. In these latter cases, there are at this time no standards that can be easily referenced.

How Should Access Control Requirements Be Identified?

The quality of an access control specification will reflect the precision with which system threats are identified [SY 1981]. It is recommended that the specification should be based as much as possible on quantitative assessments of risk and countermeasures. A risk analysis can provide valuable insight into the degree of access protection required by a database or the range of access permission that should be given to system users or subjects.

Also, if a risk assessment study can identify all data elements in a database, all owners of data in the database, and all permissions that the owners are willing to grant others with regard to their files, an extremely powerful security policy model can be developed. As a result, more comprehensive access control specifications can be derived from the model.

Which Access Control Mechanisms
Require Selection by Specification?

In general, all system changes or enhancements should be executed in conformance with a reviewed and approved specification. Likewise, all applications
and hardware, software, and communications changes should be reviewed for
security vulnerabilities.

There are at least four major system acquisition decisions that should not
be made without consideration of access control specifications. These are
decisions to acquire:

- Host computers
- Communications processors (and other communications facilities)
- Encryption systems
- Access control software packages

Host Computers

Access control mechanisms that should be considered when selecting a new
host computer should include [SY 1981]:

- Memory segmentation
- Protection of operating system from users
- Protection of users from each other
- Access control
- Password protection
- Enforcement of password changing
- Audit trails
- Warning messages
- Data encryption

Communications Processors

Features to be considered when selecting a communications processor should
include [SY 1981]:

- Protection from the user (specific features)
- Routing control
- Call-back
- Program loading
- Encryption
- Limited host memory access

Encryption Systems

Cryptographic system features to be reviewed as possible requirements are:

- System performance (i.e., encrypting speed, overhead)
- Security of the system algorithm
- Hardware or software encryption capability
- Suitability of system to perform encryption at link, network, host, or application level
- Type of key management used
- Implementation and operational expenses

Access Control Software Packages

Special features that might be considered when specifying an access control software package might include:

1. Type of architecture the package can run on
2. Operational mode such as time sharing or transaction processing
3. Performance degradation, if any
4. User response time
5. Number of simultaneous system users possible
6. Nature of self-protection mechanisms (i.e., to prevent compromise)
7. Type of access denial and alarm system (i.e., real-time monitor)
8. Quality of violation logging and reporting system
9. Specific access control features such as:
   - Verification of log-on and passwords
   - Restriction of access by protection criteria
   - Resource protection capability
   - Data display protection
   - Data structure protection
   - Type of user profile and permission system maintained

Cost will be a factor in most evaluations and recommendations. The specifications should define what is considered to be a reasonable range of acceptable cost performance. The vendor or system design response should be evaluated in light of the stated requirements and alternative solutions.

Summary

The need for good access control specifications is of primary importance. Specifications should be completed, reviewed, and approved before an organization makes any important system changes. The writing of access control specifications should be a high-priority activity that receives top management support.

Access control specifications should be prepared by a task force made up of the most qualified people available. The specifications themselves should be developed through some form of risk or threat study and should be supplemented with the use of checklists to ensure that there are no serious mistakes or omissions in the selection of protection mechanisms.

Finally, there are certain systems and products that should not be selected without the help of a security specification, including computers, communications processors and facilities, encryption systems, and access control software packages.

19. Open Networks

Chapters 19 to 23 will utilize the specification development principle described in the previous chapter. Each chapter will describe how to complete access control design specifications for a particular information system category.

Although the system designers may not have a choice, access control specifications should preferably be integrated into the design phase of a new application or hardware or software project. Security controls developed for existing systems will work, but generally will have less than ideal results.

The specifications should be developed as a direct result of the completion of the following preparatory activities:

- Creation of an organizational security policy
- Completion of an appropriate risk assessment study
- Review of the specifications for completeness and cost-performance impact
- Management approval

In addition, each chapter on access control design will address the following important questions:

- What are the major functional characteristics of this system category that should be considered in the design of access control?
- Who should decide what access controls are needed for this system category?
- Which access controls are considered most suitable for this type of system category?
- How should cost justification or risk assumption be approached for this system category?

Important Characteristics of Open Networks

Important functional characteristics of open networks that may be of particular interest to access control system designers include:

- A distributed systems architecture that facilitates database and resource sharing
- An increasing demand for user friendliness
- Use of common carrier facilities that lend themselves to wiretapping or interception of data
- Increasing implementation of local area networks (LANs) that are also capable of external communications or connection

Access Control Design Responsibility

Because the size, complexity, and geographic distribution of open networks vary tremendously, access control design responsibility will be a significant task for most organizations.

Larger organizations may have a small staff of computer and communications security experts based at corporate headquarters to provide top-level design and consultation assistance to their geographically dispersed divisions.

Corporate security policies of large organizations can be implemented much easier with a strong centrally coordinated corporate computer security staff. In addition to increased consistency in access control specifications, money can be saved by large buys of such products as access control software packages, encryption devices, and call-up and answer-back systems.

Where autonomy prevails at the divisional levels, local staffs of computer security experts and their cooperating task forces can produce the necessary access control design specifications to support their local networks and external connections.

Smaller organizations that operate open networks should probably hire outside consultants to help their in-house task force and/or system security team write the specifications. Outside assistance should be a mandatory requirement for very small companies.

Suitable Open Network Access Controls

Because of the heavy emphasis on system resource sharing and potentially vulnerable communications, open networks require a substantial amount of access control planning and implementation. For the most part, larger organizations will have the necessary resources to justify implementation of the current state-of-the-art access control mechanisms and products.

The most important specifications will be those written for central (and probably compatible) host computers. An extremely secure host that supports either a capability or kernel architecture would be a good first step in obtaining access control protection. Other important access control mechanisms are:

- A system-generated and system-controlled password system
- Communications-oriented encryption
- Call-up and answer-back systems where appropriate
- Access control software packages (depending on the selected host architectures)
- Communications processors with built-in security features
- Signature authentication systems where appropriate (via encryption)
- Protection against covert and unauthorized overt information channels
- Radiation emanation protection through the purchase of tempest-rated hardware and communications devices and shielded lines and facilities
- Database management systems that include advanced security mechanisms, such as more access control granularity and schema-subschema–view capability

Cost Justification and Risk Assumptions

Cost justification for system access control specifications should be easier for larger open-network organizations. However, the size and complexity of many of their networks and the variability in sensitivity of their different divisional and departmental systems may tax even the largest companies. This may be particularly true where the price of security might be a system with degraded performance that is less user convenient.

Security and control justification under these circumstances will require considerable corporate coordination in order to effect the economies that may be possible through the acquisition of compatible computers and communications systems and through the establishment of information access control standards and guidelines.

The challenge for management is to prevent weak links from occurring in the network while refusing requests for an inordinate amount of security by divisions or departments that have become overzealous about implementing state-of-the-art access control products.

Balancing risks and costs in open networks is not easy. Quantitative risk assessment has major limitations. Qualitative risk assessment also has its problems. Fortunately, we are not too far from the development of national and international standards and guidelines for both networks and information system access control mechanisms [e.g., the NBS data encryption standard (DES)].

The result of this standardization process should be a larger market for system security products and a commensurate reduction in cost. Advances in information and communications systems technology and related cost-performance improvements should also help.

Summary

The security of open networks is going to be a challenging problem at least for the remainder of the 1980s. Information technology and its applications are being developed faster than the security and access control mechanisms that should be accompanying the implementation of the more advanced networks.

Pressure has been put on system designers to incorporate security into information and communications systems at the design stage. The benefits of this approach are substantial. The penalties of incorporating security measures at a later stage, as a quick fix or patch, are almost intolerably high.

Network security solutions for the larger networks may be more easily justified by organizations with considerable resources. They have the advantage of centralized planning, coordination, and buying power. Smaller organizations with highly sensitive systems will probably have to struggle financially to obtain the necessary security.

The positive side is that national and international standards for both networks and access control mechanisms are being developed and will be available in the near future. As the new standards are accepted, the result should be a larger market for access control mechanisms and an improvement in cost performance. This, in turn, will make it much easier to justify the inclusion of adequate security features in open networks.

20. Closed and Limited-Access Networks

In theory, access control specifications for a closed network (i.e., no outside communications connectability) should be somewhat simpler than those for an open network. This is because access defense mechanisms should only have to protect against potential compromises from employees or authorized users, not unauthorized outsiders.

For this reason, the access control specifications needed to protect a system against intrusions by insiders in a closed network are essentially the same as those specifications that are needed to protect open networks against insider compromise.

Unfortunately, few networks can afford the luxury of total isolation or freedom from outside communications connectability. The economic and informational need to share data and system resources forces networks to open up, at least partially. Users hope this will result in the equivalent of a closed network for the most sensitive system components and an open network architecture for applications with fewer security requirements. To the extent that this can be accomplished in a practical manner, the result would be a *limited-access* network.

A good question to ask might be: Are there major differences between the specifications for a *fully closed* versus a *partially closed* network? The answer, as will be discovered in this chapter, is yes. There are a few very important differences in the approach and the security technology that are necessary to create a partially closed subnetwork within or parallel to a network that maintains some level of outside communications exchange.

Similarities and differences that occur in the following areas will be discussed:

- Important characteristics of closed and limited-access networks
- Access control design responsibility
- Suitable limited-access network controls
- Cost justification and risk assumption

Important Characteristics of Closed and Limited-Access Networks

A *closed network* system would include one or more host computers and an indefinite number of remotely located terminals, peripheral devices, workstations, and personal computers. The chief characteristics of the closed network that differentiates its access control requirements from other computer system or open network configurations are that most, if not all, of its user access resources tend to be known, tend to be locally installed, and are generally inaccessible through a dial-up or private line or other communications facility.

A reverse approach to access control specification development should work for a fully closed system. This would be accomplished by identifying those controls that would normally be implemented specifically to protect a system from an unauthorized outside access and then eliminating these requirements from the specification. The following is an example of such a list:

- Call-up and answer-back mechanisms
- External communications-oriented access control software packages
- Protection against covert and unauthorized communications channels
- Communications port protection devices
- Communications-oriented hardware and software encryption systems
- Extremely long and complex system-generated passwords

A partially closed or limited-access secure network design would probably not be practical if the designer or designers could not adequately isolate very sensitive system components from those that need much less protection. Fortunately, network architectural concepts and security mechanisms do exist that make this objective possible. These include:

- The ability to physically separate or isolate components, subsystems, and subnetworks from each other in a network
- The availability of certain access control mechanisms to provide sufficient operational confidence and integrity, to the point where the use of these systems is within the user's range of risk acceptance
- The availability of access control mechanisms that can provide both sufficient security and adaptability, thus enabling network designers to balance costs, functionality, performance, and security

These concepts are demonstrated in Figures 20-1 and 20-2. In both figures we see that, physically, it is possible to isolate very sensitive system components such as computers, databases, front-enders, terminals, and personal computers from those parts of a system that have untrustworthy outside communications connections.

In a worst-case situation, an entire computer system or subnetwork could be physically isolated from the rest of the network permanently or temporar-

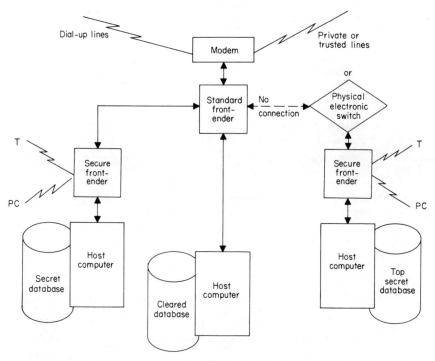

Figure 20-1 Limited-access network with standard and secure front-ender and security switch option.

ily, depending on security requirements. Granted, while disconnected, it is not logically or electronically an active network component. The point of the matter, however, is that limited-access systems are within a designer's capability, and access control specifications can be developed to provide the necessary functionality.

Access Control Design Responsibility

The access control security requirements of limited-access or partially closed networks may "push" the state of the art as much as the requirements for open networks, if not more so. This is because the dual requirements for both open and closed networks will probably conflict at some point. The need for extensive data and resource sharing for some components within a network, and almost total protection for other components in the same network, will be difficult to fulfill.

For this reason, design responsibilities should not be piecemeal or fragmented. In many cases, nonstandard or special-purpose devices will have to be specified. The best design team for this type of requirement would be a task

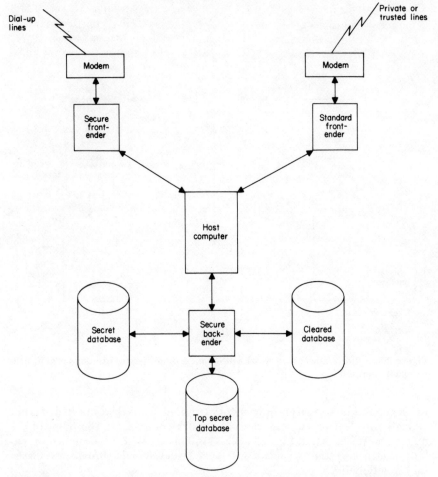

Figure 20-2   Limited-access network with standard and secure front-ender and secure back-ender.

force of company employees supplemented with outside technical consultants who are capable of expertly analyzing and testing vendor specifications and special products.

Suitable Limited-Access Network Controls

As mentioned earlier, closed network access controls and specifications will not be different from those of any other network requiring protection from abuse by insiders. The problems presented by a combination of trustworthy and untrustworthy users, computers, and communications facilities is formidable, however.

What will be needed is multilevel security with extremely powerful and dependable isolation and access control mechanisms. This is particularly true for devices that can switch access on or off through manual or electronic manipulation depending on variable requirements. Examples of such systems include:

- Secure communications processor (i.e., with integral kernel-type architectures)
- Communications switches that can provide connect and disconnect services to sensitive data and resources
- Secure back-end processors that can control access to sensitive databases

It is essential that these devices, particularly those that are software-driven or programmable, have the ability to safeguard themselves against compromise through state-of-the-art protection mechanisms.

Requirements must be generated which make it clear exactly where sensitive elements are needed and how much isolation is necessary. These requirements must be carefully compared for conformance to the manufacturer's specifications and possibly to the new NSA computer security criteria.

Another large class of communications access control devices that should be evaluated for access protection and implementation at the gateway to the network (i.e., modem or front-ender connection) includes the following:

- Call-up and answer-back devices
- Secure front-enders
- Secure modems
- Encryption devices
- Password and encryption key servers and distribution systems
- Communications and port protection systems
- Wiretap detectors

A number of systems today provide a combination of these safeguards and can be used just as effectively to protect open as well as limited-access networks. Typically, a multifunctional communications and port protection device might include the following features:

- Call-up and answer-back option
- On-line encryption-decryption
- User access code directories
- Event logging
- Auto-dial protection with a synthesized technology
- Password checking and automatic disconnect

Some systems also include such features as encrypted user terminal authentication and floppy disk scrambling mechanisms.

Cost Justification and Risk Assumptions

The decision to implement limited-access networks requires a careful balancing of risks and protection costs. The number and variety of new communications-oriented access control devices and mechanisms that are now available is impressive. Their proper use can assure security for extremely sensitive data that must reside or be processed on heavily shared computer networks. Generally, system designers will examine these tools from the following perspectives:

• The degree of protection provided
• The cost
• Any performance degradation

The results of these evaluations will indicate either that with the use of the right network architecture and protection mechanisms, a limited-access network is practical and economically feasible or that the costs of protection and the performance degradation that would accompany the implementation of sufficient access control for even a limited amount of sharing cannot be justified.

If the second conclusion is reached, the designers should specify that extremely sensitive elements of the system be physically isolated (i.e., no communications connection). The alternatives are to close the entire network, or to not implement the sensitive data systems in the first place.

Summary

The essence of access protection provided by a closed network design is that the potential problem of compromise by outsiders should be reduced to a minimum. On the other hand, a closed system without a communications connection to the outside world may be too restrictive an architecture for many computer organizations and users.

The alternative is the design of a limited-access network which can provide for controlled sharing of relatively nonsensitive information and yet offer significant protection for critical data and resources.

Access control specifications for a network can be developed only after a careful evaluation of costs, security functionality, and performance degradation. Once the system is deemed feasible, there is a large array of security architectures and access control mechanisms that the designer can use to construct the proper network.

21. Office Automation Systems

Office automation should result in material benefits to most organizations. The improvements will result from the fact that the office work is done differently in order to increase productivity. Terminal, multifunctional workstations, and personal computers will replace the typewriter. Fixed and floppy disks will be substituted for filing cabinets. The cathode-ray tube (CRT) screen should significantly reduce the amount of printed reports and hard-copy paperwork. The office's local area network (LAN) should provide more effective and expedient communication of information from one office to another. The departmental minicomputer or host computer will be shared more effectively to provide offices with more processing power and storage facilities when needed. Soon voice, data, and graphics communications will be integrated in order to improve productivity even more.

This scenario of the office of today and the office of tomorrow seems to be perfect—maybe too perfect. The problem is that the amount and the rate of change in office procedures may be too much too fast from the standpoint of system security.

Today the emphasis is on how quickly people can be trained and how soon the equipment can be delivered. As a result there are bound to be some major oversights. For instance, consider how easy it will be to overlook physical and logical access controls when designing and implementing a completely new office system.

The main advice given in this chapter is to go with office automation systems (OAS) but to go *slowly*. In addition, develop your access control and security specifications at the same time you are deciding which new office system to purchase. Do not buy products, buy solutions—*total* solutions, including internal controls and access protection. Avoid the problem of piece-meal acquisition of one new exciting OAS product after another without basing the purchases on a written OAS specification created for your particular organization.

On the other hand, automation systems can be implemented that are both modern and secure. The guidelines presented in this chapter should help you achieve this objective:

- Important characteristics of office automation systems
- Access control design responsibility
- Suitable OAS access controls
- Cost justification and risk assumptions

Important Characteristics of Office Automation Systems

Office automation systems utilize most of the same equipment (i.e., terminals, personal computers, LANs, PBXs, and various mainframes) that is used in nonoffice-oriented information systems and networks. There are, however, certain important differences in security and access control requirements for the OAS. The different security needs (or at least the different emphasis) relate to the following OAS characteristics:

- Applications
- Decentralized function
- Location
- Hardware usage and sharing
- Software usage and sharing
- Personnel background and experience
- Communications sharing

Primary office automation applications include word processing, electronic mail, electronic filing, document and text management, data processing, spreadsheet preparation, and numerous administrative functions. The possibility of unauthorized access to the files and user programs associated with automated office applications is cause for concern. For example, prior to the automation of the office (at the local level), someone typed a letter, memo, document, or financial report. The draft hard copy would normally be reviewed by the originator. If required, corrections would be made, and one or more final copies would be prepared and distributed. Normally, the master or a hard copy would be manually filed in a cabinet, letter book, or other storage container. If the information were extremely sensitive, the cabinet, desk, or container would be securely locked. If reasonable diligence were applied from start to finish, only a limited number of people would have had access to the material while it was in preparation or even after it was in final form. Generally, all such access would be of a physical nature (i.e., no electronic access) which could readily be observed by those present.

These same office functions are performed quite differently in an electronic or automated environment.

First, there may be a tendency for more people to type their own material into a system because of availability, convenience, ease of use, and rapid turnaround time. Individual capabilities are therefore significantly enhanced.

But the opportunities for mistakes, internal control violations, and unnoticed and unauthorized access to other people's data in the system are increased.

Second, sensitive data is more vulnerable in an automated office system because of the procedures that are used for data entry, filing, and storage. Three problem areas are as follows:

1. Data resides, at least temporarily, in shared systems with little or no access control protection.
2. Extremely sensitive data may reside in a shared system file for a long period of time, compared to a hard copy being locked in a filing cabinet.
3. In small offices, passwords are not seriously administered or regarded.

Third, if a local area network is used to transmit the data to another office, there is a possibility that other users of the LAN will see the communication.

Fourth, if the person to whom the correspondence is addressed is not in at the time that the electronic message or report reaches its final destination, or he or she does not choose to "open the mailbox" to see what is in it, the data will usually remain in a mailbox (i.e., storage facility) until it is finally accessed and purged. Meanwhile the data may be vulnerable to compromise.

Fifth, if a departmental or satellite computer is being used for temporary archiving or storage of documents or text until a final distribution is made or until long-term storage is arranged, the data is probably residing in a system that lacks rigorous access controls. In today's typical departmental office system, strong access controls are seldom introduced into the local minicomputers or small computers because of the expectation that only trusted users will have access. Unfortunately, considering the openness of most small offices (and even large ones), this can be a serious misconception.

Finally, the software that supports most office systems is particularly user-friendly, or easy to use. This means that, in most cases, there will be a minimum amount of internal controls embedded in the software in order to reduce user-required actions and concerns about how and why the software performs certain functions. This "invisibility" of software functionality often requires a trade-off of security and access control for convenience. For example, user *menus* (i.e., directions on how to access or use system resources shown on the CRT screen) make it possible for someone totally unfamiliar with an application to sit down at a terminal and manipulate even sensitive data.

Access Control Design Responsibility

Large organizations are beginning to centralize OAS design responsibility in corporate or divisional headquarters operations in order to establish good design and system selection decisions for their geographically distributed offices. Initially, these centralized operations focused on the development of standards for hardware acquisition to achieve interoffice system compatibility and economical purchasing power. This was allowed by the establishment of guidelines and standards for recommended OAS software acquisition.

However, most centralized system control functions have not progressed much further with their recommendations on the use of office automation systems in order to allow the offices to be creative in their approaches to OAS. It was hoped that the freedom to implement whatever style of OAS the office believed would best get their job done would result in the greatest increase in productivity. Most large organizations, therefore, are searching for an ideal balance between centralized and decentralized office system control.

From a practical standpoint, there is no reason why OAS security and access controls cannot be administered in essentially the same manner. However, problems can occur for at least two reasons. First, some large organizations have opted so completely for decentralized system decision making and operation that they are not in a position to dictate what security and access control measures their remote offices should take. Second, even if a centralized OAS control operation recommends specific access control guidelines and specifications, it is often unable to enforce them. Normally there are too many offices to check and too few people in the OAS control function to do the checking.

The answer to OAS access control for large organizations probably lies in a tough, uncompromising top management position on the subject. This should be augmented by a stronger internal audit to check the conformance of offices with access control guidelines and standards. Finally, educational material on OAS vulnerabilities and good access control specification design procedures should be sent to all offices as soon as possible, preferably before they have made too many major commitments.

From a practical standpoint, it is probably a good policy for a centralized office control official to send recommended access control specifications and guidelines to offices. The offices themselves could then decide how sensitive their systems are and the extent to which they needed to conform. This procedure for the design of access control specifications could work if the experts could help the offices prepare the specifications. A large organization should be able to justify the cost of implementing this arrangement.

A relatively small office or a group of dispersed offices belonging to a smaller organization will probably not have the luxury of being able to call upon experts from a headquarters OAS control function for advice. The development of good access control specifications for small organizations may, therefore, be a problem.

There is an answer, however. A small office can hire a consultant for the expert advice that is needed. A professional evaluation of the sensitivity of the office's information system and of the quality and type of access controls needed should be within the financial reach of even a relatively small office.

Basically, an organization that can afford OAS should be able to afford expert security advice. The increased productivity that can result from an OAS should not be threatened by the compromise of confidential data to a competitor.

What about the really small office—the one- to ten-person company? The answer to this question depends on many factors. Some very small offices may pass up an OAS for the time being, deciding that they are willing to take the risk of unauthorized data access or even total system loss. Other small offices, particularly those with a very large revenue base and which produce information as their primary product, may decide that the cost of expert security advice is just another cost of doing business that they can, in fact, afford.

Suitable OAS Access Controls

OAS security and access control specifications need to address the following four major classes of risks:

1. Risks related to a strictly local or departmental system
2. Risks associated with all the automated office systems in one facility that are interconnected with a LAN
3. Risks associated with an office system that shares communications, processing, or database resources with a remotely located host computer (i.e., where OAS access to a host is permitted through a communications network)
4. Risks related to office systems that are both connected to a LAN and are also allowed access to the resources of a remotely located host computer

Local OAS Access Control Mechanisms

Local or stand-alone office systems require access protection in at lease three main areas: physical, logical, and administrative.

Physical access protection for most office systems must be given very high priority because of the size and location of the system, and the general inadequacy of physical security in most remote (or noncentrally located) offices. For example, the theft or destruction of an entire office system would be much easier than for a well-guarded centrally located host system. Local physical protection mechanisms could therefore include:

• Computer table lock systems
• Keyboards removed and locked in safe storage
• Keyboard keys or key entry cards
• Local and central alarm systems
• Power supply locked off
• Safe storage of all removable diskettes

The protection of *logical access* can be achieved through:

• Access control software packages designed to run on personal computers
• Rigorous use of both personal and data or file passwords

- Purging of storage areas where sensitive data has resided during preparation or processing
- File or database encryption systems

    Administrative access controls could include:

- Procedures designed to assure proper password generation, distribution, use, and change
- Regular dumping of programs and data for backup and emergency reconstruction
- Restriction on diskette copying or removal from office

OAS/LAN Access Control Mechanisms

Although it may meet with resistance, the first security procedure to protect the OAS/LAN would be to keep extremely vulnerable locations or users off the LAN in the first place. Other OAS/LAN protection mechanisms might include:

- Use of a star topology instead of a ring network (i.e., in a ring network all stations usually monitor all messages in order to identify messages intended for that station)
- Use of communications encryption devices
- Classification and labeling of extremely sensitive data and reports which are prohibited from being sent over the LAN (or the data must be encrypted)
- Prohibition of all outside facility communications connections to the OAS/LAN
- Use of a communications switch to separate trusted from nontrusted network components

OAS–Host-Connected Access Control Mechanisms

Communications between an automated office system and one or more remotely located host computers will probably result in additional vulnerabilities for both the host and the office system.

In most cases, the host computer center will have considerably more physical and logical access control protection than the office system because of its abundance of resources and the experience of its employees. With the introduction of communications between the host and the OAS, the OAS now requires physical protection similar to that afforded the host. Without protection for the office system, much of the central host's protection is compromised.

Other protection mechanisms and procedures that can be used to reduce the access control weaknesses of the connected OAS might include:

- No off-loading of sensitive data from the host to the OAS

- Communications encryption
- File and database encryption
- Access control software on both the host and the OAS
- No access to the OAS database from outside or external system access but the OAS can transmit data or inquiries and receive data or messages
- Call-up and answer-back systems where required
- Physical or logical disconnection (i.e., via communications switch) of OAS from host network except during specified time periods

OAS/LAN – Host-Connected Access Control Mechanisms

The access control mechanisms discussed in the two preceding sections would also apply to OAS/LAN–host-connected systems.

Systems in this category should be scrutinized carefully because of the great potential for system compromise. One of the most serious vulnerabilities will be the OAS/LAN users who seldom access the host or any other part of the external network and tend to forget that it exists. These offices may send data through their LAN, oblivious to the fact that dial-up connections to the LAN may permit compromise of very sensitive data by outsiders operating with nothing more than personal computers and modems.

Access control specifications for OAS users, therefore, should be significantly augmented with education on how to avoid system vulnerabilities and compromises.

Cost Justification and Risk Assumptions

A balance between increased productivity resulting from office automation systems and the inconvenience and cost of required security and access control mechanisms is not easy to achieve. Most office personnel, including management, will not have the experience or enough facts at their disposal to make informed decisions in this area. Unless security experts are called in to bridge this gap, some very unwise OAS implementation decisions may be made.

At the very least, a good top management policy would be that a decentralized OAS will be supported with centralized OAS control expertise, particularly in the area of security and access control. With the full cooperation of the people who implement and use OAS, major host resources may eventually be placed at their disposal. (Most OAS users will want this resource once they reach the limits of their small systems, particularly when they want access to parts of the central host database.)

The price of this connection and resource availability should be a tight access control policy for the OAS operators and users. Anything less should not be considered acceptable. While the local OAS user may be willing to risk a local system compromise, the central host system and other OAS users should not have to share the mistakes of others. Risk assumption in this case would be reduced to the lowest common denominator: the local OAS operator and users. Local automated office systems and users that cannot or will not implement adequate access control simply should not be connected to other networks, or, at the very least, they should be given restricted access.

Summary

It is possible to achieve the productivity benefits of office automation systems without taking unnecessary security risks. However, the lack of local resources and experienced personnel can make an OAS quite vulnerable to unauthorized access. The emphasis on user friendliness makes an OAS compromise even more likely.

Larger, more financially successful organizations should employ professional computer security experts to design their new office systems. Smaller offices that believe they cannot afford this assistance will probably implement automated office systems that are extremely vulnerable to compromises and major losses. These risks may be tolerable as long as outside communications are restricted, and reasonably tight physical and logical access control procedures are rigorously followed.

22. Personal Computer Protection

The access control problems of expert, professional, and independent personal computer users was not discussed in the chapter on OAS security because of the different environmental, software, and data manipulation factors. All system users may operate the same devices, such as personal computers, terminals, or workstations. They may have stand-alone or communications-oriented systems. They may even require similar, if not identical, communications facilities. And in some cases, the degree of system sharing may even be similar.

However, an examination of typical systems in each category will reveal that the access control problems of the typical automated office system discussed in Chapter 21 are different from these other systems. Granted, differences may be only of degree or emphasis, but, on the other hand, aren't security requirements based on degrees of protection? (It is possible, of course, that redundancies might result if a particular system were in fact used for all applications—office, expert, and professional.)

This chapter, therefore, will emphasize the access control problems that the typical OAS might not have. The guidelines covered under the topics below should help identify the security and access control features to consider in the design of an expert, professional, or independent system:

- Important characteristics of expert, professional, and independent systems
- Access control design responsibility
- Suitable personal computer access controls
- Cost justification and risk assumptions

Important Characteristics of Expert, Professional, and Independent Systems

Essentially, a *personal computer* is a system designed and used to satisfy the needs of an individual—the expert and the professional—and most independent systems uniquely satisfy this requirement.

Expert System

The expert personal computer users not only use their systems to do their work, but the users are capable of modifying system software and application programs to significantly suit their operational requirements. They can use their personal computers as design tools. They can create unique products with them, if they wish. This ability to integrate all their requirements into their system for manipulation and development is what makes their application both expert and sensitive.

Professional System

The professional system users also apply their personal computers in order to get work done. The main difference between professionals and experts is that professionals generally need to acquire and use only off-the-shelf software to make use of their system. They do not need the systems experience of experts. They expect their systems to be particularly user-friendly, in order to minimize the amount of technical knowledge needed to make their personal computers productive. In a way this dependence on their systems and their lack of knowledge regarding potential vulnerabilities may make the professional systems even more susceptible to compromise than the expert systems.

Independent System

The term *independent* is used here to describe personal computer users who do not fall into either the OAS, expert, or professional categories. A good example might be the use of a personal computer in a cottage industry. The use of a personal computer at home to run a business or provide an income for an individual through some special application would be examples of the independent category. Also, the use of a personal computer at home by a company employee might fit into this category, depending upon the systems application. Strangely, of the three system categories, the independent system might be either the most vulnerable or the most secure. The vulnerability occurs because of the high probability that its environment will not be a very secure one and other internal controls will be nonexistent or extremely weak. On the other hand, depending on how many people know of the system's existence and application, the system, as a result of complete isolation, might be more secure than if it were located in a shared environment.

General Vulnerabilities of Personal Computers

Generally, all three applications of personal computers will produce the following vulnerabilities:

• There is little or no control over the operation of the system or over the user.

- There is extremely weak physical access protection (i.e., unauthorized use).
- There is significant theft and compromise potential of databases and programs residing on floppy disks.
- There is no protection of or attempt to eliminate data residue on either floppy disks, fixed disks, or internal storage. (In addition, most personal computers erase and delete commands but do not in fact erase or overwrite the magnetic recording. This is to prevent accidental file loss.)
- There is a great potential for theft of the entire physical system, including the database.
- Use of standard software and application programs (except for expert users) means that intruders will find easy access to documentation describing how the system works, making compromise easier.
- It is much harder to justify physical protection and access control software for a single computer installation.
- Lack of technical knowledge by the user (except for expert users) may result in too much reliance on friends, consultants, and vendors for support (i.e., too much systems exposure).
- Data stored in a personal computer's magnetic media or available on terminal screens or in hard-copy form is much more visible and intelligible than data handled by larger systems (as a result of more complex coding and inclusion of more programmable data controls in mainframe computers).
- When a personal computer is shared by more than one user, each user generally has complete access to all facilities, including diskettes.
- Attempts to lock up software to prevent unauthorized access to data stored on fixed or floppy diskettes is probably of little value since copies of the software packages are easily acquired elsewhere.
- Most personal computers do not have even rudimentary password or logical access control protection mechanisms.
- Most personal computers are deficient in audit and event logging software.

Personal Computers with Communications Facilities

If the personal computer system is provided with communications capability, additional vulnerabilities might include:

- Potential for unauthorized central host access (i.e., as a result of the use of automatic log-on procedure—including password—that is stored in the personal computer to make host log-on easier)
- Easy interception of data transmitted over communications lines
- Considerably reduced protection of data off-loaded on the personal computer's fixed or floppy diskette (i.e., compared to the host storage facilities)
- Ease of recording electromagnetic radiation emanating from the personal computer

- Possible impersonation of other personal computer users that log on claiming to be an authorized system user (assuming a successful user ID and password compromise)

Portable Personal Computers

Improvements in design and the miniaturization of components are resulting in increased popularity of portable personal computers. The last barrier to the use of portable computers on commercial airlines has now been eliminated, and the race for this segment of the personal computer market is well on its way.

There are advantages and disadvantages to carrying a personal computer on a trip, regardless of the mode of transportation. Traveling users will have to weigh the advantages of increased productivity and convenience against the significant potential of system loss or theft. Physical security while traveling is very difficult to maintain.

For most travelers, the loss of their personal computer, including their files and software, could be more serious than the loss of the contents of a briefcase or suitcase. For example, the loss or theft of a portable computer system or several of its floppy disks could result in a much more serious situation than the loss of hard copy because of the following:

- The floppy disks (or other storage devices) could contain far more data than the average traveler would carry in his or her briefcase.
- Data generated during the trip might not have been copied or backed up yet.
- The data might be the most current status of an organization, a plan, or a program, and, therefore, extremely sensitive.
- Since the person is traveling, there might be a considerable delay in the reconstruction of the data, which could have serious effects on the organization or on the individual mission.
- The possibility of data or file manipulation without the traveler's knowledge could be great because of the amount of time that the personal computer might be left unattended during the trip (e.g., left temporarily in a hotel room or other facilities during meals or meetings).
- If the person plans to use the system in a communications mode during the trip, the lines used will probably be more vulnerable to wiretapping or compromise than the facilities at the home base.

It appears, therefore, that people who contemplate a significant use of portable computers while traveling should either make special arrangements for the protection of their equipment when it is not in their personal possession or should refrain from storing or placing sensitive data into the systems file during the traveling portion of their trips.

In addition, because of the relative value of the device itself, individuals who carry them on public conveyances should seriously consider the possibility of their being stolen.

If a computer is concealed in a briefcase, the chances that it will be stolen are lessened. However, risks will escalate as a result of using or demonstrating the personal computer in public.

Access Control Design Responsibility

Access control design responsibility for personal computers will vary considerably depending on whether the system is:

- Purchased for personal use by an individual
- Purchased for individual or departmental use with the acquisition authorization generated by an employee or local manager (i.e., assumes no centralized personal computer acquisition and control function)
- Purchased for individual or departmental use with the acquisition authorization generated by a centralized personal computer acquisition and control function

Individual Systems

For systems purchased by individuals, access control needs will obviously be determined by the people buying the system. Unless the individual is already an experienced computer user, access control needs will probably be completely overlooked or minimized. The best advice that can be given to the inexperienced new system buyer is to:

1. Evaluate maximum loss potential from a system compromise or theft.
2. Visit any public library and read about the subject before making a system selection decision.
3. Ask a computer vendor for advice and for other sources of assistance.
4. At the very minimum, plan on the worst happening sometime and take appropriate precautions such as:
   - Reasonable physical security, including possibly a local alarm system
   - Regular copying of valuable data onto diskettes which are then transferred to another building and locked up securely in some form of safe storage area
   - Buying insurance as needed and as available

Locally Authorized Systems

Systems locally authorized for individual or departmental use should be carefully reviewed by local management before acquisition is permitted. In a larger organization, the centralized data processing department and electronic data processing (EDP) audit team should be consulted for access control and security guidelines. If such assistance is not available, other personal computer users already operational in the company can provide their own access control specifications or guidelines for review and consideration. A brief visit from an outside consultant or someone from the organization's general accounting firm could be a valuable source of advice.

Very sensitive personal computer applications should be supported with a written review and management decision with regard to how access control and security is going to be provided for the personal computers. These guidelines should be included in the department's personal computer training material and implemented along with the installation of the personal computer itself.

Centrally Authorized Systems

Installations of personal computers acquired by individuals or departments in large organizations should comply with the specifications and guidelines established by a centralized system acquisition and control function. There will always be those who feel that this arrangement may detract from local autonomy and productivity, and in a very few instances, they may be right. However, in general, most large organizations are finding that the price of this much autonomy is greater than they can afford.

The organizations that have developed corporate guidelines and standards for internal information systems have had good reasons for doing so; in general, better and safer systems have been the result. This same assistance and expertise need to be made available to the new users of personal computers in the organization. As a matter of fact, communications or network facility connections should not be allowed for personal computers unless authorized access controls have already been implemented.

Finally, all parties concerned should directly or indirectly benefit from the imposition of this level of information protection and discipline.

Suitable Personal Computer Access Controls

The Checklist Approach

Personal computer users, even with limited resources, should create their own security and access control specifications. The more sensitive the system, the more carefully the following list of access controls should be examined for solutions to compromise threats:

PHYSICAL ACCESS PROTECTION

- Equipment table locks
- Removable keyboard that is secured in locked storage area
- Valuable diskettes copied and stored off premises

- Local diskettes with valuable data stored in locked cabinet
- Local alarm system (i.e., on doors and windows)
- System power access lock
- Company or personal identification information engraved on main hardware system
- Securing of entire area (i.e., good locks on doors and windows)
- Electronic security devices
- Special ID markings on all boards and modules to detect unauthorized substitution
- Locked files for system documentation and hard-copy printer output

LOGICAL ACCESS PROTECTION

- Read-only permission for specific files
- Passwords for selected files
- Use of a purge routine to eliminate data residue in files
- A menu-driven software system to control user access at log-on
- Personal password authentication scheme
- User passwords not stored in system itself
- Installation of an access control software package designed for personal computer
- File encryption
- Use of a user-protect disk package
- Redesign or implementation of a more secure personal computer operating system
- Combination label and password disk protection scheme
- Installation of a special-purpose secure front-ender designed just for personal computers
- Use of compilers that create machine code only
- Secure database package for personal computers
- Special data compressive routine to protect data
- Use of program destruction routines which operate if an unauthorized access takes place

COMMUNICATIONS PROTECTION

- Communication encryption
- Authentication through digital signatures
- Dedicated or private communications lines
- Possible implementation of a star-type network to overcome the security weaknesses of ring and bus-type networks (too many possible listeners)

- Use of fiber optics for the communications carrier to avoid message interception
- For short distances use of coaxial cables over twisted pairs because they radiate less

HOST-RELATED PROTECTION

It would be short-sighted to overlook how personal computers and accessible central host computers can supplement each other's access control and security. Although connecting personal computers and host computers in a network increases the vulnerability of each system, it also affords the opportunity to enhance each system's security through the implementation of the following protection mechanisms:

- Off-load files from the personal computer to a host for back-up protection
- Call-up and answer-back facility on the host front end to validate that a message is in fact coming from a specific personal computer
- Use of the host access control software to authenticate personal computer users
- Generation of sensitive hard-copy outputs only on the host printers if the mainframe's physical security and internal controls are significantly better than those of the personal computer
- Where extremely sensitive data must be shared with other network users, the originating personal computer user can send the data (i.e., probably in encrypted form) to the host database so that the more powerful host access control mechanisms can screen the other users who want access to the data
- The use of a secure front-ender at the host or communications switch can be used to authenticate all personal computer users on the network as they attempt to communicate with each other or with the host

Cost Justification and Risk Assumptions

In large organizations the process of system cost justification and risk assumption should be a management-coordinated, shared responsibility. In general, what is best for the organization should be best for the individual—assuming that there may be differences in objectives or in willingness to take risks with valuable company data.

The decentralization of information system resources in an organization is a reasonable thing to do, as long as the informational assets are properly safeguarded and effectively and efficiently utilized. Individual computer users may or may not be in a position to make the best decision as far as information access protection is concerned. Comparison of their recommendations against basic corporate or central staff guidelines should not be a problem in most organizations. Too much information control is generally better than too little.

For the individual personal computer owners or users, the balancing of information protection costs and risks will normally be influenced by cost factors. Without professional advice, most personal computer users may have a difficult time placing a monetary value on their personal software and database.

As mentioned earlier, the relative isolation of many of these systems may work to the user's advantage as far as security is concerned. However, as even these systems move into network connections, the individual users will discover that the isolation factor is no longer working in their favor. This will be a good time for them to reconsider the balancing of cost protection versus risk of loss.

Summary

A personal computer used by an individual or even shared by a group of individuals will not generally have the numerous safeguards that can be implemented on larger systems. In addition, with the trend for each individual to have his or her own personal computer or terminal, even the most basic internal controls that might otherwise be applied may be eliminated from consideration. This is because most expert, professional, and independent systems will probably be exclusively accessed by just one person.

The solution to this problem as advocated in this chapter is for the personal computer users in larger organizations to call upon the experience and resources of their centralized data processing department and EDP audit functions for assistance with the development of access control specifications. Individual system users, on the other hand, can use a checklist approach to security. All personal computer users, however, should give their utmost attention to the physical security requirements of their system because this appears to be the most vulnerable area in these systems today.

23. The Home Computer

The distinction between the home computer and the personal computer is rapidly fading. There are only a few clear-cut differences today, and even these too will undoubtedly fade. Eventually, the major difference will be more in the computer's application rather than in hardware, software, or cost differences. The telephone is a good example of this product evolution. There are homes that have more modern, elaborate telephone and communications systems than do some small businesses.

In addition, many home computers do word processing and run some very elaborate business- and finance-oriented application programs. However, even if these applications were run on more powerful microcomputers, there might still be another important distinction. Most home computer users acquired their systems for pleasure, and not for profit. This denotes an amateur, not a professional. Professionals generally earn their livings from their own activities and often pursue higher standards of performance than amateurs.

If one overlooks the emotional (and financial) factors, the compromise or loss of an amateur's home computer should not be as consequential as a similar loss suffered by an expert or professional system user. Naturally, this conclusion might be totally unacceptable to more than a few home computer owners.

We grant that this is not a totally defendable position. Therefore, this chapter lays the groundwork for a special treatment of security and access control problems faced by home computer users. The following important issues will be covered:

• Important characteristics of home computers
• Access control design considerations
• Suitable home computer access controls
• Cost justification and risk assumptions

Important Characteristics of Home Computers

By today's definition the home computer is not supposed to cost as much nor be as powerful as a personal computer. A home computer is supposed to cost less than $1,000 and is supposedly used primarily for entertainment.

Three factors, besides the purchase price or costs of replacement, influence rising concerns about security and unauthorized access to home computers:

1. Since only about 65 percent of the computers in homes are used primarily for playing games [DR 1984], a significant number of systems are used partially or entirely for more serious purposes.

2. Communications modems cost between $70 and approximately $600. The ability to connect a home computer to a network that offers access to extremely important financial and technical services means that we will probably see an increasing volume of more serious (i.e., nonentertainment) home computer applications.

3. The rapid improvement in cost performance of computers meant for the home means that in the near future we will see home computers with the power of today's personal computers. There is no reason to believe that the more experienced home computer users will continue to use their systems primarily for entertainment. More serious and practical applications should become commonplace.

Access Control Design Considerations

The more common nonentertainment applications of home computers are similar to those of the small automated office system. These include word processing, budgeting and financial planning, and other spreadsheet applications.

As home computer applications begin to resemble those of a small office, more personal and sensitive data is going to be put on the system. Home computer users should begin to look a little more closely at how they intend to protect their personal privacy.

This issue takes on even more significance when family members, friends, and even the children of friends and neighbors learn to use the system. Common sense and the desire for personal privacy dictate that even home computer users, particularly those that intend to share a system, should consider establishing certain rules of access or privacy for their systems.

In most homes, an informal but realistic approach to preventing unauthorized access to such applications as dad's and mom's investment portfolio will probably suffice. In addition, young and old alike should respect reasonable privacy rules regarding any personal correspondence produced with the computer's word processing system and temporarily stored on one of its floppy disks.

As more serious network applications become available through a modem and communications connection, such as videotex and remote purchasing and banking, system access rules may have to be implemented with more rigor.

Finally, as home computer users start inputting home business and professional data (e.g., a teacher putting student grades on a system), security and access control become still more consequential. At this level of application, a written set of access rules for the home computer should not be considered overkill.

Suitable Home Computer Access Controls

Most of the access controls covered in Chapters 21 and 22 can be applied to the home computer system depending on the nature of the system's applications, whether or not it is shared, and whether or not a modem and communications are available to the system.

The first concern of the home computer user should be the physical security of the system. Equally important should be a procedure for maintaining backup data and programs off the premises.

Logical access control will be difficult for the more basic or smaller home computers and probably not justifiable except for shared systems. Even standard personal computer users can have difficulty implementing a high level of protection in this area. By the time the home computer user faces the fact that he or she has serious logical access control problems, it may be time to advance to a more powerful personal computer with potentially stronger access control features.

Cost Justification and Risk Assumptions

By today's standards, most home computer users spend less than $1,000 for their systems. The vast majority of the owners, as mentioned earlier, use their systems primarily for entertainment. This class of user should probably seek protection through a special or regular homeowner's general insurance policy.

As the home computer owner starts inputting sensitive or valuable data in a system, the user must weigh not only the value of the physical hardware and software but also the cost of loss of compromised data. If the maximum possible loss would truly be a hardship (i.e., considerable difficulty replacing the system and reconstructing the data), then consideration should be given to how much additional money should be invested in physical security and insurance protection (if available).

Once the maximum loss potential clearly exceeds a user's reasonable ability to recover from the loss, the choices may be to:

- Upgrade the computer to one with more protection features and increase physical protection simultaneously
- Remove the sensitive applications residing on the system and put them on a

system belonging to a service bureau (after careful investigation). If communications protection does not pose a problem, the home or personal computer can be used to access the application through a data network. If safe communications poses a problem, and it can be justified, encryption can be added to the system. If the cost is a problem and convenience is not, then the user might personally visit a service center or receive and transmit data through the mail.

It should also be obvious at this point that the type of user described above is no longer a typical home computer user. The result is that the user has moved into some higher category of computer systems dependence and potential vulnerability.

Summary

A true home computer user who spends less than $1,000 for a system and uses it almost entirely for games does not have an access control problem of consequence. The main risk of loss to the user is associated with the cost of replacing the physical system. This risk should be covered, if possible, with an insurance policy.

Of the approximately 35 percent of home computer users who run word processing and financial applications on their systems, each must look at their own system risks to determine their maximum vulnerability or exposure to loss. If the system is shared and/or has communications capabilities, then the user must perform an even more careful analysis.

Most home computer users in this category will probably find that increasing the physical security of their systems and carefully backing up their data will satisfy their protection needs. If dependence on their systems exceeds this category, and they would have serious difficulty recovering from a maximum loss situation, they will probably need outside assistance, such as can be provided by a computer service company. They may utilize such services either on-line or off-line depending on their vulnerability to communications compromise.

Finally, at this level of system dependence and risk exposure, they no longer are a typical home computer user. Their applications and protection requirements are more like those of a personal or office systems computer user.

Implementing and Monitoring Access Control

COMPUTER SECURITY AWARENESS PROGRAM

PLANNING PHASES

LOGICAL ACCESS CONTROL PLAN

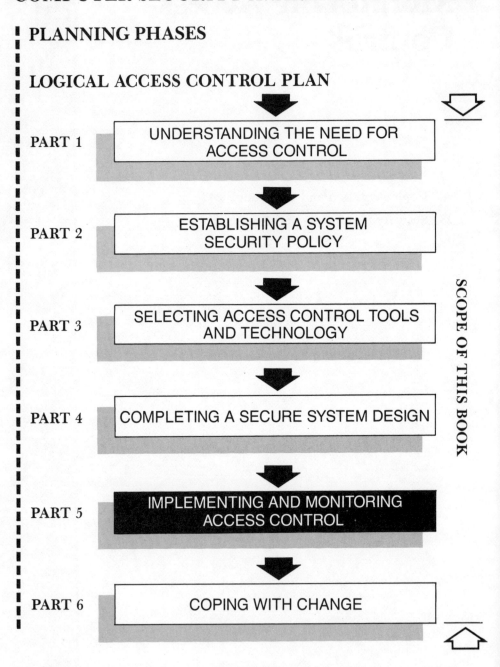

24. Implementation and Checkout

The implementation of a secure access control system based on a carefully constructed design specification is a process that can utilize significant resources. For large organizations, this effort will include management reviews and approval; creation or revision of policy and procedure manuals; meetings with sales people representing various security products and services; documenting and mailing out requests, proposals, or functional specifications to vendors; product demonstrations and evaluations; technical reviews and product selection meetings; and finally implementation and checkout.

For smaller organizations or small system users the period of time from the recognition of a need for better information system access control to the achievement of the objective may be considerably shorter than that required by larger organizations. The possibility of less stringent security requirements and reduced system size, complexity, and approval processes can be an advantage to a small system user when it comes to the implementation of access controls.

Another major difference between larger and smaller systems is documentation. Generally speaking, the larger, the more complex, and the more sensitive the system, the more important it is to thoroughly document security plans.

However, regardless of system size or configuration, there is a pattern to the implementation and checkout of an access control system. In the case of a large information system or network, the process may be quite formal and rigorous; the process for smaller systems will be less formal. Even if done informally, however, the implementation and checkout of a new or revised access control system should include:

- Communication of security objectives and implementation plans to the users of the system
- The initial implementation of new access controls on a pilot or test basis
- Full implementation based on a phased approach
- A thorough checkout or test of all access control mechanisms in an operational environment

247

• Periodic reviews and tests of access control features to locate control circumvention or new vulnerabilities

Communication of Security Objectives and Plans

In all organizations the implementation of a new or revised system security policy should start with a formal announcement of management objectives and plans. The announcement should be followed by a computer security educational program designed to clarify the responsibilities of all individuals who must comply or in any way support the new or modified access control systems. Many organizations have implemented what they call a security awareness program to ensure that every employee involved in the new activity knows the requirements.

Actual implementation of the security awareness program is conducted by a systems security officer (SSO). If there is no such position, then someone else who is qualified to hold this special communications and educational position should be appointed on at least a temporary basis. The communications and educational program will probably involve three classes of individuals:

• System owners
• System operators
• System users

System owners, for instance, could be the organization that hired a facility management company to run its system. System owners are not always system users or system operators. They may in fact own the hardware and software as an investment or provide the facility for one of their operating divisions. Their level of involvement in system security will be limited primarily to review and approval functions.

System operators, in the case of a large host system or network, must be thoroughly briefed. Their access control responsibilities, along with those of the system security officer (if there is one), will include all major security functions, such as compromise prevention, detection, and correction. Under normal conditions, the correction function should include executive involvement.

System users will probably require the most education and detailed instruction on how and why certain access control mechanisms have been installed.

With very small systems, where the owners, operators, and users are a small group of individuals, the implementation process will be less formal. For extremely sensitive systems, an outside security consultant could be brought in to ensure that access controls are properly implemented and checked out.

Implementation of Pilot Systems

The more sensitive and complex, and the larger a system is, the more need there is to implement major access control improvements on a test basis. The major advantages to this implementation process, of course, are that the results of system testing will not cause major problems in production or disrupt the existing system. The pilot system should not only be considered as a test vehicle, it should also be regarded as an excellent training and learning process for both system operators and users.

The pilot system should be tested against preestablished specifications. The test, in other words, should check out the access controls against all important design and performance criteria.

In very large and sensitive networks, the test plan itself must be carefully designed in order to fulfill its objectives. It is even possible that two test plans may have to be developed—one for the pilot test and one for an operational test. Ideally, after passing its pilot test, the new security processes or mechanisms should be given a thorough operational test before final acceptance.

Phased Implementation Approach

If numerous logical and physical access controls are going to be implemented in a relatively short time frame, such as in a new information system or network going on-line, a phased access control implementation plan will probably work best. Of course, this same reasoning could be applied to the entire system as well.

In a phased approach, the following mechanisms might be implemented one at a time at a frequency that permits each new procedure or access control device or process to be thoroughly tested before acceptance and before installing or making the next level of security operational:

- Installation and checkout of any modifications to operating system access control features
- System log-on and identification function installed and checked out
- Password system installed and checked out
- Access control software package (if any) installed and checked out
- Database management system security features tested
- Port protection devices (if any), such as call-up and answer-back, installed and checked out
- Encryption system installed and checked out
- Total access control system integration checkout (does it all work together without any conflicts, unexpected system degradation, or new vulnerabilities)

The major advantage to the phased approach is that by introducing a few variables into the installation and test process at one time, problems can usually be pinpointed more easily. The final or integration phase should test system safeguards with every possible type of compromise, including multiple and simultaneous attacks.

Final Operational Checkout

The checkout of new security and access control mechanisms in an operational or production environment must be done with considerable care. Consideration should be given to when test controls should not be attempted. Examples might include:

- During periods when new hardware or system or application software is being installed
- When any tests of system hardware or software are being made
- When vital production jobs or operations are being executed
- When extremely sensitive live data is being processed

The operational checkout should be performed by the most competent team of individuals that can reasonably be assembled to do the job. The team leader should tightly control all schedules, test plans and activities, and documentation. An outside expert or consultant should be considered to help with the final operational security integration test, if no such individual is available within the organization. The following should be totally clear to the team members before the operational testing begins: exactly what the test plan is, who is to perform which test, and how results are to be documented.

During operational testing, participation by system users should be included. User feedback should be included with test documentation.

During these test periods, many organizations are beginning to use what is termed "tiger-team testing." This is the use of unorthodox and highly creative procedures to try to compromise part of the information system or network. This procedure should be left to experts on the subject in order to minimize major operational interruptions, data contamination, or data loss.

Periodic Reviews and Tests

Most information systems continuously undergo change and enhancement. It is always possible that even after an access control system has been thoroughly tested and checked out, new vulnerabilities might appear. At the very least, as new users enter the system, new communications devices and lines are connected, and new hardware and software modules are added, the possibility of new and unexpected weaknesses should be considered.

The best process for handling these possibilities is the periodic review and test of system safeguard mechanisms. Frequently this activity can be accomplished by the internal EDP audit team or the EDP audit team of the organization's outside accounting firm. Even these security audits should be supplemented periodically by an expert review of security controls.

Probably the biggest danger to installed access controls, other than a hardware, software, or communications facility change, is the intentional circumvention of safeguards by operational employees and system users to overcome inconvenience or inefficiency. Periodic reviews and tests should check on these possibilities.

Summary

An important phase of computer security development is how to plan and efficiently carry out the implementation phase of an improvement plan for information systems access control. The objectives of the access control plan should be communicated to system owners, operators, and users. A pilot test of access controls should be completed before full-scale implementation of the new procedures and protection mechanisms.

The implementation of safeguards, particularly for large systems or networks, should be carried out in orderly phases to permit better testing and problem diagnosis. Access control mechanisms should be tested eventually in an operational environment, but this must be done with great care to prevent damage to live programs, data files, and operational schedules. Finally, system safeguards should be periodically tested for new vulnerabilities.

25. Security Monitoring and Feedback

Access control monitoring uses a combination of manual and automated procedures to prevent, detect, and report on actual or attempted compromises of an information system or network. *Feedback* is the information that is used to trigger automatic or manual countermeasures. This chapter discusses how monitoring and feedback can be used to provide continuous surveillance of user and process accesses to an information system.

The following procedures and technologies that might be used to facilitate system monitoring and feedback are covered in this chapter:

- The need for access monitoring
- Approaches to access monitoring and feedback
- Active versus passive monitoring
- Recognizing unauthorized access
- Security and access violation reporting
- Follow-up investigations and action

The Need for Access Monitoring

The job of keeping an information system secure is continuous and never-ending. After system access policies and specifications have been defined and security mechanisms and procedures installed, the real job of maintaining system security has just begun. Both anticipated and unanticipated security problems can and do occur. Examples of events that can trigger these problems include:

- Errors or omissions in the access controls that have been installed
- System changes that result in new vulnerabilities
- Legitimate users trying to circumvent controls for both harmful and benign purposes
- External parties trying to test system safeguards or penetrate the system for a variety of unauthorized and illegal activities

253

The only safe assumption that can be made about computer security, therefore, is that any system (but particularly those connected to a network) may be attacked at any time. A monitoring and surveillance system is the most logical mechanism to use against these potential abuses.

Approaches to Access Monitoring and Feedback

Monitoring access to an information system is usually implemented through protection mechanisms built into special access control software packages or into basic computer hardware and software functions. Often a combination approach is taken to add layers of security protection to a system.

The monitoring and feedback system is in itself a key access control mechanism, but certainly is far from being the whole of computer security. For example, access control and violation reporting mechanisms are often built into encryption and port protection systems and communications front-enders. The system accounting package outputs are often reviewed by EDP auditors and system security officers for evidence of violation. In addition, there are numerous physical safeguards, backup procedures, application program controls, and database security mechanisms that play a part in total system security.

The access control monitoring and surveillance system is the key, however, to preventing, detecting, and reporting on potential and actual violations. Even these systems are of limited use, however, without human interaction and intervention. The reasons are as follows:

- Access rules may change, and at least one person (preferably two) must be able to make those changes to the access control system.

- Since unauthorized access is basically a human-factor problem, serious violations must be dealt with personally by the appropriate people, such as managers, security officers, law enforcement personnel, and attorneys.

- Computer-generated violation reports often cannot interpret the difference between errors and intentional compromises, nor can they determine how serious the penetration was if one is identified.

The flow of a typical access control monitoring and feedback system is shown in Figure 25-1. The primary functions implemented in this system include:

- Compromise prevention
- Compromise detection
- Automatic compensatory response
- Violation feedback and reporting

The typical full-feature access control software package provides all these functions. There are, however, important differences associated with the more comprehensive systems. For example, the design philosophy of some systems permits access only if the access meets predefined rules. Other systems would

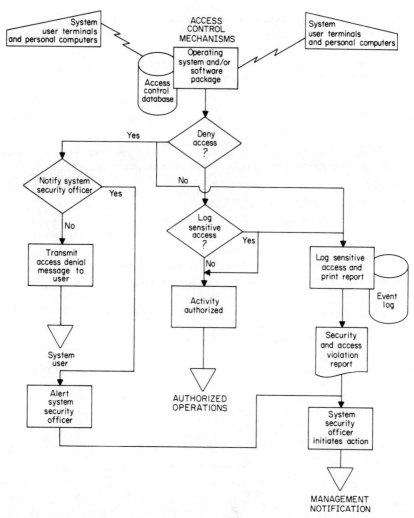

Figure 25-1   Access monitoring and feedback system.

deny access only if an illegal access attempt was identified. The general violation reports of some systems are of very little value because it is difficult to detect errors from actual compromise attempts, while some systems provide encryption data which directs the reader's attention to the more probable or actual violations.

Active versus Passive Monitoring

Some access control monitors simply deny access, depending on how many times an invalid password or other transaction is presented to the system.

Although undoubtedly a valuable security tool, this is a limited approach to access monitoring and surveillance.

Most comprehensive access monitoring and feedback systems provide both real-time access protection (i.e., compromise prevention and detection) and passive protection (i.e., violation reports). The objective of this dual approach to access monitoring is to:

- Minimize unnecessary inconvenience to users through too many access denials of legitimate transactions
- Establish a realistic approach to handling the large number of unintentional errors users make when logging on or using a system
- Provide an adequate database for violation reporting that should aid the successful investigation of a serious security breach
- Allow even suspected transactions to occur, which cannot for some technical or other reason be canceled but which can be dealt with immediately by human intervention
- Allow time for management to authorize the implementation of a "trap" for the purpose of gathering more evidence for investigation and/or legal action

Recognizing Unauthorized Access

System default or access-denial mechanisms should replicate the organization's preestablished security policies. Unfortunately, many apparently illegal access attempts may only be user errors, while many apparently legitimate accesses to extremely sensitive objects may in fact be compromises. The problem of what to look for and how the system should react to the stimuli is an exceedingly difficult problem for both security monitor designers and system users.

Unauthorized Process Actions

Not all system activity is initiated by a resident human being using a computer, terminal, or console. Many system accesses can be triggered by automated "decisions," which in turn generate computer programs or cause an existing program or device to perform a set of operations. These operations may require access to sensitive resources in the originating computer or even another network computer. Access monitors, therefore, need to include not only access rules for human users but also rules that should be followed when processes request access.

Unauthorized User Actions

As indicated earlier, because of the frequent errors made by people in their attempts to access a system, it is difficult to distinguish between authorized and unauthorized activity. For this reason, the following transactions or events should be noted for possible inclusion in a violation report or investigation:

- All system access denials
- Accesses to sensitive data or resources
- All sign-ins and sign-offs
- Memory-bound violations
- Unauthorized access to privileged instructions
- Sensitive resource utilization
- User profile or permission changes
- System reconfigurations
- Sensitive data communications
- Modifications to security parameters
- All system user changes
- All hardware or software changes

A security violation investigation cannot be carried out successfully without this information. In addition to built-in controls designed to immediately block actual or likely system compromises, logging of sensitive events is the most important feature of a good monitoring and feedback system.

Security and Access Violation Reporting

Thousands of organizations have implemented some form of access control monitoring and feedback system in the United States. However, the value of these systems, particularly the violation reporting function, has been seriously questioned by many users. A typical criticism is that the violation or security reports contain too little or too much detail and are deficient in violation pattern analysis.

Reports with Insufficient Detail

Monitoring and feedback systems that provide too little detail in their security or violation reports probably were not designed with reporting as a high-priority specification. Unless users of these systems have the expertise and the resources to modify the software themselves, they will have to evaluate more suitable access control software packages that contain a more comprehensive reporting function for violation event logging.

Reports with Too Much Detail

The main gripe of systems security officers, investigators, and EDP auditors about the reports presently produced in the United States by the "better" access control software packages is that they contain too much detail. The criticism is leveled primarily at the lack of exception information that would make the daily violation report easy to read and understand. System designers respond that if the security people could define exactly which events constitute the serious system violations they want reviewed, they could produce a more useful report. Marketing people respond by saying that this is not a practical solution, since each customer's needs differ so much that this degree of selectivity is not possible in a "canned" package. Even the organizations that have designed and implemented their own access control and feedback system find fault with the security and violation reports their systems produce.

The problem is that there are simply too many user transactions that can access sensitive data and too many unintentional errors made in these transactions. This situation prevents the creation of the classic "exception report" that security officers and EDP auditors expect. This is particularly true for systems that experience extremely large volumes of daily user transactions.

How then should security and access violations be effectively reported? Computer security experts are beginning to think that the answer may lie in pattern recognition and variance reporting.

Reports Based on Pattern and Variances

The experts say that security and access violation reports containing *only* data relating to high-probabililty violation events may be possible, but they need more time to test their theories.

It is claimed that the application of artificial intelligence to computer use patterns will produce this breakthrough. In other words, certain events or user transactions occurring at abnormal times or under abnormal conditions have a much higher probability of being an unauthorized access than the other system activity that occurred that day. The experts contend that by accumulating a history of normal authorized activity over a sufficient period of time, certain statistical inferences can be made about every type of transaction that might occur in the system, even the illegal ones.

Monitoring and feedback systems that implement this approach have not yet entered the commercial marketplace. It is possible that the commercial market may have to wait while the large systems users, with the resources and the time, implement and prove their theories on a system-by-system basis. Eventually, with the bugs worked out, the pattern and variance reporting theory may be introduced as a package that, at least partially if not wholly, solves the problem of security and access violation reporting.

Follow-Up Investigations and Actions

The mission should now be completed. With the evidence in hand that proves someone broke the law or violated company policy by an authorized computer access, all that is left is to take the necessary corrective action. This should be the happy ending or, at least, the conclusion to another incident of unauthorized computer access or abuse.

Unfortunately, many people who have suffered computer abuse say that this is not the scenario that occurs after doing everything "by the book" to end unauthorized system activity. Some reasons given include:

- Nothing can be done because in the process of gathering the evidence it was tainted or contaminated.
- The holes in the system that permitted the unauthorized activity cannot be plugged because of technical problems or cost.
- We do not want the information to get out because others may attempt a similar break-in and succeed.
- We cannot prosecute because the law does not clearly cover this crime, and we would probably lose the case.
- We do not want any bad publicity.

Reasons such as the above reflect one of the major problems in dealing with computer abuse. It is called *lack of professionalism*. What differences would professionalism make? Professionals or experts in the field of computer security and access control would design the following into the organization's computer monitoring and surveillance system:

- Internal controls that should prevent someone or some process from contaminating the event logs that contain the evidence of abuse.
- Proven access control mechanisms that themselves cannot be corrupted and which offer the degree of protection defined in the organization's security policy and access control specifications.
- A carefully constructed security and violation report that is as exception-oriented as possible and that highlights those variances which are the best-known indicators of unauthorized computer access activity.
- Controls that function in such a way as to conceal from the penetrator the fact that his or her unauthorized access has been discovered and that appropriate countermeasures are being taken (e.g., authorities notified and telephone traces initiated).

Above all, discovered unauthorized activity must be communicated as quickly as possible to appropriate levels of management. Even systems security officers may not know the full implication of a penetration of a particular database. For really serious computer abuses, corrective action should not be a system security officer's function, but a top management function. This is especially the case where vital organizational assets are threatened and disciplinary or legal action may be required.

Summary

There are crucial steps that should be taken to implement and maintain an access control monitoring and feedback system. Although a monitoring system is just one facet of total systems security, it is a key element because it is the primary prevention, detection, and violation reporting mechanism.

Typically, access control monitoring either is performed by an add-on access control software package or is embedded in the host computer hardware and software system. The monitors usually operate in two modes: an active mode that can actually block unauthorized access or activity and a passive mode which simply logs such activity and includes it in some form of daily violation report.

Access monitors must intercept and log all sensitive system access and activities which, if compromised, would harm the system or its users. Security and access violation reports are critical elements of the system, but generally are not very useful because they are too detailed and do not adequately pinpoint dangerous variances. Improvements in violation reports are anticipated with breakthroughs in dangerous activity pattern recognition.

The real benefit from the implementation of a security monitoring and surveillance system is its ability to block unauthorized access when and where possible and to report the balance of possible abuse in a form that permits rapid and effective action against the culprits. The actual implementation of corrective action in cases of serious or potentially dangerous abuses should be a high-level management function.

Coping with Change

COMPUTER SECURITY AWARENESS PROGRAM

PLANNING PHASES

LOGICAL ACCESS CONTROL PLAN

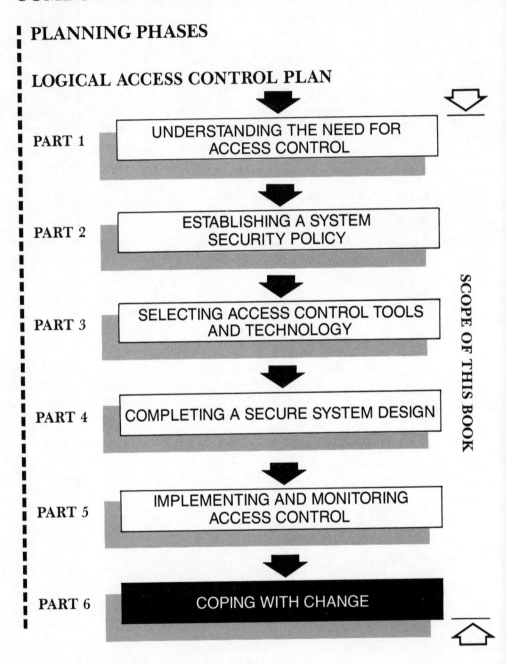

PART 1 — UNDERSTANDING THE NEED FOR ACCESS CONTROL

PART 2 — ESTABLISHING A SYSTEM SECURITY POLICY

PART 3 — SELECTING ACCESS CONTROL TOOLS AND TECHNOLOGY

PART 4 — COMPLETING A SECURE SYSTEM DESIGN

PART 5 — IMPLEMENTING AND MONITORING ACCESS CONTROL

PART 6 — COPING WITH CHANGE

SCOPE OF THIS BOOK

26. Keeping Up with Technology

This chapter discusses why solutions to computer abuse are not keeping up with the continuous advancements and applications of computer-related technology. Generally speaking, computer abuse is technology-driven. This means that there has been a tendency for computer users to implement the latest information systems products with little regard for the consequences of possible abuse or compromise.

Unfortunately, improvements in cost performance, productivity, and functionality are higher on most computer users' priority lists than security, privacy, and confidentiality. This does not mean that users who implement more advanced systems are necessarily making a bad decision. Rather, it indicates that either the users don't take the time to evaluate threats or, if they do, they are consciously willing to tolerate the risks.

In this chapter the position is taken that the above approach carries with it a number of unnecessary risks. With proper planning, specification development, and, in some cases, minor modifications to the system design, some security problems can be avoided. Specifically, computer users should be able to cope with technological change and simultaneously achieve access control security by following these guidelines:

- Define and quantify possible system risks
- Specify feasible safeguards within the current state of the art
- Maintain surveillance over system changes with the help of monitors and system users
- Implement security in phases

Define and Quantify System Risks

The best way to cope with system vulnerabilities introduced with new technology is through advanced planning. *Advanced planning* is simply the screening of the new technology or products for greater or possibly new compromise potentials.

A review of what has caused vulnerabilities in computer systems and networks in the past may also help. For example, security compromises have become more common as systems have achieved higher cost-performance and functionality goals in the following areas:

- More data stored in much smaller memory devices
- More rapid access to data
- Easier access to databases from remote terminals and personal computers
- Easier and more efficient sharing of system resources
- More user-friendly access, thus greatly increasing the user base

In addition, many new systems application concepts have evolved as the result of cost-performance and functionality advances. For example, the following system user concepts were developed more as a result of advances in technology than as initial design goals:

- Random access processing
- Time sharing
- Multiprogramming
- Multiprocessing
- Transaction processing
- Network processing
- Distributed processing
- Word processing
- Electronic mail
- Artificial intelligence

The introduction of each of these new system concepts resulted in new forms of computer abuse or an increase in frequency of abuse. In all probability, access control problems and other security problems could have been anticipated and avoided as the new systems were implemented, if designers and system users had done their homework.

Clearly, there is a need to do a better job of risk evaluation before implementing a new computer or network concept. Risk definition and quantification may at times be difficult but certainly not impossible for most systems. A complete risk definition is not expected. Systems *survival anticipation* might be a better description for the type of analysis and specification needed.

For example, the question What does it take to survive? may be more meaningful to a bank, a government, an airline, or a small time-sharing and data service company than the question How do you measure the potential cost of a computer crime, privacy violation, or a game that a student might play?

The state of the art of the definition and measurement of computer abuse is adequate to determine the likelihood of surviving one or more compromises. After this determination has been made, needed safeguards should be specified and implemented. The point is that great precision or a large statistical database is not generally required in order to formulate a valid system security and access control strategy. And most importantly, the best time to plan system security strategy is when the plan for the new system is in its initial stages.

Specify Feasible Safeguards

After the estimation of the potential compromise or impact of a new product or technology, the next step is to specify a solution. The solution may not offer 100 percent protection. It should, however, reduce risks to acceptable levels. It should also be realizable within the current state of the art and available when the new system goes on-line. In addition, it should be demonstrable in one form or another (e.g., a model or working system).

Unfortunately, in comparison to other computer-oriented technological accomplishments, computer security technology seems to be progressing at a much slower pace. Unacceptable cost performance and a lack of consumer demand were the two main reasons for this lack of progress.

In addition, complete solutions to certain computer access control problems today must wait for technological breakthroughs in the following areas: more practical security kernel mechanisms, better biometric (positive user identification) systems, more secure database management systems or mechanisms, and better protection mechanisms for software and personal computers.

There are many solutions to most of the classic access control problems. Some are very technology-dependent; others are not. The new port protection devices such as those offering call-up and answer-back facilities and encryption can be used very effectively. The use of the new "smart card" for more positive user identification is also an important breakthrough. Improved access control software packages are an excellent way to upgrade security. In many cases, major system violation problems can be solved just by a slight improvement in the user password system. The fact of the matter is that system users, with the help of computer security experts, have a rather large array of products and mechanisms to choose from.

Maintain a Surveillance System

In order to cope with changes to system hardware and software, a monitoring and feedback system must be implemented that can be modified to meet changing system security needs. Most information systems and networks are constantly undergoing changes or improvements. It is a misconception to believe that because a security surveillance system was effective in preventing unauthorized activity when it was installed that it still is as effective in a technological environment that has been undergoing constant upgrading and enhancement.

System changes and expansions introduce new opportunities for penetration and compromise. The design of security features into the system changes and a frequent review of the current capability of the surveillance mechanisms are two ways to maintain adequate, continual system access protection.

Implement Security in Phases

Major computer systems and networks are usually implemented in phases. This permits adequate testing and debugging and assures users of better total systems quality and more dependable access during implementation.

Whenever possible, system security mechanisms should be introduced in concert with the new subsystems. Part of every major system's qualification process should be a security and access control procedure which assures that planned protection features are functioning as expected. If access control tests are conducted on a phase-by-phase basis along with tests of other system enhancements, major omissions or faults in the mechanisms are likely to be identified before serious abuses can occur.

Summary

The need to match the implementation of computer systems and networks with appropriate access controls is of primary importance. Historically, one of the most difficult problems in computer security has been the inability to keep up with the rapid introduction of new computer products and applications.

Problems of coping with technological changes, as far as unauthorized system activity is concerned, can be resolved by following four important guidelines: (1) define and quantify risks during the system design phase, (2) specify feasible safeguards that are within the state of the art that can be demonstrated and tested, (3) implement and be prepared to change the access control monitoring and surveillance mechanisms as the information system itself undergoes upgrade or change, and (4) implement other security mechanisms in concert with the implementation phases of all major subsystems.

27. Security Guidelines and Standards

There is a widespread effort by numerous governmental, professional, and commercial organizations to develop guidelines and standards in the area of computer security and access control. Special computer security technical committees and working groups are sponsored by such organizations as the National Bureau of Standards (NBS), the Department of Defense (DOD) Computer Security Center, the International Standards Organization (ISO), the International Federation of Information Processing (IFIP), and the Institute of Electrical and Electronic Engineers (IEEE), to name a few.

Many large corporations have also addressed the need for internal guidelines and standards, initially focusing on procedural matters such as password or physical access control standards. Most companies, however, anticipate assistance from both governmental and professional standards development projects. One example of a security standard already adopted by many commercial organizations is the National Bureau of Standards data encryption standard (DES).

Although the focus and scope of the work being done by these organizations vary considerably, the objectives are quite similar. Most of the committees or groups are working toward the development of computer security guidelines and standards that will satisfy practical security problems and that are technically attainable, cost-justifiable, flexible, and measurable.

In this chapter it is suggested that these standards and guidelines will eventually have a tremendous impact on computer abuse. Without them, every computer user and every organization is individually responsible for creating their own secure systems. This approach can be expensive and wasteful because of the unnecessary duplication of efforts. In addition, without guidelines and standards, few organizations will ever achieve a consistent way to measure the degree of security that they have attained. This will result in information systems that are either extremely vulnerable or too secure, neither of which is desirable.

The difference between security guidelines and security standards will be discussed in this chapter, as will some of the more important guideline and standard development work that is being done in this area by:

- The National Bureau of Standards
- The DOD Computer Security Center
- The International Standards Organization
- Other contributing organizations

Guidelines versus Standards

The main difference between guidelines and standards is that *guidelines* are designed to indicate the best way to avoid difficulties or to attain a given objective. Guidelines are usually in the form of recommended procedures as opposed to being mandatory requirements. *Standards* may be derived from general principles, measurements, specifications, or attributes required by law, established by custom, or issued by a regulatory authority. They are normally "must do" or "shall do" specifications.

For example, an organization could establish a standard that all data transmission must be encrypted. This might be a very unwise thing to do, however, because of cost, system overhead, and the fact that much of the data to be transmitted is really not sensitive enough to warrant encryption. In this case, the standard might state instead that all computer and data communications systems access shall be controlled. A guideline might recommend that encryption be considered as a solution to the protection of extremely sensitive data transmissions. Another guideline might recommend that the NBS data encryption standard (DES) be considered among the available encryption alternatives.

Guidelines may also lead to the development of standards and may be used to assist with their implementation. Frequently, no one organization, professional association, or government agency is the sole developer of a set of guidelines or standards. Also, it is not uncommon to see one organization develop guidelines in an area, while another organization may be the official source of the related standards.

This situation seems to prevail in both data processing and computer security and access control guidelines and standards. One of the interesting phenomena of this process is that the organization that produces the initial set of guidelines or standards may not be the official or even the historical source of guidelines or standards in a particular area.

For example, many times government agencies adopt guidelines and standards that are developed by professional associations and vice-versa. The reason for this exchange is that a lack of time and limited resources can dictate that there may be little value in repeating the research required to create professionally acceptable guidelines and standards, when another organization has already made this investment. In addition, we often see the same individuals involved in the development projects regardless of the organizations represented because they are often jointly sponsored by both government agencies and commercial companies. Each sends representatives to advise the other so the best possible guidelines and standards result. This is what has happened in the evolution of computer security and access control guidelines and standards.

National Bureau of Standards

The National Bureau of Standards is the technical arm of the Secretary of Commerce charged with the development of federal standards under the Brooks Act (Public Law 89-306).

The chief goal of the National Bureau of Standards is to "strengthen and advance the nation's science and technology and facilitate their effective application for public benefit." The NBS has sponsored research studies, workshops, and seminars on almost every aspect of electronic data processing (EDP). Many NBS projects are designed to provide EDP standards, guidelines, and technical advisory services which subsequently lead to more effective computer utilization.

Contributions of the NBS to the state of the art in computer security and access control have occurred primarily through its internal programs and joint sponsorship of computer security–related workshops, seminars, and study reports. NBS activity in this area has been directed toward the satisfaction of both government and nongovernment security needs.

The primary NBS computer security responsibility, however, is to seek new technology to satisfy federal automatic data processing (ADP) security requirements. Its Institute for Computer Sciences and Technology then distributes the technology in the form of federal information processing standards (FIPS) and guidelines. The work of one NBS-sponsored activity, Task Group 15—Computer Systems Security, has been extremely productive.

Examples of guidelines already published by the NBS include the following:

- "Computer Security Guidelines for Implementing the Privacy Act of 1974"
- "Guidelines for Automatic Data Processing Physical Security and Risk Management"
- "Guidelines for Security of Computer Applications"
- "Guidelines for Computer Security Certification and Accreditation"
- "Guidelines for Evaluation of Techniques for Automated Personal Identification"
- "Guidelines for Automatic Data Processing Risk Analysis"
- "Guidelines for Implementing and Using the NBS Data Encryption Standard"
- "Guidelines on User Authentication Techniques for Computer Network Access Control"
- "Guidelines for ADP Contingency Planning"
- "Guidelines on Integrity Assurance and Control in Database Applications"

NBS guidelines, of course, may be more generic than those that would be developed by a specific organization for an internal application. The quality of the NBS guideline documentation, however, is generally outstanding and can serve as a starting point or model for the development of specific organizational guidelines. A more complete list of NBS computer security documents was published in August 1984 [CO 1984b].

Probably the most notable NBS computer security standard is the data encryption standard. NBS also assisted the American Bankers' Association with the development of a new message authentication code (MAC) standard. The earlier Financial Institution message authentication standard X9.9 was developed by the American National Standards Committee on Financial Services, X9, operating under the American National Standards Institute (ANSI). It was published by the X9 Secretariat of the American Bankers' Association in April 1982 [FI 1982].

A working group of the International Standards Organization (ISO) Committee on Banking Procedure (TC 68) developed a proposal for an international standard on this subject. The new American national standard was submitted to the ISO working group, and may be used to develop an international standard similar to the U.S. standard.

The data encryption algorithm (DEA) is currently being used to generate a MAC. (The DEA is actually the DES; the DES is implemented in hardware and the DEA is implemented in software.) The complete authentication process involves the computation, transmission, and validation of a MAC. The MAC is used to validate the authority of a sender (a bank customer or correspondent bank) and to verify that the contents of the message (i.e., a bank transfer) has not been altered in transit. The MAC is added to a message by the sender and transmitted to the receiver. The message is accepted as authentic by a receiver if the DEA and a secret key produce a MAC that is the same as the one received. Counterfeit or modified messages will fail the test.

This standard is an excellent example of how government agencies, professional associations, and commercial institutions can cooperate to develop useful information security standards.

The DOD Computer Security Center

In 1981, the DOD Computer Security Center assumed the responsibilities established by the DOD Computer Security Initiative in 1978. The main responsibility was to ensure the availability of trusted automatic data processing systems for use in the Department of Defense.

The new organization is continuing to concentrate on the development of trusted computer systems. It focuses its efforts mainly on how to transfer technology from various sources into more secure computers and networks. Its most significant achievement to date has been the development of a product evaluation procedure that is used to certify the level of security or trustworthiness possible in a particular computer system.

The evaluation procedure and criteria can themselves be considered standards. Products that meet the established criteria (or standards) are certified because they satisfy specific security requirements. The emphasis is on product security standards as opposed to procedural or administrative standards.

Another example of a DOD-developed security-oriented product standard is the one used to qualify products under the Tempest rating. The objective is to achieve a given level of security by defining what constitutes a safe or unsafe amount of electromagnetic radiation from a computer or communications product.

Although the above requirements or specifications may not be officially labeled as standards, it would appear that they really are de facto standards. In essence, products that meet certification requirements have met DOD standards. It is the hope of the DOD that both government agencies and commercial organizations will benefit from their efforts in this area.

The International Standards Organization

Various working groups belonging to the International Standards Organization (ISO) met and concluded that there is a need to generate a set of standards for security enhancement within the open systems interconnection (OSI) architecture. It was felt that the security requirements for various OSI layers should be implemented within a common architectural framework and not as independent solutions to individual system user problems. It was also declared that the need for security standards within the OSI stemmed from the following three situations:

- The increase in shared networks which contain information with various protection requirements.
- The existence of data protection legislation in various countries that requires that suppliers of data processing services be able to demonstrate the integrity and privacy capabilities of their system.
- The desire of various organizations to implement OSI standards that contain protection enhancements for existing and future systems (i.e., to make the systems more secure).

The work of the ISO ad hoc group on security is taking on real significance as the group identifies international computer and network security requirements. Their proposal to define security standards for the various OSI layers is beginning to take shape and will probably materialize sometime during 1986 to 1987. Initially, this group proposed standards that would help to reduce vulnerabilities in the following areas:

- Integrity
- Confidentiality
- Authentication

- Access control
- Availability
- Signature service
- Traffic flow security
- Information channel control

Their proposal to produce standards in these areas understandably excluded their also trying to develop standards in the areas of physical security, personal identification methods, operating systems security, security audit analysis, and control of electromagnetic radiation.

According to the ISO working group report, access control addresses the restriction of rights or capabilities of one entity to access other entities, functions, or services in an OSI network. The report identified the following three areas which require access control requirements:

1. User authentication
2. An authorization list (i.e., that defines types of access and resources)
3. The process of securely managing the authorization list

The ISO security report also focused on the potential benefit of producing encryption standards for the various layers in the OSI model.

The interest of the ISO working group in producing security-related standards for OSI architectures at a relatively early stage is an excellent example of the correct way to design security into a system. This early inclusion of security requirements in the OSI model should produce more secure networks and save system operators and users the time and resources it would take to reimplement their systems to make them more secure.

Other Contributing Organizations

Other professional associations have formed computer security working groups and are undertaking projects that have led or will lead to better computer security and access control guidelines and standards. Foremost among these associations are:

- International Federation for Information Processing (IFIP), Technical Committee for EDP Security, TC-11
- Institute of Electrical and Electronic Engineers (IEEE), Technical Committee on Computer Security and Privacy
- Association of Computer Machinery (ACM)
- American Institute of Certified Public Accountants (AICPA)
- Institute of Internal Auditors (IIA)

It would be improper to leave this subject without mentioning the considerable contribution being made by private industry to computer security and access control guidelines and standards. This includes both user organizations and producers of computer hardware and software.

The development of computer security standards is not a one-way street. That is, guidelines and standards are not made by government organizations and professional associations and then handed down to industry. Neither is the opposite true. Rather, government organizations, professional associations, and businesses need each other's assistance in order to develop, implement, and validate new computer security guidelines and standards. Only if good ideas are tested and used in practical applications will they be of value. The best and most effective guidelines and standards will evolve in this fashion.

Summary

The importance of computer access control guidelines and standards cannot be overemphasized. Government agencies, professional associations, and industry must work together to produce guidelines and standards that will eventually solve computer abuse problems.

Although individual companies and government agencies will develop and implement their own guidelines and standards, much of their work will be shared. A cooperative approach will eliminate the duplication that uses extra time and resources.

Guidelines and standards take many forms: Some focus on more secure procedures and administration, while others relate primarily to technical or hardware and software requirements. Some efforts in this area, such as the security product certification work being done by the DOD Computer Security Center, may not even appear to be related to the development of guidelines and standards, when, practically speaking, the certification procedures are themselves de facto standards.

Guidelines and standards, therefore, work together to produce both the procedures and the hardware and software technology that will be needed to prevent unauthorized access to both current and future computer systems and networks.

28. A Future for Computer Security Technology

There are people who perceive computer security and access control technology as being chronically slow to develop. There is another group that contends that computer security technology has always been ahead of its time and, therefore, has suffered from a lack of buyers. It is suggested in this chapter that both ways of looking at computer security technology, including access control, are correct. It simply depends on one's perspective.

If a government agency is looking for solutions to very serious national security problems, such as multilevel security access control, it may focus on the lack of efficient computer-oriented security tools. A manufacturer, potential producer, or vendor of computer security technology may point out how difficult it has been to sell enough of the computer security products already in existence to make a reasonable profit. A representative of any one of a large number of commercial organizations may point out the cost, overhead, and complexity of available computer security products and declare an intention to wait for something more worthwhile to come along. The government wants more secure information systems regardless of cost. Industry is not sure it needs more information security and is not certain how much it would pay for it, even if its needs could be established. It is no wonder potential suppliers looking at the market for new information security tools are perplexed about how and when to invest in new products in this area.

Eventually, however, the passage of time, changing technology, and a continued rapid increase in the number of computer users will resolve many of the above questions and issues. There should be many technological improvements in computer security in the future. The following sections discuss the reasons that support this conclusion.

Computer Security Awareness

The perceived need of the potential computer security buyer must be changed before there will be an increase in market demand for new products and technology. Computer security awareness is already increasing, and this trend should continue for the following reasons:

- As a result of computer abuse the frequency and magnitude of financial losses will probably increase.
- Press coverage and internal publication of losses and ways to avoid computer system compromise will increase.
- Both government and commercial organizations will sponsor and maintain more internal computer security awareness programs.
- Educational institutions will improve on their academic offerings in computer abuse prevention, EDP auditing, and secure computer systems design.
- Top management will recognize and desire to do something concrete about the increasing computer abuse problems.
- Computer crime and privacy laws, other legislation, and regulations will be enforced more rigorously, adding weight to the consequences of computer abuse and the need for users to install adequate prevention mechanisms such as access controls.

Government Certification of Computer Security Products

The DOD Computer Security Center's certification program can have a significant impact on the purchase of more secure computers and access control mechanisms by both government and industry. The reasons for this are as follows:

- Federal agency regulations may stipulate that government computer systems that contain sensitive data have to be protected by properly certified security products or mechanisms.
- The increased sales (or potential sales) of such products to government agencies should reduce unit costs to the point where such products will become more attractive to prospective industrial buyers.
- State and local governments may voluntarily (or involuntarily if required by federal regulations) follow the lead in installing more information security mechanisms, thus adding strength to market demand.
- Many commercial organizations will probably specify that their new computer product acquisitions must also meet government certification requirements. This will occur because buyers will have more confidence in the protection features of certified products. It will also occur because many defense contractors will be required to provide certified computer products in order to assure adequate protection of classified data that must be processed in support of their weapons contracts.
- Even if the government certification program does not pass the test of time (i.e., is discontinued sometime), the benefits of the research efforts in this area are bound to have long-term positive consequences in the promotion of more secure information systems.

Competitive Responses to Government Certification Requirements

Once it becomes clear to the possible suppliers of new computer security mechanisms that the market demand for these products will be sustained, the number of competitive offerings in this area should materially increase. As a result, improvements in cost-performance and product attractiveness should also occur, thus precipitating still more market demand.

All segments of computer security technology will benefit from this increased demand and competitive response. The following hardware and software should be made more secure:

- Mainframe operating systems
- Database management systems
- Access control software
- Port protection devices
- Encryption systems
- Secure communications processors
- Biometric and personal identification systems
- Stand-alone secure minicomputers and microcomputers

The above products have characteristics that can help protect access to a host computer, database, or network. In addition, a combination of the above products will generally be needed to provide layers of protection or total systems access control.

Today, there are still certain cost-performance, cost-benefit, and technical or operational problems with most of these mechanisms from a user's point of view. Also, as explained above, no single product or group of technologies can solve the entire problem of computer access control or provide 100 percent systems security. What can be expected, however, as a result of increasing competition, is a combination of cost-performance improvements. In addition, more security capabilities will be introduced in a single package (i.e, port protection, encryption, and biometric checking), which will also result in better cost performance.

Security System Options

Another development certain to have an impact on the market for computer security tools is the approach that some suppliers will take to sell security technology to the more skeptical commercial prospects.

This approach involves the separation and/or unbundling of security software packages or features. The advantages to customers are that:

1. They only pay for what they get.
2. They only have to select or turn on the security features they want, when they want them (i.e., convenience improvement).

3. They can adjust the application of their security tools so as to minimize or achieve a more ideal system overhead (i.e., resulting from security procedures).

This approach to solving computer security cost-performance problems has the added advantage of allowing suppliers to continue to compete with other vendors on strictly a cost-performance basis for the business of those prospects not interested in security. (It will also give those prospects the opportunity to determine more precisely how much or how little system security actually costs.)

Development of Computer Security Guidelines and Standards

As was explained in the previous chapter, the development of computer security and privacy guidelines and standards at all levels (i.e., federal, international, government, and nongovernment) should make the implementation of computer security and access control a less challenging experience for most organizations.

These new guidelines and standards should have a definite impact on future computer security technologies and products. In addition, as the industry and products mature, we should see more consistent application of the new products, which, in turn, can greatly increase market demand.

Communication Networks and Distributed Systems

Modern data communication networks make the automation of information management and data processing much easier for large, widely dispersed organizations. Improvements in cost control, productivity, and information resource sharing are forcing an increasing number of large corporations to implement data communication networks and distributed systems. Unfortunately, many of these networks are vulnerable to various forms of unauthorized system access. The market is essentially wide open for new technologies and products that will make these distributed systems and networks safer. More secure products that should be of interest to these prospective buyers are:

- Office automation systems
- Database management systems
- Network processors and guards
- Host computer front-end guards
- Host computer gateway guards (i.e., alongside standard front-ender)
- Encryption hardware and software
- Port protection systems

The ideal technology would offer exactly the right amount of protection at the right place. It would enhance rather than detract from a company's ability to implement a distributed system at a national or even international level. It would enable management to fine-tune security performance and modify security to match changes in system architecture, application, or sensitivity.

All these requirements hold promise for the future of computer security technology.

Summary

The future for improvements in computer security and access control technology is bright because of the many forces at work that should motivate the potential suppliers of the new products to create new computer and network-oriented security tools.

The most important factor that should influence the market for better computer security is the customers' perception of their need for more information systems protection. This perception should grow and change significantly, at least for the remainder of this decade, for reasons such as increases in financial loss experience, news coverage, education on the subject, management edicts, and new laws and regulations.

Other factors that should influence a greater demand for new security technology and products are government certification programs, competition by suppliers trying to establish a lead in market share, introduction of optional security features, development of more computer security guidelines and standards, and the need for more information protection by large companies wanting to expand and modernize their distributed systems and communications networks.

Underlying the above requirements for better information systems security and access control technology is the great increase in the number of people who are becoming computer users. There is definitely a relationship between the number of people given computer access and the number of incidents and severity of computer abuse.

The development and use of computer security technology should become increasingly more important as we progress further into our information age. The conclusion, therefore, is that the future for information security technology is extremely bright.

Finally, we can, and will, find ways to maintain progress toward more beneficial and safer uses of computers and communications networks. Our goal should be that computer abuse must not be allowed to block the advances being made toward a better society through the introduction of new information and communications technologies.

Bibliography

[AN 1972] Anderson, J. P.: "Computer Security Technology Planning Study," ESD-TR-73-51, prepared for Deputy for Command and Management Systems, HQ Electronic Systems Division (AFSC), L.G. Hanscom Field, Bedford, Mass., October 1972, vols. 1, 2.

[AN 1984] "Announcing the Standard for Password Usage," FIPS Pub. "Draft," National Bureau of Standards, Gaithersburg, Md., August 1984.

[BE 1973] Bell, D. E., and L. J. La Padula: "Secure Computer Systems," ESD-TR-73-278, Mitre Corporation, Bedford, Mass., November 1973–June 1974, vols. I–III.

[BE 1976] Bell, D. E., and L. J. La Padula: "Secure Computer Systems: Unified Exposition and MULTICS Interpretation," MTR-2997, rev. 1, Mitre Corporation, Bedford, Mass., March 1976.

[BE 1983a] Bemey, Karen: "Washington Takes On Computer Crime," *Electronics*, Nov. 17, 1983.

[BE 1983b] Becker, Hal B.: *Information Integrity*, McGraw-Hill, New York, 1983, p. 112.

[BL 1979] Block, Victor: "New Privacy Bills Aimed at EFT Communications," *Infosystems* (Washington Info), Hitchcock Publishing Co., Wheaton, Ill., November 1979, p. 18.

[BO 1980] Bonyun, D. A.: "The Secure Relational Database Management System Kernel—Three Years After," *IEEE Computer Security and Privacy Proceedings*, Oakland, Ca., Apr. 14–16, 1980, pp. 34–37.

[CL 1983] Claybrook, Billy G.: "Using Views in a Multilevel Secure Database Management System," *IEEE Computer Security and Privacy Proceedings*, Oakland, Ca., Apr. 25–27, 1983, pp. 4–17.

[CO 1973] "A Comparative Study of IBM, Honeywell, UNIVAC and Control Data Operating Systems," RISOS (Research in Secured Operating Systems), ARPA Order No. 2166, University of California, January 1973.

[CO 1975] *Computer Security Guidelines For Implementing the Privacy Act of 1974*, National Bureau of Standards, FIPS-PUB-41, U.S. Department of Commerce, Springfield, Va., May 30, 1975, p. 3.

[CO 1981] Coppotelli, D. J.: "Emerging Corporate-Wide Information Security Strategy," *Computer Security and Privacy Symposium Proceedings*, CY 22-00, Honeywell Information Systems, Phoenix, Ariz., Apr. 7–8, 1981, pp. 9–11.

[CO 1983a] "Computer Systems Access Control Software," *Data Processing & Communications Security*, Madison, Wis., September–October 1983, pp. 22–24.

[CO 1983b] "Computer-Related Fraud and Abuse in Government Agencies," U.S. Department of Health and Human Services, Washington, D. C., June 1983.

[CO 1984a] "Computer Disk, 12 Years Work Stolen at Convention," *The Arizona Republic*, May 7, 1984, sec. B1.

[CO 1984b] "Computer Security Publications," *NBS Publications List 91*, National Bureau of Standards, Gaithersburg, Md., August 1984.

[DA 1981] Davida, George I.: "A Database Encryption System with Subkeys," *ACM Transactions on Database Systems*, vol. 1, no. 2, June 1981.

[DE 1982] Denning, D., J. Schlorer, and C. Wehrle: "Memoryless Inference Controls for Statistical Databases," *IEEE Computer Security and Privacy Proceedings*, Oakland, Ca., Apr. 26–28, 1982, pp. 38–43.

[DE 1983] *Department of Defense Trusted Computer System Evaluation Criteria*, CSC-STD-001-83, Department of Defense Computer Security Center, Fort George G. Meade, Md., Aug. 15, 1983.

[DI 1976] Diffie, W., and M. E. Hellman: "New Directions in Cryptography," *IEEE Transactions—Information Theory*, vol. I, no. 6, 1976, p. T–22.

[DR 1984] Dreyfuss, Joel: "What Will Send Computers Home," *Fortune*, Apr. 2, 1984.

[FA 1983] Fam, B. W., and J. K. Millen: "The Channel Assignment Problem," *IEEE Computer Security and Privacy Proceedings*, Oakland, Ca., Apr. 25–27, 1983, pp. 109–112.

[FE 1978] *Federal Agencies Can and Should Do More to Combat Fraud in Government Programs*, Comptroller General's Report to the Congress, GGO-78-62, Washington, D.C., Sept. 19, 1978, p. 1.

[FE 1981] Fernandez, E. B., R. C. Summers, and C. Wood: *Database Security and Integrity*, Addison-Wesley, Reading, Mass., 1981, p. 218.

[FE 1984] "Few Takers for Embedded Protection," *Computerworld*, Framingham, Mass., Mar. 12, 1984, p. 115.

[FI 1982] *Financial Institution Message Authentication X9.9*, American National Standards Committee X9—Financial Services, American Bankers Association, Washington, D.C., Apr. 13, 1982.

[FL 1981] Flinn, J. W.: *Guide to Designing and Implementing Computer Systems Security*, TX02, Honeywell Information Systems, Phoenix, Ariz., 1981, pp. 1–8.

[GO 1974] *Government Looks at Privacy and Security in Computer Systems*, NBS Technical Note 809, National Bureau of Standards, Washington, D.C., February 1974, pp. 8–10.

[GR 1984] Graubert, Richard: "The Integrity Lock Approach to Secure Database Management," *IEEE Computer Security and Privacy Proceedings*, Oakland, Ca., April 29–May 2, 1984, pp. 62–74.

[GU 1983] *Guideline for Computer Security Certification and Accreditation*, National Bureau of Standards, FIPS Pub. 102, U.S. Department of Commerce, Springfield, Va., Sept. 27, 1983, p. 12.

[HI 1975] Hill, R. H.: "Long-Range Computer Security Objectives," *Computer Security and Privacy Symposium Proceedings*, DE 20, Honeywell Information Systems, Phoenix, Ariz., Apr. 29–30, 1975, pp. 73–77.

[HO 1980] "Honeywell's SCOMP Aims to Keep Data Secure," *Mini-Micro Systems*, March 1980, pp. 37–38.

[IN 1983] *Industrial Security Manual for Safeguarding Classified Information*, DOD 5220.22-M, Superintendent of Documents, U.S. Government Printing Office, Washington, D.C., January 1983.

[JE 1980] Jeffrey, Seymour: *Proceedings of the Third Seminar on the DOD Computer Security Initiative Program*, National Bureau of Standards, Gaithersburg, Md., Nov. 18–20, 1980, p. B–2.

[KA 1973] Karcher, P. A., and R. R. Shell: *MULTICS Security Evaluation*: *Vulnerability Analysis*, ESD-TR-74-XXX, Electronics Systems Division (AFSC), L. G. Hanscomb Field, Bedford, Mass., June 1974.

[KI 1983] Kirchner, Jake: "Privacy Plan Developed for Videotext," *Computerworld*, Framingham, Mass., July 11, 1983, p. 1.

[KO 1980] Koenig, R. C.: "Advances in Information Classification," *Computer Security and Privacy Symposium Proceedings*, DM 35, Honeywell Information Systems, Phoenix, Ariz., Apr. 15–16, 1980, pp. 119–124.

[LA 1971] Lampson, B. W.: "Protection," *Proceedings of the 5th Princeton Conference on Information Science and Systems*, Princeton, N. J., March 1971.

[LO 1979] Lobel, J.: "Risk Analysis Results," *Computer Security and Privacy Symposium Proceedings*, MEDW-359-801, Honeywell Information Systems, Phoenix, Ariz., Apr. 2–3, 1979, pp. 79–84.

[MA 1984] Madron, T. W.: "Software Piracy: How Serious Is It?," *Computerworld*, Framingham, Mass., Feb. 20, 1984, p. 69.

[MI 1980] Miranda, S. M.: "Aspects of Data Security in General-Purpose Data Base Management Systems," *IEEE Computer Security and Privacy Proceedings*, Oakland, Ca., Apr. 14–16, 1980, pp. 46–58.

[MI 1982] Minnesota, State of: Proposed Computer Crime Bill 609.522 (H.F. No. 356), Chapter No. 534, 1982 Session Laws, Minnesota Statute 609.

[MU 1976] Munson, B. R., and C. M. Smith, Jr.: "The Study of Data Base Management Systems with Bibliography," *Data Base Directions—The Next Steps*, NBS Special Pub. 451, National Bureau of Standards, Washington, D.C., September 1976, p. 125.

[MU 1982] *MULTICS Data Security*, GA01-00, Honeywell Information Systems, Phoenix, Ariz., 1982.

[NI 1979] Nibaldi, G. H.: *Proposed Technical Evaluation Criteria for Trusted Computer Systems*, M79-225, Contract No. AF 19628-80-C-0001, Mitre Corporation, Bedford, Mass., Oct. 25, 1979, pp. 1–2.

[OE 1980] "OECD Guidelines Governing the Protection of Privacy and Transborder Flows of Personal Data," *Recommendations of the Council of Europe*, adopted at its 523d meeting on Sept. 23, 1980.

[PA 1984] "Password Usage Standards," National Bureau of Standards Pub. "Draft," National Bureau of Standards, Washington, D.C., 1984.

[PR 1974] *The Privacy Act of 1974*, Public Law 93–579, 93d Cong., S.3418, Dec. 31, 1974.

[PR 1984] *Proceedings of the 198– Symposium on Security and Privacy*, Oakland, Ca., sponsored by the Technical Committee on Computer Security and Privacy, IEEE Computer Society, Silver Spring, Md., 1980–1984.

[RE 1984] *Report of Ad Hoc Meeting on Security*, WOI Ad Hoc Group on Security, International Standards Organization, prepared for ISO (TC 97/SC16/WGI) after meeting in Washington, D.C., Mar. 12–16, 1984.

[SA 1983] Savner, D. A., and B. D. Weiss: "A Hard Stand for Software Protection," *Computerworld*, Framingham, Mass., Sept. 26, 1983, p. 24.

[SC 1975] Schiller, W. L.: "Notes on Approach for Design of a Security Kernel for the PDP-11/45", ESD-TR-75-69, Mitre Corporation, Bedford, Mass., May 1975.

[SE 1976] *Security analysis and Enhancements of Computer Operating Systems*, NBSIR 76-1041, National Bureau of Standards, Washington, D.C., April 1976, p. 3.

[SE 1979] Sessions, M. V.: "The Security and Privacy of Data Management Systems," *Computer Security and Privacy Proceedings*, MEDW-359-501, Honeywell Information Systems, Phoenix, Ariz., Apr. 2–3, 1979, pp. 99–101.

[SY 1976] Sykes, D. J.: "Data Encryption Standards and Applications," *Computer Security and Privacy Proceedings*, DE 89, Honeywell Information Systems, Phoenix, Ariz., 1981, pp. 91–93.

[SY 1977] Sykes, D. J.: "Implementation of the NBS Encryption Standard," *Computer Security and Privacy Symposium Proceedings*, DF 84, Honeywell Information Systems, Phoenix, Ariz. Apr. 19–20, 1977, pp. 61–65.

[SY 1981] Sykes, D. J.: "Generating Secure System Specifications," *Computer Security and Privacy Symposium Proceedings*, CY22-00, Honeywell Information Systems, Phoenix, Ariz., Apr. 7–8, 1981, pp. 91–93.

[WE 1972] Westin, A. F., and M. A. Baker: *Databanks in a Free Society*, Quadrangle Books, New York, 1972.

[WE 1983] Westin, A. F.: "New Eyes on Privacy," *Computerworld*, Framingham, Mass., Nov. 28, 1983, pp. 11–18.

[WI 1984] "The Wizard Inside the Machine," *Time*, Apr. 16, 1984, pp. 56–63.

[WO 1974] Woodward, F. G., and L. Hoffman: "Worst Case Cost for Dynamics Data Element Security Decisions," *Proceedings of the ACM Annual Conference*, Association for Computing Machinery, 1974.

[WO 1983] "Working Draft for an Addendum to ISO 7498 on Security," International Standards Organization, TC 97/SC16, Secretariat, ANSI, October 1983.

Index

Database security (*Cont.*):
 selecting the DBMS, 173–175
 set mechanism, 167
 view concept, 167–171
Dedicated systems, threat to, 17
Default principle, 127
Degaussing, 175–176
Diffie, W., 200
 (*See also* Encryption)
Disaster recovery, 12
Distributed system, 25
Distributed systems architecture (DSA),
 183

Eavesdropping, 78, 195
 (*See also* Encryption)
Electromagnetic radiation, 6, 105–106
Electronic data processing (EDP) audits,
 80
Electronic fund transfer (EFT) and
 videotex, 44–45
Electronic mail security, 186
 (*See also* Office automation systems
 security)
Electronic surveillance (*see* Physical
 security)
Encryption:
 cryptoanalysis, 194
 cryptographic concepts, 194
 data encryption standard (DES), 196–
 199
 database encryption, 201–202
 Diffie and Hellman, 200
 dummy traffic insertion, 185
 eavesdropping, 78, 195
 electronic signatures, 201
 interception, 6, 195
 key distribution center (KDC), 200
 key management, 199
 open systems interconnection (OSI),
 184–185
 public key systems, 199–201
 types of: end-to-end, 196–197
 file, 201–202
 header, 185
 link, 195–197
 work factor, 194

Federal Bureau of Investigation (FBI), 2,
 27, 183

Federal information processing standard
 (FIPS):
 data encryption standard (DES), 198
 Publication number 102, 15
Federal Privacy Act of 1974, 39
 (*See also* Computer privacy)
Floppy disks, 53
Fraud, computer, 29–32

Hacking:
 414s, 1, 2, 4, 5
 Los Alamos National Laboratory, 1
 Pepsi-Cola, 1
 Security Pacific Bank, 1
 Sloan-Kettering, 1
 Telenet, 1
Hellman, M. E., 200
 (*See also* Encryption)
Home computers:
 access controls for, 242–243
 characteristics of, 242
 control cost justification for, 243–244
 vulnerability of, 18
Honeywell:
 distributed systems architecture
 (DSA), 183
 DM-IV, 171–172
 DPS/6, 151
 DPS/7, 151
 DPS/8, 151
 GCOS III, 146, 150, 172
 I-D-S/II, 171
 Multics, 84, 141, 148–156
 SCOMP, 143, 151, 158
Host computers and microcomputer
 access, 94–95

IBM (International Business Machines),
 131, 133, 146, 171, 183–184, 198
IEEE (Institute of Electrical and
 Electronic Engineers), 163
Industrial espionage, computer-oriented,
 33
Industrial Security Manual (ISM), 63–
 65
 (*See also* Information classification)
Information classification:
 categories of, 61–65
 and classified information,
 government, 63–64
 confidential, 64

ABOUT THE AUTHOR

Jerome Lobel is manager of computer security for Honeywell Information Systems, and has been recognized as one of the leading international experts in the area of computer security and privacy for over seventeen years. He has directed or participated in the design of many of America's most sensitive computerized information systems. A leading educator in the field, currently teaching the subject as a member of the faculty in the Department of Computer Science at Arizona State University, he has chaired numerous conferences and seminars and has had more than thirty articles published.